MAKARIOS

Archbishop Makarios III, first President of Cyprus

MAKARIOS

A Biography

STANLEY MAYES

To the people of Cyprus, Greeks and Turks, who deserve a better future

First published 1981 by
THE MACMILLAN PRESS LTD
London and Basingstoke
Companies and representatives
throughout the world

Photoset in Great Britain by
REDWOOD BURN LTD
Trowbridge & Esher

British Library Cataloguing in Publication Data

Mayes, Stanley
    Makarios
    1. Makarios III. *Abp of Cyprus*
    2. Cyprus – Presidents – Biography
    3. Bishops – Cyprus – Biography
    956.4′504′0924   DS54.9
    ISBN 978-1-349-16502-5   ISBN 978-1-349-16500-1 (eBook)
                                DOI 10.1007/978-1-349-16500-1

Contents

List of Plates

Preface

There have been many books about the Cyprus problem but few – and these somewhat fragmentary – about the man who for nearly thirty years was most identified with that problem: Archbishop Makarios III, later the island-republic's first President. Perhaps this is not surprising since Makarios had little private life: both as prelate and as politician he was always a public persona.

When Makarios first became generally known outside Cyprus in the mid-1950s it was in the character of a nationalist leader opposed to a colonial regime, who condoned, if he did not actually encourage – in spite of his cloth – the activities of a terrorist organisation called EOKA, the creation of Colonel George Grivas. To the average British serviceman in Cyprus and his family, with him or back home – in fact, to most people in Britain fed on a popular press – 'Black Mac' was a religious fanatic, a Rasputin-like figure, a priest who approved of murder. To the British politicians who tried to negotiate with him or circumvent him the Archbishop was a wily Byzantine, a master of equivocation, almost impossible to pin down. The Turks and Turkish Cypriots, with their longer experience of subject Greeks who outmanoeuvred their rulers, simply 'knew' that Makarios could never be trusted. Mainland Greeks saw him first in the tradition of their own national liberation struggle, then as a liability who bedevilled their foreign relations and repeatedly brought them close to war with Turkey.

The British hoped they could eliminate the Archbishop's influence by deporting him to the Indian Ocean. But the violence in Cyprus increased and no Greek Cypriot would negotiate without Makarios. After many abortive attempts at a solution Britain finally agreed to a settlement worked out between Greece and Turkey, with power unequally but inequitably shared

vii

between the two ethnic communities in the island. Apart from the sovereign bases retained by Britain, Cyprus became independent. It was not what Makarios had proclaimed as his only goal – Enosis, the union of Cyprus with Greece. That, like partition, was permanently ruled out. Grivas wanted to fight on, believing that Makarios had betrayed their struggle, but he was eased out of Cyprus with a plethora of Greek honours.

My earlier book dealing with these events, *Cyprus and Makarios*, began as a study of an 'insoluble' problem. It was half-written when suddenly, in February 1959, the Zürich and London agreements cut the Gordian knot but left many fraying loose ends and a double sense of frustration. I recorded then my pessimism about the settlement. But for a time it seemed to work and Cyprus dropped out of the headlines.

By the end of 1963 the constitution had broken down and Cyprus was divided into two armed camps, the one supported militarily and diplomatically by Greece, the other by Turkey. After some months of intercommunal violence, the brunt of which was borne by the Turkish Cypriot minority, a United Nations peace-keeping force established an uneasy truce which lasted until General Grivas, who had returned to command the Greek Cypriot forces, broke it in 1967 with a savage onslaught on the other community. He was again forced to leave the island under a Turkish threat to invade.

Rid of Grivas for the second time, President Makarios now felt strong enough to open negotiations with the Turkish Cypriots, aimed at giving them limited autonomy. But his insistence on Greek majority rights precluded any agreement, and the talks dragged on for six years. In the meantime the situation had been complicated by the accession of a military dictatorship in Greece which disliked Makarios's growing independence of Athens and hoped to do a new deal with Turkey. The 'Colonels' sent Grivas back to Cyprus and, in collusion with three 'diehard' Bishops, he organised a second EOKA to undermine Makarios's position and achieve Enosis, or at least the union of most of the island with Greece. The new terrorist campaign lost most of its momentum when Grivas died in January 1974. But six months later the Greek 'Colonels' carried out a *coup* against Makarios and drove him into exile for the second time in his life. Nikos Sampson was set up as a puppet-President, whereupon Turkey seized the opportunity she had been waiting for for eleven years and launched a massive invasion. Cyprus was split into two by the 'Attila Line', more than a third of the Greek Cypriot population became refugees and the Turkish-occupied north presently declared itself a Turkish Cypriot 'state'. Makarios returned as President but died broken-hearted two-and-a-half years later, with his country still divided and occupied. It remains so still.

I first met Makarios in the mid-1950s, in the company of other journalists, as he passed through London on his way to lobby the United Nations. In spite of my basically pro-Greek sympathies – though I believed the Turkish Cypriots had a case – I found him a faintly sinister figure. A six-months stay in Cyprus in 1944 and a later reconnaissance on the eve of EOKA violence in 1955 had done nothing to persuade me that the majority of Greek Cypriots, in spite of their desire to be thought of as Greeks, wanted actual political union with Athens. My assessment of the Archbishop in *Cyprus and Makarios*, published in the week that the island achieved its unsought independence after so much bloodshed, was predictably harsh.

Later I had more opportunities to get to know him as a person as much as any Englishman could. From 1969 onwards I visited Cyprus regularly and was usually accorded a long private session with the President in which I was now able to converse with him in Greek about the current situation. I also met many of the other actors in the drama – among them Clerides and Denktash, the Greek and Turkish Cypriot negotiators in the intercommunal talks; the rebel Bishops; the socialist leader Dr Lyssarides, a close confidant of the Archbishop and his personal physician; Nikos Sampson, the ex-EOKA killer who became the 'Colonels'' puppet-President; and Kyprianou, the Archbishop's eventual successor as Head of State. I became increasingly fascinated by the complexity of Makarios's character as well as charmed by his simple dignity, his consideration for others and his impish sense of humour. I decided to embark on a full-scale biography and told him of my project. He promised help with it, although it was in no sense to be an official 'Life' and he must have been aware of the strong criticism I had often made of his policies in my earlier book and in hundreds of broadcast talks and newspaper articles; it was a measure of his magnanimity.

My last interview with Makarios was in July 1977. He looked old and tired but no one guessed the end was so near. I left him a searching list of questions about obscure or disputed issues. He promised x *Preface*

smilingly to let me have the answers as soon as possible. I never got them: a week later he was dead.

Apart from a strong sense of personal loss and my belief that only Makarios could have solved the problem which he had done so much to create, that he was already cautiously moving towards such a solution, my book has suffered in that it could not include his final judgment of events. The facts are as accurate as I have been able to establish from the available sources. A definitive biography will be possible only when the governments of Britain, Greece, Turkey, the United States and Cyprus have yielded up their official secrets and the politicians – and the secret agents – have written their memoirs. But the time that has elapsed since Makarios's death allows some perspective on his life. In the recurring, almost annual cycle of a new round of intercommunal talks, more deadlock, another sterile debate at the United Nations and then a fresh initiative by the UN Secretary-General to get talks started again, the Cyprus problem still seems 'insoluble'.

Makarios was partly the prisoner of a role he inherited, partly the victim of outside forces which he did not appreciate until it was too late to resist them successfully. His career seems to me to have been a tragic failure and if some will not agree with that judgment I hope this book will be accepted as a sympathetic, if critical study of a remarkable personality whose final place in history is not yet certain.

February 1980   STANLEY MAYES

Acknowledgements

My thanks are due in the first place to the late President Makarios himself, for without the regular interviews he granted me and the long off-the-record conversations we had, especially during the last years of his life, I should never have felt any competence to tackle this biography. I am also grateful to members of the Archbishop's family: his only sister, Mrs Maria Hadjicleanthous, his nephew (Maria's son), Mr Andreas Neophytou, and his uncle, Mr George Mouskos, who gave me details of incidents in Makarios's life or insights into his character.

Then, on the official level, I should like to acknowledge the generous help I have had over a number of years from the Government of Cyprus: from Mr Militiades Christodoulou, Director of the Public Information Office and his staff generally, but in particular from Mr Peter Stylianaki, who even after his retirement from the PIO has never spared himself in his efforts to get me the contacts and material I needed. The friendship of Peter and his wife, Nelly, is something I greatly treasure.

I am also grateful to Cyprus's former High Commissioner in London, Mr Costas Ashiotis, and to the High Commission's former Press Counsellor, Mr George Lanatis, for their help in arranging some of my visits to Cyprus.

I should like to record my thanks to Mr Patrocilos Stavrou, Under-Secretary to the President, who in his special position as archivist to President Makarios supplied me with texts of speeches and documents which I had difficulty in obtaining elsewhere.

I have been fortunate in knowing most of the political leaders in Cyprus for a long time. I am grateful especially to President Spyros Kyprianou, Mr Glafkos Clerides, Dr Vasos Lyssarides, Mr Ezekias Papaioannou and Mr Tasos Papadopoulos for the useful discussions of Cyprus and its problems that I have had with the over the years. I have always been kept well-informed of Turkish Cypriot opinion by Mr Rauf Denktash, to whom I should also like to express my thanks for interviews and hospitality.

I am also indebted to the late Abbot Chrysostomos of Kykko Monastery and to Father Maximos and his brother-monks for the hospitality I have enjoyed in their company and for their reminiscences of Kykko's most famous son.

I am grateful to a number of people who helped me (after Makarios's death) with information about particular periods of his life: among them Mr George Prodromou, Headmaster of the Pancyprian Gymnasium, who showed me the school record of the future Archbishop and President in great detail; Mr Walter G. Muelder, Dean Emeritus of Boston University School of Theology, for his communications about Makarios's post-graduate studies and his recall to Cyprus as Bishop; and Mr Andreas Azinas, the present Commissioner for Cooperative Development in Cyprus, who played an important part in the organisation of EOKA. I should also like to thank John Dickie, Diplomatic Correspondent of the *Daily Mail*, for the loan of a now rare copy of *Makarios in Exile* (not in the British Museum or the London Library) and Mr P. M. Charalambous, who lent me Lawrence Stern's *The Wrong Horse* and supplied me with additional bibliography.

Almost last, but by no means least, I want to thank my old friends, Ruth Jordan and Nissim Kivity (wife and husband), for originally prodding me into writing this book; Baqer Moin of the BBC's Persian Section, for drawing The Macmillan Press's attention to a work in progress; and Miss Merle Hughes for her sustained interest and painstaking effort in typing my manuscript.

Finally, I must express my gratitude again to the Public Information Office in Cyprus for permission to reproduce plates 1, 2, 3, 4, 5, 6, 8, 11, 12, 14, 15, and 16, out of the hundred or more which Mr Peter Stylianaki and Mr Panos Hadjiyannis so kindly found for me. For the frontispiece and plates 7 and 10 I owe my thanks to Popperfoto. And I am especially grateful to Mr Spyros Papayeoryiou and to his publishers Ladias and Co. of Athens for allowing me to reproduce as plates 9 and 13 two highly significant photographs from *Makarios: poreia dia pyros kai siderou* (Makarios: through fire and sword).

PART ONE

SEED-TIME

1 Goatherd and Acolyte

In August 1913 that confused and many-sided scramble for territory known to history as the First and Second Balkan Wars ended with the Treaty of Bucharest. It marked a further stage in the break-up of the Turkish Empire. Under the agreements worked out that year Serbia, Montenegro and Bulgaria all made substantial gains at Turkey's expense. Albania emerged as a new and independent state. The Sultan and the European Powers also recognised Greece's annexation of autonomous Crete, her right to southern Epirus and part of Macedonia and her sovereignty over more islands in the Aegean, including Samos, Chios and Mitylene, which lie close to the coast of Turkey. Within a matter of months the small kingdom of Greece almost doubled its size and population.

It is unlikely that much of this filtered through to the village of Ano Panayia in the hills of western Cyprus, beyond an awareness that Greece, the motherland, was fighting against age-old enemies – Turkey and Bulgaria – and redeeming her lost children. It was there on 13 August, three days after the signing of the Treaty of Bucharest, that the wife of a peasant-farmer gave birth to a son who was to become Archbishop of Cyprus, the leader of a new national struggle, and eventually President of a reluctant republic. His whole career was to be bound up with the question of whether Cyprus too should become part of Greece.

Ano or Pano ('Upper') Panayia lies some 2700 feet above sea-level in a fold of the western slopes of Mt Troodos, which dominates a third of the island. Below the village the ground falls away through dusty orchards and olive-groves and neat terraced vineyards to the district-town and little port of Paphos some twenty-five miles distant. Around and above it are magnificent forests of

Aleppo pine, variegated with dwarf golden oak and silver plane-trees. Here and there on the uplands are bare patches which were constantly made larger by the marauding goat until there was legislation against it in 1913. In these clearings the villagers sowed their sparse wheat or pastured the sheep and goats that provided them with meat and milk and also hides and fleeces. It was a hard life, but the villagers were not poor as poverty is known in the Eastern Mediterranean.

Ano Panayia was – in 1913 – almost entirely a Greek Cypriot community. A population map based on the 1960 census showed only one Turk then living among more than a thousand Greeks in the year that Cyprus became independent. Yet just below Ano Panayia there were some wholly Turkish Cypriot hamlets and, until circumstances forced them apart, the two communities were dotted like currants and sultanas in a cake all the way down to the coast, as they were in most other parts of Cyprus. Paphos itself was mixed and nearly a third of its population was Turkish Cypriot.

Life in Ano Panayia revolved around the pattern of the working year and the festivals of the Church. The very name of the village enshrines the universal Greek epithet for the Virgin Mary – Panayia, the All-Holy. The Church was the centre and the supreme authority. It regulated men's lives even more than parental discipline, and far more than the local policeman or the occasional government official who toiled up the winding mountain-road on mule-back to see that the *mukhtar* – the term retained from Turkish times for the village 'president' – was doing his job properly. Sometimes there were other, grander visitors – the Bishop of Paphos, or even the Archbishop of Cyprus himself – who would come to visit the Monastery of Chrysorroyiatissa which stands in a superb setting a mile and a half beyond the village.

According to Greek Cypriot tradition Chrysorroyiatissa was founded in the year 1152 by a hermit-monk, Ignatios, who built a shrine here to house the luminous, wonder-working icon of the Panayia washed ashore below from the coasts of Asia Minor; like others in Cyprus, it was said to have been painted by the Evangelist St Luke. Today the icon is hidden by a silver-gilt cover except for a few square inches of smoke – blackened paint exposed to the kisses of the faithful. The most likely etymology of 'Chrysorroyiatissa' makes it mean 'Our Lady of the Golden Breasts' – a description which may well owe something to that older object of veneration –

'golden Aphrodite' – who rose from the sea in luminous foam at Paphos.

Christodoulos Mouskos, the father of the child who was to become Archbishop Makarios III and the first President of Cyprus, had a small piece of land outside the village planted with vines, but chiefly he got his living from the goats he pastured on the uplands. His brother George remembered him (in 1977 – perhaps with the exaggeration of age) as having about a hundred head of livestock. Christodoulos and his wife lived in a one-storey house near the centre of the village. The single large room was partly divided by a stone wall which left the smaller rear part for the yoke of oxen or sick animals that needed attention. The front part had a fire-place in one corner and a high wooden platform diagonally opposite, which served as a bedroom or storage space. A chair or two, a table, a chest, a row of cooking-pots and utensils and some woven cover-lets were almost the only furnishing. Outside, in the walled court-yard, there was a privy and an oven for making bread.[1]

Michael – the future Makarios – was the couple's first child, and doubly welcome because he was male. His mother would have rejoiced to take part, two days after the birth, in the great festival of the Virgin which brought so many visitors to Chrysorroyiatissa. She could not because of her ritual uncleanness rather than through weakness after labour; Cypriot village women are tougher than most. Even after forty days, when the child was baptised in the village church, his mother stayed at home according to Greek Cypriot custom. The godfather renounced the devil on behalf of the infant and spat ceremoniously on the floor three times in token of this renunciation. Afterwards there was much feasting with the slaughter of some choice victim from the family herd.

Michael Christodoulou ('son of Christodoulos') Mouskos was a year old when the First World War broke out. It had little direct impact on Cyprus except that, as Turkey entered the war on the side of Germany, Britain formally 'annexed' the island in November 1914. Since 1878, when Disraeli acquired Cyprus from the Sultan in order to safeguard the imperial route to India, Britain had continued to recognise Turkish sovereignty over the island. This enabled her to answer to all the demands of the Greek Cypriot Enotists – those who persistently clamoured for Enosis, the union of Cyprus with Greece – that the island was not hers to give. Now, in spite of some protest from the leading Enotists in Nicosia, the annexation was generally welcomed by Greek Cypriots as the last stage in 'national rehabilitation' before a magnanimous and freedom-loving Britain ceded the island to Greece. The Turkish Cypriot leaders 'loyally' accepted the change and begged the High Commissioner to see that the island was not handed over to Greece but became permanently part of the British Empire.

In October 1915 Britain did, in fact, offer Cyprus to Greece. It was a desperate attempt, when the war was going badly, to persuade the vacillating and pro-German King Constantine to fulfil Greece's treaty obligations to Serbia and bring her into the war on the side of the Allies. The Zaimis Cabinet however was unwilling to abandon Greece's neutrality and the offer lapsed. But the end of the First World War, which saw Greece among the victorious Allies – Venizelos, the great Liberal statesman, had eventually brought her in – also saw a recrudescence of the Greek Cypriot demand for Enosis in application of the principles for which the war had been fought.

The war was over and the Allies were engaged in the more acrimonious business of peace-making when the young Michael Mouskos first went to school at the age of six. In that remote corner of Cyprus, now a British possession, the curriculum in a Greek Cypriot primary school was virtually indistinguishable from that of any 'demotic' school in Greece. One of the first High Commissioners appointed after Britain's acquisition of Cyprus in 1878, Colonel (later General Sir) Robert Biddulph, had advocated the teaching of English throughout the island as the first step in educational advance. However, Gladstone, who had succeeded Disraeli as Prime Minister, was a noted philhellene, and even his Colonial Secretary, Lord Kimberley, thought that English, though obviously necessary, should not become 'a language for general use in any way on a level with the two ancient languages of the island'.[2] If Lord Kimberley was somewhat vague about the relative antiquity of Greek and Turkish, he at least had no desire to deprive either Cypriot community of its cultural heritage. So two Boards of Education were set up, one under the control of the Greek Cypriot archbishop, the other supervised by the Turkish Cypriot *mufti*. Each laid down the curriculum for the schools in its own community, chose the text books, allocated the government grants-in-aid and fixed the conditions of service for the teachers, who were appointed by local education committees. They approximated as much as possible to the system on the parent mainland.

So in those early years Michael would not have been aware that he was living outside Greece or anything but Greek. The stories he was told were of Greeks and Persians, Greeks and Turks – Marathon and Thermopylae and 1821 – not of the British Empire. The Greek flag flew over the church and the school and from every house on all 'national' occasions – and on many others. The Union Jack might appear over the *mukhtar's* office on King George V's birthday and Empire Day or when some English official honoured the village with a visit. The only newspapers that came to Ano Panayia, often several days late, were Greek, published in Nicosia and as pungent as any in Athens. Yet down the road were Turkish Cypriot children who played the same games but spoke a different language, though some of them also knew Greek. The coffee-shop where their fathers flicked their *komboloi*-beads as they gossiped or played *tric-trac* (backgammon) was a familiar sight, even if it stood in the shadow of a mosque, not the church.

For the Greek Cypriot villagers their chief complaint was that, even after Britain had formally annexed Cyprus, they still had to pay her 'tribute' equal to the surplus revenue previously claimed by their Turkish overlords. Britain justified this originally with the argument that there had been no change of sovereignty, but the money was used to pay the interest due to the mainly British and French bondholders who had financed the Ottoman Loan of 1855, on which Turkey subsequently defaulted. Greek Cypriot bitterness about the 'tribute' was not assuaged by the fact that it was presently offset in part by government grants-in-aid for development. Yet the taxes paid to the Porte before 1878 had been collected by the Church with the aid of Turkish policemen.

Michael was a bright and lively boy. Someone who once shared a bench with him in the village school told the writer that the future archbishop was always good and obedient, but this is belied by other reports of youthful naughtiness. Years later, on a visit to his birthplace, Makarios reminded an old villager of how he had once boxed his ears for cutting down some of his bamboo canes. Certainly Makarios was good at his lessons, though these were not exacting. He was expected to take his share of the family chores and often he would stay up on the mountain in the *mandra* where the goats were penned; this was his father's home for a large part of the year.

From here Michael would run down the two or three miles to school or church, and return to the *mandra* in the afternoon. His boyhood on the craggy slopes of Troodos gave Makarios a physical toughness that was to stand him in good stead all his life.

After some five years – an unusually long gap – the Mouskos family was increased by the birth of another boy, Yiacovos (or Yiacoumis). Then, when Michael was ten, a girl arrived and was baptised Maria. Their mother, Eleni, survived the birth of her third child only by a few months; she died, ill and exhausted, in April 1924. It was a cruel experience for the sensitive Michael, and a bad blow for his father who was left with three young children to bring up, one of them still a baby. He coped for a few months as best he could and then, with the understanding of his neighbours, quietly married Anastasia Yeoryiou in order to have a woman in the house. She proved a good stepmother and had no trouble with Michael. In due course she bore Christodoulos another son, George.[3]

The gaps in the ages of the children did not make for close companionship between Michael and his siblings, but family ties were strong – as always among Greeks – though the eldest boy was soon to leave home. Years later, when Makarios had become President as well as Archbishop, his brother, Yiacovos, regularly acted as his chauffeur and Maria, though married, regarded herself as a kind of unofficial 'housekeeper' to her famous brother and kept an eye on his welfare. Neither ever presumed on the relationship and their position in Makarios's later background was a reminder of his humble origin.

Makarios had an uncle by marriage, Polykarpos – the husband of his mother's sister – who served as priest in the little church at Ano Panayia. (A Greek Orthodox cleric may marry before he is ordained as priest, but if he does so he is debarred from further advancement in the Church.) The young Michael would often go to help his uncle prepare for services or to take part in them as an acolyte or *papadaki* (little priest). The elaborate ritual of the Greek liturgy, the sonorous voice of the priest, the smell of incense, the dull gleam of icons in the candle-lit gloom all made a strong appeal to an impressionable boy. Sometimes Michael would go along the road to Chrysorroyiatissa and talk to the monks in the sequestered calm of the tree-lined courtyard, always a blaze of colour in summer. The Church was not remote from everyday life. The married priest and his wife toiled in the fields like other villagers. At

Chrysorroyiatissa the miracle-working icon had a special power to help those accused in the courts or awaiting sentence. Rupert Gunnis, the historian of Cyprus's churches and monasteries, says in his book published in 1936 that 'even the youth who has stolen goods worth but a few piastres from his master will pray to the icon that he shall not be found out'. The Greek guide-book to Chrysorroyiatissa vouches for the first statement but rejects the second as an exaggeration.[4]

The normal prospect for a boy reaching adolescence in Ano Panayia was to leave school and go to help his father full-time in preparation for becoming the family breadwinner. Michael loved the countryside but he did not relish a life of herding goats or tending vines. Sometimes, when he was younger, he would play at being a priest, wearing a pair of his father's black baggy breeches, the Turkish *vraka*, round his shoulders and swinging a dried gourd as a 'censer'. There were other stories of his beating his schoolfellows at every game, of his claiming that one day he would be Governor of Cyprus and even more, and of his killing two fierce snakes – like Heracles in his cradle – that seem more apocryphal than true.[5] More seriously, the village schoolmaster believed that such a bright pupil must have the chance of further education. There was a gymnasium or Greek secondary school in Paphos, but going there was impossible because the boy would have nowhere to live. The Church was the only way of escape from the drudgery of peasant life. Christodoulos was disappointed that his eldest son would not be following in his footsteps, but he was persuaded by the schoolmaster to apply for Michael's admission to Kykko Monastery some fifteen miles away over the mountain, to be educated in the school there and to train to become a priest.

One day in September 1926, when Michael was thirteen, his father took him and his school-friend, Antony Erotokritou, another likely lad, over the rough tracks to Kykko. The schoolmaster was waiting at the monastery and presented them to the Abbot, Cleopas. After talking to the boys he presently indicated that Michael was acceptable as a novice, but rejected Antony as being too small and looking too young, though they were the same age. The schoolmaster pleaded for both of his pupils, but they were sent back to their village to await instructions. At the beginning of October Michael alone was summoned to Kykko. He went with mixed feelings, but a few weeks later Antony was sent for, and subsequently another boy from Ano Panayia joined them.[6]

At first Michael was a little homesick, but when he climbed the hill above the monastery he could see the houses of his village gleaming in the distance across the valley.

2 Cloistered Monk

Kykko Monastery stands on a triangular, wind-swept site some 3800 feet above sea-level; from it there are impressive views across to the highest peak in Troodos eight miles away. The monastery dates from about 1100 and is the largest and richest foundation in Cyprus; it ranks in prestige in the Orthodox world with St Catherine's in Sinai and the monasteries of Mt Athos. Kykko acquired its great wealth largely through the gifts of pilgrims – many of them from Tsarist Russia – who came for centuries to venerate the miracle-working icon of the Panayia presented to it by its first patron, the Byzantine Emperor Alexios Comnenos; the icon is another reputedly painted by St Luke. In more recent times Kykko has depended on the revenue from its large estates and investments in Cyprus. It has several monastic dependencies (*metokhia*), of which the best-known is the great square Metokhi on the outskirts of Nicosia, not far from the ruins of the presidential palace, the former Government House.

Today Kykko has only a handful of monks and usually not more than two or three novices, though it can accommodate a thousand visitors when they come for the great festivals of the Church and the attendant fairs. The present buildings are of no great antiquity since the monastery has often been destroyed by fire. But there are stone cells where you must stoop to enter by a door in a three-foot-thick wall, yet will find electric light, running water and even a shower and a modern w.c. among the amenities inside. When Michael Mouskos became a novice in 1926 the community of monks was much larger and their life more primitive and self-contained. The journey down to Nicosia – two hours now by car – required a couple of days on the back of a mule; it was not lightly undertaken and seldom permitted.

Michael Christodoulou – he now dropped the name Mouskos – joined the other boy-novices in the routine of the monastic life. Winter and summer they were woken by the harsh clanging of the bell in the tower between the two courtyards, to dress hurriedly and attend the first service in the church at half past five. Then there was a frugal Greek breakfast, at which the boys would serve the abbot and his monks with tiny cups of black coffee, dry rusks and occasionally cheese or hard Cypriot sausages, afterwards scrambling for what was left. There were lessons in the morning, and then work about the monastery buildings or in the kitchen garden – drawing water from the well, cleaning out the refectory and the cells, gathering herbs and salad vegetables, whitewashing the stone walls and seeing to the supply of candles of all sizes for religious and domestic use. The midday meal would most often be beans cooked in the heavy oil of Cyprus, with bread and olives and more cheese. Meat was seldom eaten except at Easter and other festivals and fish was practically unknown. The boys would play while the monks took their siesta. Then there was the afternoon service at four o'clock and afterwards, in the summer months, an hour or two of daylight before the evening meal and an early bed. Only the most studious would go back to his books by candle-light at the end of a long day.

The boys had discarded their village clothes of shorts and shirt when they entered the monastery. Now they wore the Turkish *vraka* or baggy trousers and, on formal occasions, a black cassock and the novice's small round hat.

Michael Christodoulou was something of an odd one. He preferred going for long solitary walks to playing with the other boys. He studied well, without difficulty, but was often pert in his manner and inclined to answer back. Chrysostomos, who later became Abbot of Kykko, kept many memories of the years during which, as *ephoros*, or supervisor, he was responsible for the education and training of the young Michael, who also acted as his personal servant.[1] On one occasion when Michael was clearing away in the refectory he dropped some plates and broke them. Chrysostomos made him promise to be more careful. A few days later he saw the boy crossing one leg over the other, playing some game as he carried a pile of dishes; he told him to put them down and then cuffed him. Michael complained indignantly that it was unfair: he had not been punished when he did break something, and now he was hit when he had not broken anything. Chrysostomos gently reminded the young sophist that he had broken his promise; that was the reason for the cuff. Michael accepted the explanation, evidently with that respect for precision balancing an awareness of the value of ambiguity, which he displayed so much in later life.

On another occasion Chrysostomos fancied sausages for breakfast. Michael told him there were none left. Chrysostomos was sure he had seen some: what had happened to them? Michael explained, with no trace of embarrassment, that he had given them to the monastery cats because they were hungry. Makarios's affection for animals and his interest in natural history were uncharacteristic of the Greek Cypriot; they were part of his inherent gentleness.

In class he was quick at repartee. He grew bored when his fellow-pupils were slow to grasp the intricacies of Greek grammar. Once the teacher, seeing his impatience, said: 'Michael, you don't agree with my method of instruction?' 'Oh no', he answered: 'It's the grammar that doesn't agree!'

Occasionally the novices were allowed to visit their families. The three boys from Ano Panayia would borrow mules from the monastery for the journey and ride triumphantly into the village, to the great admiration of their younger brothers and sisters and the secret pride of their elders, especially the schoolmaster.[2]

If the immediate purpose of the school at Kykko was to prepare young Cypriots for the life of a priest or monk, its overriding mission – like that of the monastery itself and of the whole Church of Cyprus – was to keep alive the flame of Hellenism in an island which, almost throughout its history, had been subject to foreign domination. The earliest Greek-speaking settlers – Mycenaeans – reached Cyprus probably around the middle of the second millennium BC. Thereafter the local Greek element never disappeared, though the island was dominated successively by Egyptians, Assyrians, Phoenicians, Persians, Ptolemaic Greeks, Romans, Byzantine Greeks, Arabs, Franks, Venetians and Turks before the arrival of the British.

The Church of Cyprus traces its origin back to the Apostle Barnabas, a Greek Cypriot, who together with St Paul converted the Roman governor of the island to Christianity in AD 45. Four centuries later an astute Archbishop of Cyprus, Anthemios, managed to throw off patriarchal control from Antioch and to get the Byzantine Emperor Zeno to confirm that his Church was independent ('Autocephalous'). Since then the Archbishop of Cyprus has ranked in dignity with the Patriarchs of Constantinople, Alexandria, Antioch and Jerusalem. Every holder of the office has enjoyed the right, conferred by the Emperor Zeno, of wearing a cope of imperial purple, carrying a gold and silver sceptre instead of a pastoral staff, and signing his name in imperial red ink.

The Church of Cyprus suffered badly during the Frankish (Lusignan) and Venetian periods, between the twelfth and the sixteenth centuries. Its property was confiscated and its hierarchy subordinated to the Latin Church. However, when the Turks took Cyprus in 1571, they restored the Greek Church to its former position and, following their usual practice with subject peoples, made the Archbishop responsible for the good behaviour of his flock and subsequently for collecting the 'tribute' for the Sultan. From this developed the concept of the Archbishop as Ethnarch (the 'national leader').

By the middle of the eighteenth century the Archbishop of Cyprus generally exercised more power than the Turkish Governor who was, in theory, his overlord. In some cases he used it to improve the condition of his people by bargaining with the Ottoman Government at the Porte; in others he and his bishops were more rapacious than the Turks in screwing the last piastre out of the peasant. Greek Cypriot propagandists have claimed that the Church was always in the forefront of a struggle for freedom and – after 1821, when it first became possible – for Union (Enosis) with an independent Greece. The truth is not so simple. In 1785 part of the Turkish garrison in Cyprus revolted because of a collective fine imposed by the Porte on both communities for an earlier riot. The revolt was put down after more than a year only when Archbishop Païsios and two of his bishops had appealed to the Sultan for help. In 1804 Archbishop Chrysanthos had to get troops from Constantinople to suppress another Turkish rising – this time in protest against excessive taxation levied by the Greeks.

When the mainland Greeks launched their War of Independence against Turkey in 1821, Archbishop Kyprianos promised them money and supplies but excused himself from joining more actively in the revolt on the grounds that Cyprus was too far from Greece and too close to Turkey. The Greek revolutionary organisation then asked that the Cypriots should make a specially large contribution to the war effort since they had virtually governed themselves for so long. Unfortunately some revolutionary propaganda from the mainland fell into the hands of the Turkish Governor of Cyprus who suspected the worst and had Kyprianos and his bishops executed, in spite of arguments from the Sultan that the Christian inhabitants of Cyprus had never been 'guilty of the slightest disloyalty to our government'.

These three archbishops – Païsios, Chrysanthos and Kyprianos – all helped to maintain and extend the predominantly Greek character of Cyprus by building schools, restoring churches and monasteries and generally improving the administration of the island in the interests of their community. They did much to erase from the minds of Western travellers the earlier reputation of the Cypriot clergy for ignorance, tyranny and self-indulgence. And Kyprianos and his bishops became – undeservedly – the first martyrs in the cause of Enosis.[3]

For the next fifty years the Archbishop's temporal powers were strictly regulated by the Porte. The desire for Enosis burned fiercely among Greek Cypriot teachers and lawyers who had been to Athens and seen the new Greek state. The Church encouraged their belief that they should be part of it. But there was no political agitation for Enosis while the Turks were ultimately masters; there was no forum for it and the mass of the Greek Cypriot population was apathetic. However, when Britain took over the administration of the island from 'the sick man of Europe' in 1878, the Greek Cypriot hierarchy and the intellectuals warmly welcomed the change. They expressed the hope that the freedom-loving British, who had ceded the Ionian islands to Greece in 1864, would soon do the same with Cyprus. The Turkish Cypriots prayed they would not.

Gladstone said perceptively in 1880 that, 'since the bulk of the people of Cyprus are Greeks', the more Britain did to improve their lot, the quicker would be the growth of Greek national sentiment and of their desire for union with a free Greece. Once the island had obtained for the first time – in 1882, at the insistent demand of the Archbishop – a representative assembly, its nine elected Greek Cypriot members constituted themselves a permanent Opposition, judging every legislative proposal by the extent to which it might shorten the path to Enosis. The three elected Turkish Cypriots and the six nominated members of the Council invariably blocked any attempt by the Enotists to get more control of the island's affairs, and the High Commissioner, afterwards the Governor, had the casting vote. Cyprus had lost much of the strategic value which Disraeli saw in it after the British occupied Egypt (in 1882), but no government at Westminster for nearly eighty years could contemplate relinquishing the island, except in dire necessity. The British attitude to the Greek Cypriot clamour for Enosis was justified by the young Winston Churchill when he visited Cyprus as Under-Secretary of State for the Colonies in 1907: 'I think it is only natural', he said, 'that the Cypriot people who are of Greek descent should regard their incorporation with what may be called their mother country as an ideal to be earnestly, devoutly and fervently cherished.' He went on to say: 'On the other hand, the opinion held by the Moslem population of the island that the British occupation of Cyprus should not lead to the dismember-ment of the Ottoman Empire ... is one which His Majesty's Government are equally bound to regard with respect.' For years afterwards the Enotists ignored the second statement and wilfully misinterpreted the first to mean that all Cypriots were Greek. But the Churchillian argument lost much of its force when Britain annexed Cyprus and later made it a Crown Colony.

It was a long time before the Church of Cyprus recovered the power it had lost. This was not only because the British refused to recognise the Ottoman concept of the Archbishop as Ethnarch or leader of a subject people. When the relatively mild Sophronios died in 1900 the archiepiscopal throne remained empty for nine years. The Bishop of Paphos, as statutory Locum Tenens, should have arranged the election of a new archbishop, but he had prede-ceased Sophronios. For nearly a decade the political passions of the Greek Cypriots were mainly focused on the often violent feud between the supporters of the two remaining bishops, Cyril of Kitium and Cyril of Kyrenia. Each in turn eventually succeeded to the Throne of Barnabas. But another long gap in its occupancy fol-lowed in 1933.

In 1931, while Michael Christodoulou was still a novice at Kykko, the agitation for Enosis flared into sudden violence. There were several reasons for this. The general economic depression in the West had also affected Cyprus. When the colonial government introduced a Bill to increase taxes and customs duties in order to offset the trade deficit, the Greek Cypriot members of the Legislat-ive Council – with the support for once of a Turk – voted it down. The Governor, Sir Ronald Storrs, thereupon resorted to an Order-in-Council to put the measure through. The Greek Cypriots were already smouldering with resentment over the recent statement in London by the Chancellor of the Exchequer, Mr Philip Snowden, that an accumulated Cypriot surplus was being used as a sinking fund for the Ottoman Loan which Britain had guaranteed in 1855. All the petitions and memorials on the subject of Enosis that Greek Cypriot organisations had addressed to the British Government with such monotonous regularity, only to have them rejected with the stock answer that the subject was not for discussion, were now so much combustible material waiting for a spark.

The Greek Cypriot members of the Legislative Council debated for a long time what form their protest should take. Eventually, on 17 October, they met to consider a manifesto drawn up by one of their number, the militant Bishop of Kitium, Nicodemos, probably with the help of the Greek consul-general in Nicosia, Alexis Kyrou. Because of the strong language of the document, which denounced British rule as 'this abomination' and called for its overthrow, some of the Council members accepted it in principle but insisted that they should look at the manifesto again in a week's time. However the bishop jumped the gun, published the manifesto, tendered his resignation from the Council and on 20 October delivered an impassioned address at the Limassol sports ground and 'Enosis' Club, calling for civil disobedience. The audience's response was cautious, but a blown-up account of the meeting reached Nicosia and convinced the other Greek Cypriot members of the Council that the bishop was stealing a march on them. A demonstration was hastily organised and suddenly on the evening of 21 October a large crowd began to move towards Government House. It was led by the chief priest of the popular Phaneromeni Church – Dionysios Kykkotis (a 'graduate' of the monastery) – who carried a Greek flag. The march had begun as an emotional gesture rather than an act of insurrection. There was nothing new in the people shouting 'Enosis' slogans. But when the police – who included Greeks as well as Turks – tried to disperse the crowd with their batons, tempers were lost, stones were thrown, blazing rags were pushed through the broken windows, and in a few minutes the old pre-fabricated hut that had been sent out from England in 1878 to act as Government House went up in flames. The myth of resistance rose from its ashes.[4]

Several people were wounded – one youth fatally – when the police opened fire. As the news spread, violence broke out in other towns and many of the villages. The Governor brought in extra troops from Egypt, but there was little difficulty in suppressing the scattered, uncoordinated riots of an unarmed people. Six persons were killed, more than 2000 were subsequently convicted of 'offences connected with the disturbances' – which included looting – and ten were banished from Cyprus indefinitely. Foremost among them were Bishop Nicodemos of Kitium, his milder colleague, Makarios of Kyrenia, and Dionysios Kykkotis, the priest who had led the march on Government House; there were also two Communist leaders and a certain Savvas Loïzides, who was to reappear nearly a quarter of a century later in a more determined effort to achieve Enosis.

The news of the Nicosia riot reached Kykko as an epic story of the people defying tyranny and striking a blow for freedom, with its hero a priest who had once been a novice at the monastery. Michael Christodoulou, now just eighteen, wrote on a wall in the monks' kitchen: *Zito i Enosis*, Long Live Union [with Greece], and added his initials. Years afterwards, as President, Makarios would say with a twinkle in his eyes that disavowed any real involvement at the time: 'That was my first political statement'.

Two years later, at the somewhat advanced age of twenty. Michael Christodoulou was sent down to Nicosia to complete his formal education at the Pancyprian Gymnasium. His two friends from Ano Panayia went with him and all three lodged in the Kykko Metokhi. Each of them now took the surname Kykkotis to show their spiritual brotherhood. Michael's leaving certificate from the Kykko school gave his final examination grade as *arista* (excellent). He was entered in the fourth class – the third from the top – along with some secular sixteen-year-olds.[5]

The Pancyprian traces its origin to a school founded by the unfortunate Archbishop Kyprianos in 1812; it was inaugurated as the island's principal Greek secondary school in 1893. The gymnasium is housed in a long, low building, in pseudo-classical style, opposite the old ramshackle archbishopric which with its appendage has become, since Independence, a triple museum dedicated to Greek Cypriot folk art, icons and the National Struggle. The handsome modern archbishopric also faces the school but is separated from its predecessor by the 'cathedral' church of St John. For more than half a century the archbishopric and the Pancyprian Gymnasium were the twin poles of a battery that constantly charged the Greek Cypriot community with the powerful current of nationalism.

Most of the teachers in the Pancyprian were graduates of Greek universities – Athens or Salonika. The curriculum they followed was, by an early decision of the British Government, under Greek Cypriot control and virtually identical with that of any gymnasium in Greece. The history taught was the history of Greece, not that of England or the British Empire, and there was special emphasis on the role of Cyprus in classical and Byzantine times and under the Turks. The teaching was generally old-fashioned and academic, with much learning by rote and little discussion or analysis, though Michael Kykkotis proved an argumentative pupil. There was little open Enosis propaganda at this time but a clever teacher could instil a sense of continuous struggle when he traced the history of Greek and Greek Cypriot subjugation to foreign overlords or pointed to the steady geographical expansion of the modern Greek state.

The young monk showed no particular interest in the politics of Enosis while he was at the Pancyprian. He was chiefly concerned to acquire that extra learning which would give him status and authority in a society where *o morphomenos anthropos*, the educated man, is regarded with particular respect. He also welcomed the opportunity to perfect his speaking of the Greek language, in the purist but pedantic *katharevousa* form which he admired for its rhetorical possibilities. At an early age he had been impressed by the power of sermons delivered from the pulpit.

Michael Kykkotis spent three years at the Pancyprian, moving up annually from one class to the next with excellent grades. His final report from the 'Sixth' showed that he got – in the system of Greek marking – 10 out of 10 for Religion, French and History, 9 for English and 8 for Ancient Greek and Mathematics – his lowest marks in any subject. His conduct was 'most proper' (*kosmiotati*) or, as we should say, 'excellent'.[6]

After finishing at the Pancyprian in the summer of 1936 Michael returned to Kykko, where presently he was put in charge of the monastery school. He had sobered down since his earlier exuberance as a young novice and now, in his mid-twenties, he acquired the reputation of being a strict but good teacher whose commendation was always valued. In his free time he still showed a love of solitude and preferred taking long walks with a book among the pinewoods of Kykko to sitting and gossiping at the café with the other monks. Opinion was that he would go far, but he expressed no particular ambition except to study in Athens.

The Church of Cyprus was now in very poor shape and the Enosis movement at its lowest ebb. Two of the three bishops had been deported after the 1931 disturbances. The third, Leontios Leontiou of Paphos, had been no less militant than the others but he had escaped deportation because he was out of the island at the time of the riots; he was allowed to return the following year. Although it was now 'sedition' to advocate a change in the sovereignty of Cyprus, Leontios defied the Governor's edict and continued to preach inflammatory sermons, for which he was charged, convicted, bound over and more than once put under police supervision and restricted to the town of Paphos. But his was almost a lone voice in the island. The Archbishop, the mild and moderate Cyril III, died in 1933. Leontios, as Locum Tenens, should have held elections to the archiepiscopal throne but he refused to do so while his fellow bishops were exiled. So the Church's political leadership declined. Nationalist passions had been further damped down by the abolition of the Legislative Council, the imposition of direct rule and the passing of a series of repressive laws. These forbade the flying of the Greek flag and the playing of the Greek national anthem except on appropriate occasions, restricted the ringing of church bells and prohibited meetings of more than five persons without the permission of the district commissioner. Political organisations were banned and there was also a strict censorship of newspapers and books. The Governor took over the ultimate control of primary education and from 1936 onwards secondary schools in Cyprus received government grants only if they conformed to standards and regulations laid down by the British Director of Education. Almost all the Greek gymnasia, including the Pancyprian, preferred to keep their independence and not compromise their Hellenism. However the agitation for Enosis had now shifted to the groups of exiles in London or Athens. And the Church of Cyprus received another blow when two new laws of 1937 disqualified any person deported or convicted of sedition from being elected archbishop and stipulated that the choice must also have the approval of the Governor. The Throne of Barnabas stayed empty.

The new director of Kykko monastery school had introduced a livelier method of instruction than he had known there himself, but he soon found the environment too cramping for his energies. After a year of teaching the young novices he succeeded in getting himself appointed to the post of secretary to the monastery council, which had its offices at the Metokhi in Nicosia. Here, apart from attending to administrative matters at which he was most competent, he was able to urge upon his superiors his desire to go to Athens to study theology.

But first there was one important step to take. On 7 August 1938, just before his twenty-fifth birthday, Michael Christodoulou Kykkotis was ordained deacon by the Locum Tenens, Bishop Leontios, in Phaneromeni Church. Now the long-time novice broke his last links with the laity, shed his old names and entered the Church as Deacon Makarios. It was a good choice of name. It had a serene and spiritual sound – Makarios means blessed – and it flattered the old exiled Bishop of Kyrenia who bore the same name and was much admired by the young deacon.

There was a vacancy for him in Paphos, where the people of his own district might have come to see and hear him. But the following month Makarios had gained his point and was off to enrol as a student in the theological school of the University of Athens with a meagre grant of about seven pounds a month from Kykko Monastery. It was September 1938. The war-clouds were gathering over Europe. Chamberlain had just returned from Munich with the promise of 'Peace in our time'.

3 Student at Large

In 1938 Athens was still a small, semi-oriental, semi-Balkan city of barely 500,000 inhabitants. There were no tourist tavernas in the unspoilt Plaka below the Acropolis, and the waiters sauntered with their trays and complete unconcern across the roads around Constitution Square. But it was bewildering enough for the young Makarios who had never seen anything bigger than Nicosia.

He found suitable lodgings with a friendly landlady and began to explore the city. There were beautiful old Byzantine churches that surpassed any in Cyprus. He climbed the Acropolis and scrambled over the rocks of the Areopagus nearby to see where St Paul, the companion of his own Church's founder St Barnabas, had later preached to the Athenians about 'the Unknown God'.

Years afterwards Makarios spoke of his admiration for the sculpture of Athens, but he seems to have been impressed less by the classical austerity of the statues and reliefs in the museums and on the Acropolis than by a sculptured tomb in a modern cemetery which bore the somewhat sentimentalised marble figure of a sleeping girl – 'so life-like', he said, 'that you feel at any moment you will see her breathing'.[1]

The main part of the University of Athens is housed in a polychrome neo-classical building midway between Constitution and Omonoia Squares. Here for the next four years Makarios attended theological lectures and studied the early Fathers of the Church. He developed a particular interest in Origen, the third-century Alexandrian Greek philosopher-theologian, who often fell foul of his superiors and was eventually denounced for heresy. Makarios was inclined to share Origen's view that sinners would not be punished in hell for ever and that good must eventually triumph over evil. He also respected the Alexandrian for his reputedly prodigious memory and ability to dictate to eight scribes simultaneously.[2]

Makarios was at the beginning of his third year at the theological school when Mussolini's forces invaded Greece, in October 1940. The Italians were soon pushed back into Albania but in April 1941 the full weight of the German war machine was thrown in and the Greek Government capitulated. Makarios, as a British subject, might have been interned. He tried to return to Cyprus but the ship on which he was due to sail was bombed and sunk by the Germans, so he had no alternative but to stay and endure the occupation. He lived through the grim winter of 1941–2 when people died on the streets of Athens from cold and hunger. Once he had a bad attack of bronchial pneumonia. Makarios's peasant toughness and the austerity to which he had become accustomed at Kykko enabled him to survive, but he claimed later that he had been too weak to consider joining the Resistance.

Makarios graduated from the theological school in the summer of 1942. From 1941 he had helped to support himself by officiating as deacon at the normally fashionable Church of St Irene down in Aiolou Street near the Acropolis. But he continued to study and in 1944, around the time of the liberation of Greece by the Allies, he entered the law school of Athens University. The future was still uncertain, he was in no particular hurry to go back to Cyprus and, as with so many Greeks, the subtleties of the law fascinated him.

On 13 January 1946 – another of the significant '13s' in his life – Makarios was ordained priest and archimandrite at St Irene's Church. He was now thirty-two. He was appointed to the working-class parish of St Paraskevi in the port of Piraeus and managed to combine his ministry there with his legal studies. But this did not last long. Suddenly, in the opening-up of travel and educational facilities after the Second World War, Makarios as a bright young priest was awarded a scholarship and a grant from the World Council of Churches to pursue his theological studies further in the United States. He left for Boston, Massachusetts, in September 1946.

Before he set out on this long adventure Makarios returned to Cyprus to see his family and friends. It is surprising he had not done so earlier – as soon as the German occupation of Greece had ended – given the normal Greek's attachment to his family and the warmth of Makarios's nature. He had been away for eight years. His old mentor, Chrysostomos, and the other monks at Kykko were delighted to see the prodigy they had produced. He was invited to preach a number of sermons and to speak on the 'National Question' – Enosis. Makarios's vibrant voice, his command of language, his knowledge of Greece and what she had suffered, and his obvious erudition made an impression that lasted after he had gone back to Athens to sail for America.[3]

It was during his last year in Greece that Makarios first met Lt-Col George Grivas, the man with whom his name was to be linked for so long in the militant campaign for Enosis.[4] Grivas had been born in 1898, the son of a prosperous corn-merchant in the village of Trikomo, not far from Famagusta, the eastern port of Cyprus. At the age of eleven he was sent to the Pancyprian Gymnasium where he did little to distinguish himself academically but tried to compensate for his very small size – he was well under average height – by hardening himself as an athlete. He claimed to have won the 100, 200 and 400 metre races as well as the high jump in his last year at the gymnasium.

Grivas grew up in the period of the Balkan Wars and his whole ambition was to become a soldier and fight for a 'Greater Greece'. He went to Athens in 1916, gained a commission and first saw active service in the disastrous Greek expedition into Asia Minor in 1922 – a chauvinistic attempt to recover ancient Greek lands encouraged unwisely by the Allies. Grivas went through the traumatic experience of a crushing defeat by the Turks. In 1940, when Italy invaded Greece, Grivas was posted as chief of staff to the 2nd Army Division. Again there was ultimate defeat, this time by the Axis powers. In 1943 he formed a secret organisation of Royalist officers and NCOs, which he called by the Greek letter 'X' (*Khi*). Its aim was not to harass the occupation forces but to be ready to neutralise the main Greek resistance movement, the Communist-led EAM, when the Germans left. After the liberation of Greece in 1944, Grivas's *Khi* became notorious as a paramilitary organisation of fascist thugs who brutally tried to impose their own kind of order on the Greek countryside. When Grivas turned *Khi* into a political party it failed to secure a single seat in parliament.

The meeting between the young Cypriot priest and the fiery little colonel with the lean, hungry look and the Groucho Marx moustache came about because Makarios had written some articles for the *Khi* newspaper, attacking Communism from a Christian standpoint. This, it must be remembered, was after the

Communists had failed in their first post-liberation attempt to get control of Greece – thanks to British intervention – but were preparing for the next 'round'. Grivas was already embittered by his own lack of recognition and by what he saw as British indifference to the Communist danger in Greece. But he had not yet formed any plan for liberating his native Cyprus from the British yoke or for countering the threat there from the Communist-led AKEL, which had profited by the Church's weakness to make itself the only effective political movement in the island. There were still strong Greek and Greek Cypriot hopes that in the post-war atmosphere Britain must surely recognise the justice of the demand for Enosis. Greek Cypriots had been exhorted to fight 'for Greece and freedom'; it was not surprising if they identified the two goals. In 1946 Grivas and Makarios were no more than fellow-Cypriots meeting casually in their common motherland.

The voyage to the United States was a nightmare. To save money Makarios had booked the cheapest passage possible on a cargo boat. He found himself sharing a cramped space near the engine-room with members of the crew and the ship's cat. In spite of his fondness for cats, the animal's nocturnal prowlings, together with the changes of the watch and the noise of the engines, made sleep almost impossible. The dirt and the clinging smell of hot grease were also a great trial to Makarios, who was always fastidious about personal cleanliness. Fortunately there was a well-to-do American Greek travelling cabin-class, who struck up a friendship with the young priest and got him moved to a more private and comfortable berth. The ship spent three weeks 'tramping' round Mediterranean ports before it started the voyage proper. There was a violent storm near the Straits of Gibraltar and Makarios found himself giving priestly consolation to a young Greek bride who thought her last hour had come. The voyage took seven weeks, but the relief of being on dry land again was tempered by the overwhelming impact of New York. Makarios was met by a woman from the Methodist Society which was sponsoring his visit and settled in a hotel. He waited there miserably for several days, not having understood – with his then very limited English – that he was expected to make the next contact. The noise and bustle of New York terrified him and made the once bewildering Athens seem like a quiet, friendly town.

When the Methodists found him again they explained that he

could not begin his studies at the theological college in Boston until the new term started in January. He was sent to their Fellowship Centre at Wallingford, near Philadelphia, to spend the next two or three months becoming acclimatised. The atmosphere was friendly. The young Methodist ministers, training in practical subjects as well as in theology before going off to serve in poor parishes, impressed Makarios with their down-to-earth Christianity. They helped him with his English and the director of the Centre took a particular interest in the shy and modest young Cypriot, showing him how to shop and find his way about. Makarios had Christmas dinner at the director's house, where a Greek American family had thoughtfully been included among the guests. He was surprised to see everybody – even the men – helping to clear away and wash up after the meal: it was so different from Cyprus – and Greece – where the household chores are entirely reserved for the women.[5] Makarios began to find the American way of life very attractive.

At thirty-three he was a good-looking, personable young man, of a little more than average height and without that formidable stature that his archbishop's headgear later gave him. He had left the *rasa* – the black, swirling robes of the Orthodox cleric – and the stove-pipe hat behind him in Athens. Now, clean-shaven except for a neat but thick moustache and without the Greek priests' 'bun', he looked like a 'nice young curate', even to the Protestant 'dog-collar' which he took to wearing. His hair was somewhat thin and receded from a high, intelligent forehead, but the clever brown eyes, already slightly hooded, had a warmth and humour in them that conveyed great charm. His hands were soft and well-manicured and his dress invariably neat. Both in Greek and in English he spoke slowly, as if savouring the words. Later, except in flights of oratory, this was to develop into a slightly 'prissy' manner, though he compensated for it by the attentiveness with which he listened to the other speaker.

The year and a half that Makarios spent at Boston were uneventful. He followed the theological lectures as best he could and continued to read indefatigably. He came to know several Greek American communities and was not without social life. Women found him attractive because of his gentle courtesy, but as an ordained priest of the Orthodox Church marriage was now forbidden to him. He had friendships with women in the United States which continued after his return to Cyprus. But there is no evidence that he ever lost his virginity.[6]

Meanwhile the political situation in Cyprus was changing. In October 1946, as Makarios was about to make his first acquaintance with the United States, the British Secretary of State for the Colonies in the new post-war Labour Government, Mr Arthur Creech-Jones, announced that the Governor of Cyprus was to summon a representative Consultative Assembly to work out a new and more liberal constitution for the island. There was also to be a ten-year programme for economic development and social welfare. The 1937 laws about the election of an archbishop were to be repealed and those deported in 1931 were to be allowed to return.

Bishop Leontios of Paphos, the Locum Tenens, and his Ethnarchy Council immediately rejected the offer of a constitution. The Greek Cypriot political parties which had been allowed to emerge during the war to encourage morale joined in the denunciation and, together with the Church, demanded Union with Greece as the only acceptable solution. Creech-Jones replied that no change in the sovereignty of Cyprus was contemplated.

The Bishop of Kyrenia returned to Cyprus in February 1947; his fellow exile, the Bishop of Kitium, had died in Palestine some years before. Eventually the long-overdue elections for an archbishop were held and on 20 June Leontios, the Locum Tenens, was swept to victory largely by a left-wing vote. But the man who had fought for Enosis so long from the foot of the throne occupied it only for five weeks. He died on 26 July, after a short and sudden illness. The old but still vigorous Bishop of Kyrenia, the only Metropolitan left, was presently elected Archbishop as Makarios II and set himself to rally the so-called 'nationalist' forces against the left-wing AKEL.

The election of Leontios had left the see of Paphos vacant. AKEL suddenly remembered the bright young priest who had preached so eloquently and was now studying in America. Makarios was told he would have the full support of the Left as the most suitable candidate for the Paphos bishopric. But the Nationalists were backing Cleopas, the Abbot of Kykko, and Makarios declared he could not think of opposing his spiritual father.[7] In fact, he was not at all interested in the idea of becoming a bishop.

Some months later, in the spring of 1948, when Makarios was in his second year at Boston, he received a telegram from Cyprus informing him that he had been elected Bishop of Kitium.[8] This time it was by the Nationalist vote in opposition to the candidate put forward by the Left. The news was not at all welcome. Makarios was enjoying life in the United States and engrossed in his studies on 'the sociology of religion'. But the more influential members of the Holy Synod – his namesake, Archbishop Makarios II, the former Abbot of Kykko, Cleopas, now Bishop of Paphos, and the new Abbot, Chrysostomos, Makarios's old teacher – wanted this talented young man to impart a new drive to the campaign for Enosis.

Reporters appeared at the theological college. 'Are you the secretary to Bishop Makarios?' they asked the bland young man sitting at his books. 'No, I am Makarios', he said. 'How old are you? Are you married? Why have you not got a beard?' He was besieged with questions. The next day there were headlines: 'College Student Elected Bishop'.

PART TWO

HARVEST

4 The Bishop's Throne

Makarios was reluctant to accept his election as bishop for several reasons. He wanted to complete his studies at Boston. He had hopes of becoming a professor of theology at Athens University. Alternatively there was the possibility of staying on in the United States and serving as priest in one of the many Greek communities there. The American way of life had made a strong appeal to him, in spite of his Orthodox Church background and his personal austerity. Cyprus was a very small pond to return to after swimming so free.

Makarios had to be persuaded by the Holy Synod that it was his duty to respect the verdict of the people. (In theory, Cypriot bishops are chosen democratically; in practice, the hierarchy usually decides on the man it wants, though he must also have strong political backing from the Right or the Left.)[1] Makarios insisted that he should remain a few more weeks at Boston to round off his work. This also gave him time to start growing a beard again, which he was loth to do. Since the beard became so much a part of his physical image later – a gift to cartoonists even when they made it the wrong shape – Makarios's dislike of growing one may appear odd. It seems to have been due partly to his fastidiousness about his person, partly to a certain obstinate nonconformity, and it went back to his youth. Lord Caradon, formerly Sir Hugh Foot, the last Governor of Cyprus, recalls the story Archbishop Makarios told against himself after a celebration dinner at the Kykko Metokhi in 1960 to mark the end of the long-drawn-out haggling between himself and the British Government over the independence agreements. Makarios looked across benevolently at Abbot Chrysostomos. He told the company how his early mentor and spiritual father had once beaten him towards the end of his novitiate

31

because he refused to grow a beard in preparation for his life in the Church. Neither blows nor pleading made him change his view that he was not ready to take this step. In despair Chrysostomos had called for a taxi to take Michael Mouskos back to his village in disgrace. Then, at the last moment – according to Makarios – his old tutor had broken down and thrown his arms around him: 'My boy, come back', he said. 'I cannot let you go.'[2]

Such brinkmanship was later to become a familiar part of Makarios's technique in the difficult situations he encountered, both as Archbishop and as President of Cyprus. In 1948 he had little idea of what lay ahead of him as Bishop of Kitium, outside his religious functions, excepting the commitment to promote the struggle for Enosis. The immediate practical problem – apart from the beard – was for the bishop-elect to appear in Cyprus properly dressed. He sent a telegram to his old landlady in Athens asking her to bring his *rasa* and the stove-pipe hat to the airport. He made a quick change in the plane and stepped out a presentable young Greek priest, even if the beard was still rather small. He stayed in Athens for a while to let it grow longer, and then, when he was satisfied that he was ready for his new role, he flew to Nicosia. He still refused to wear a 'bun' and was the first Cypriot bishop to cut his hair.

There were two ceremonies to be undergone. Both took place on 13 June 1948 – again that auspicious 13! First, in the morning, he was consecrated bishop at the 'cathedral' Church of St John in Nicosia – and it was a long service. Then, in the afternoon, he drove in procession to Larnaca and was enthroned in the cathedral of the diocese before a large crowd of people eager to see their new Metropolitan. For his enthronement address Makarios took as his text the words of St Paul: 'my strength is made perfect in weakness'. He felt that his youth and inexperience required such an approach to his new tasks. He recalled the previous Bishop of Kitium, who had died in exile many years before, and he promised he would try to follow the example of his predecessor's life. Afterwards there was a reception at the Bishop's palace. The guests stayed late. Eventually, at the end of a tiring but uplifting day, Makarios was left alone and wandered through the house that had been unoccupied for so long. The next day he read the reports of his enthronement in the newspapers. One of them ended: 'At last, after many years, the lights of the Bishop's House are shining again'.

Larnaca is built on the site of the ancient Kitium, which gives its name to the bishopric, but the other town in the diocese, Limassol, is larger and more important; it also has another residence and offices for the bishop in a somewhat gloomy building in the centre of the town. The diocese was a part of Cyprus Makarios scarcely knew at all. He planned a programme of visits and within a year had been at least once to every village under his spiritual authority, riding on a mule or a donkey where the roads gave out. He instituted a fund for the clergy, to give each priest a decent stipend. He persuaded a local industrialist to endow an orphange in Larnaca and organised a Brotherhood of Friends of the Poor. The Bishop's palace was in a sad state of decay; Makarios put in hand substantial renovations but his style of life remained simple and unaffected.[3]

Even these activities failed to satisfy Makarios's appetite for work. However, his older namesake, the Archbishop, had other employment for him. Makarios II had already launched a campaign to recover the political initiative from the Left, which had profited by the Church's long paralysis and begun to show an interest in self-government. This had naturally been encouraged by the colonial government, which hoped that by promoting trade unions and cooperatives it could channel away much Enotist sentiment. In 1932 – the year after the banishment of the bishops – Cyprus had only one trade union. By 1944 there were ninety. The number of Cypriots organised in cooperatives rose from a few hundred in 1932 to 37,000 in 1940.[4]

The ban on political parties was lifted early in the Second World War to encourage national sentiment and raise morale. The Left was quick to take advantage of this. In October 1941 the hard core of the old Communist Party of Cyprus (KKK), which had been proscribed in 1933, set up a new Working People's Reform Party, known from its Greek initials as AKEL. It attracted a considerable number of Greek Cypriot intellectuals and professional people as well as trade unionists and members of cooperatives. AKEL soon had a strong popular base in the wide range of welfare activities it organised through the more left-wing trade unions, surpassing anything the government or the right-wing trade unions could offer.

In 1946 a left-wing coalition dominated by AKEL won control of four of the six town councils in Cyprus. This was a serious challenge to the Nationalists and their hopes of Enosis. AKEL had warmly supported the idea of 'national rehabilitation' – in other words, union with Greece – when it looked as if the Communist-led Left would take over in Athens at the end of the German occupation. However, as Greece came under a succession of post-war right-wing governments described by the Left as 'monarcho-fascist', AKEL's enthusiasm for Enosis and its own extinction faded.

When the new Governor of Cyprus, Lord Winster, invited a number of organisations and individuals to take part in a Consultative Assembly to advise on the shape of a new constitution, the Ethnarchy, as we have seen, immediately rejected the offer. AKEL, after some hesitation, accepted it. The Turkish Cypriots also agreed to take part. But the Consultative Assembly soon became deadlocked when the Greek Cypriot members demanded full self-government, which was clearly not intended by the Governor's terms of reference. Months later, in May 1948, the Commonwealth and Colonial Office produced a more elaborate version of the Creech-Jones proposals. They offered a constitution in which the elected representatives of the larger community, the Greek Cypriots, could always outvote the combined forces of the Turkish Cypriots and the nominated British members of the legislature, so long as their aims were not prejudicial to the Turkish Cypriots or to the interests of Britain. Bills affecting defence, external affairs, finance, minorities and the constitution were not to be introduced without the consent of the Governor, and there was to be no discussion of the island's status. The proposed constitution was only a first step in self-government for a people who had had little experience of political responsibility. But even to many who were not thinking of Enosis it was an affront; it seemed designed for a people just emerging from the jungle rather than for civilised Greeks who had invented democracy.

Three weeks before Makarios's enthronement the Consultative Assembly accepted the government's proposals by eleven votes to seven. Of those who voted in favour of the new constitution six were Turkish Cypriots who had been individually invited to join the Assembly. The minority vote against the proposals came from the elected left-wing mayors and the trade union representatives – all Greek Cypriots. In these circumstances Lord Winster had no option but to report failure.

Although the left-wing Greek Cypriots ostentatiously withdrew from the Consultative Assembly, the Church was quick to exploit their embarrassment at ever having seemed ready to abandon the 'national cause' for the sake of a delusive self-government. In July 1948 the Archbishop reorganised the old Ethnarchy Council – which included laymen as well as clerics – to make it more effective for promoting the struggle for Enosis. Subsequently a smaller Ethnarchy Bureau was created as its 'inner cabinet' and executive arm. The young and talented Bishop of Kitium became its first chief.

Makarios threw himself into the work of the Ethnarchy Bureau with great zest – more, it seems, to unite Greek Cypriots under the leadership of the Church than with any expectation of achieving the age-old dream of Enosis. Unlike the Archbishop he was not fanatically anti-Communist. As a churchman he could not accept the ideology of the Left but he knew that many of those who voted for AKEL were far from being Marxists. He had no personal antipathy towards AKEL's leadership – men like the Moscow-trained Ezekias Papaioannou, its secretary-general, or Andreas Ziartides, who ran the left-wing trade unions – but he saw the Church as upholding the true values of Cypriot Hellenism. In fact, at this time, when Greece was locked in a deadly civil war between the Nationalist forces and a Communist-led guerrilla army backed by Greece's northern neighbours, there was even the possibility that Greek freedom might be extinguished on the mainland. It was all the more important, therefore, in Makarios's eyes, that Cyprus should preserve its national identity. The Turkish Cypriots were merely an irrelevance. What mattered was to create a political leadership that could effectively challenge a colonial government which denied the Greek Cypriots their rights as part of a great nation.

So, in April 1949, when the Ethnarchy denounced Communism as the enemy of the nation, the Church and the cause of Enosis, Bishop Makarios's part in this was mainly tactical. Municipal elections were scheduled for the following month. Amid mutual accusations of 'betraying' and 'enslaving' the people, AKEL lost control of the Nicosia town council to the Right – keeping Famagusta, Larnaca and Limassol, while the Nationalists held on to Paphos and Kyrenia. The Church-backed candidates won eleven out of the fifteen smaller municipalities and received 60 per cent of the total vote. This was a great blow to AKEL which had dropped the demand for 'self-government' and was now advocating Enosis as fervently as the Right.

In the same month as the elections Makarios, as chief of the Ethnarchy Bureau, launched a new illustrated periodical, *Elliniki Kypros* (Greek Cyprus) dedicated to the campaign at home and abroad for Enosis. Its editor was the writer and critic, Nikos Kranidiotis, who later, on the proclamation of the Republic, became the Cypriot ambassador to Greece, a post he still held at the time of Makarios's death. The colonial government allowed *Elliniki Kypros* to make its impassioned demands for Union with Greece until long after EOKA's campaign of violence had got under way. It was suppressed only when Makarios was deported to Seychelles in 1956.

The Greek Cypriot Right tried hard to get Athens to take up the 'national cause'. Makarios went to Greece and saw King Paul and a number of political leaders. But there was little response from a Greek government preoccupied with a civil war.

In September 1949, when the Nationalists were getting the upper hand in Greece and the Left in Cyprus knew it could count on no support from that quarter, AKEL tried a new tactic. It suggested to the Ethnarchy that they should jointly take the 'Cyprus question' to the United Nations. The Church rejected this proposal outright. Although it already had ideas of 'internationalising' the issue, it had no desire to enlist the help of the Communists. However, AKEL went ahead on its own. On 23 November it sent a memorandum to the UN Security Council and the General Assembly, denouncing British rule in Cyprus and suggesting that, if there was any doubt about the genuineness of the Greek desire for Enosis, the United Nations should conduct a plebiscite in the island. At the same time AKEL began to collect signatures to support this petition. The Ethnarchy was suddenly afraid of losing the initiative and the right-wing press told the people not to sign.

Then, on 1 December, the Ethnarchy Bureau announced that, under Bishop Makarios's chairmanship, it had taken cognisance of a decision by the Holy Synod *on 18 November* – five days before publication of the AKEL memorandum – that the Church should hold a plebiscite. It still needed a full meeting of the Ethnarchy Council and an encyclical from the Archbishop – proclaiming a plebiscite for 15 January 1950 if the Governor had not decided to hold it himself – to launch the scheme properly.

There is no proof as to which side thought of a plebiscite first.

The idea had been mooted several times before, but had never been taken up. What seems clear is that AKEL forced the hand of the Church by beginning to collect signatures. The Church plebiscite was certainly the 'brainchild' of Makarios.[5] After accusing the Ethnarchy of appropriating its idea, AKEL adroitly cancelled its collection of signatures and ranged itself solidly behind the Church's decision as though it were a victory for the people.

On 12 December the Archbishop wrote to the new Governor, Sir Andrew Wright – Lord Winster had been relieved of his post at his own request – challenging him to hold an honest plebiscite or to accept one organised by the Church. The Governor replied with the usual disdain of the British colonial official for unwelcome mass petitions and referred to a statement by the Greek Foreign Minister as implicitly disapproving of the Ethnarchy's intention. Sir Andrew pointed out that the proposed 'plebiscite' was no more than an attempt to reopen a question which His Majesty's Government had repeatedly said was 'closed'. People, he added, would be asked to vote for something when they knew that their action would have no effect. Many names would be collected because people would be reluctant to refuse their signatures. The Governor concluded with a warning about the danger of public disorder and subscribed himself 'Your humble servant'.

The Archbishop rejected these arguments and Makarios began to organise the 'plebiscite' with a new sense of the power that his position gave him. Sheets for signature were displayed in the churches for a week from 15 to 22 January. There was no secrecy. Bishops, priests and local committees exhorted the people to demonstrate their unquenchable desire for Enosis by adding their names. All Greek Cypriots aged eighteen or over, male or female, were eligible to make the declaration. Whole families signed together, sometimes in tears. Public order was exemplary.

The result was never in doubt. Of the 224,727 Greek Cypriots considered eligible to 'vote', 215,108 were reported to have expressed their desire for Union with Greece. This represented some 95.7 per cent of the chosen 'electorate', or about three-quarters of the whole adult population of Cyprus. The Turkish Cypriots made no attempt to disrupt the proceedings, but they sent a memorandum to the United Nations, declaring they would never allow Enosis since it would ruin Cyprus economically and probably lead to civil war.

The Ethnarchy communicated the result of the 'plebiscite' to the

Governor and called on Britain to respect the people's will in accordance with the liberal principles she always proclaimed. The British Government replied again that the question was closed. Later the Minister of State for the Colonies, Mr John Dugdale, told the House of Commons that the so-called 'plebiscite' proved nothing; in any case, he added, British public opinion, and the Labour Party in particular, disliked plebiscites and referenda because they did not seem to conform to the principles of true democracy.

The British Government made great play with stories of intimidation during the 'plebiscite'. It was said that some priests had threatened to cut off families from the sacraments if they failed to sign. Probably these stories were exaggerated. But in a small, shut-in community it was virtually impossible for a Greek Cypriot to withhold his name without future ostracism, unless he could plead that as a civil servant he would be victimised by the colonial government.

The Archbishop had told the Governor that he would now use 'all internationally-recognised legal means' to achieve the liberation of his people. In mid-February 1950 Bishop Makarios announced that a 'national delegation' would go to Athens, London, other European capitals, the United States and the United Nations to enlighten world opinion. The quiet student of theology was emerging as a politician, eager to measure the strength of his ancient Church against the secular forces that refused national justice.

It was expected that the Bishop of Kitium would lead the delegation himself, in view of his role in organising the 'plebiscite' and his experience abroad. Instead the mission was entrusted to the older Bishop of Kyrenia, Kyprianos, who was known for his fanaticism in the cause of Enosis.

The mission left Cyprus on 14 May and was away for several months. Then something happened which could not have been foreseen but was not completely unexpected. On 28 June the old Archbishop died, at the age of 80. The right-wing 'Committee for the Coordination of the Cypriot Struggle' at once pronounced in favour of Bishop Makarios as his successor. The only possible rival was the absent Bishop of Kyrenia. Bishop Cleopas of Paphos was considered too retiring to be a candidate. However, as Locum Tenens, he issued an encyclical ordering the names of those who held doctrines in conflict with those of the Church – i.e. Communists – to be struck off the electoral rolls. How far, if at all, this affected the result is not clear. The extreme Right lobbied hard in support of the Bishop of Kyrenia. AKEL may well have reckoned that, in spite of his anti-Communism, Kyprianos would be easier to outmanoeuvre than the formidable young Bishop of Kitium. However, Makarios had made an impact on many Greek Cypriots not close to the Church with his youth, his energy, his learning and eloquence and, above all, his personal magnetism – the element so essential to a popular leader. In due course the people chose their local representatives, who then nominated delegates to sit with the bishops and abbots on the electoral board. Eventually, on 18 October 1950, the Bishop of Kitium was elected Archbishop as Makarios III by a majority claimed to represent 97 per cent of the Greek Cypriot people. There were rumours of prolonged gerrymandering behind the scenes. Whatever the truth of these, the Bishop of Kyrenia was convinced that his 'important' mission abroad had conveniently kept him out of Cyprus during the election campaign while his successful rival had all the resources of the Ethnarchy Bureau at his command. Kyprianos never forgave him for this and later became one of Makarios's most bitter opponents.

Makarios was only thirty-seven when he ascended the Throne of Barnabas and so became head of a small but rich and powerful Church which had established its independence fifteen hundred years earlier. He was also Ethnarch – the 'leader of his people' – a title the British had disregarded as an anachronism though the office had again become a political reality. Even the best-organised party in Cyprus, the Communist-led AKEL, had been forced to accept that it could not challenge the Church on its own ground, however much it might denounce individual churchmen or their supporters as reactionaries bent on keeping the people 'enslaved'.

It is difficult to imagine the feelings of Makarios III as he put on the imperial purple of Byzantium and wielded the gold-and-silver sceptre of the Archbishop for the first time. Only two years before he had been a modest young student, aspiring perhaps to a college post in theology. Now the accident of history had thrust a responsibility upon him which he had not consciously sought. It gave him a power that had defied successive overlords for centuries, yet had not set Cyprus free. In the changed circumstances of the modern world everything was possible. At his enthronement Makarios proclaimed that he would fight, however long and difficult the struggle, for the national rehabilitation of Cyprus through the desired union with Greece. The scholar and churchman had become a politician fired with the ambition to win a place in history as the man who brought nearly half a million Greeks back into the national fold.

5 'Enosis and Only Enosis'

Archbishop Makarios saw two important tasks ahead of him at the beginning of his reign – and both were political. The first was to consolidate the power of the Nationalists, the second to 'internationalise' the Cyprus question so that it was no longer a domestic issue between the Greek Cypriots and Britain. The nature of an Orthodox Church – static and ritualistic – made it unnecessary for an archbishop to spend much time on purely religious or ecclesiastical matters, apart from regular celebration of the liturgy, the observance of festivals and the requirements of private prayer. The Church of Cyprus had again assumed a national responsibility – and this was paramount. Oscar Wilde's Canon Chasuble claimed that his sermon on the meaning of the manna in the wilderness could be adapted to almost any occasion, joyful or distressing. Archbishop Makarios could – and did – use every opportunity to make *his* sermons political speeches on the theme of Enosis.

He took enormous care over his sermons, composing them like poems; in fact, the best of them, when written out in short lines, have the structure of free verse. The language was simple and the imagery always vivid and direct. Often it was built around the idea of a toiling, suffering people who thirsted for freedom and longed to be free of a foreign yoke. Then, changing the metaphors, Makarios – especially in the later years – would transform his hearers into soldiers on the battlements, constantly alert against attack, standing firm against every shock, closing the ranks as some of them fell to a martyr's death, never lowering the flag. To a foreign ear the clichés might chink like the small change of a much-debased currency, but to a Greek Cypriot crowd, hearing Makarios speak from the pulpit or from a platform on the walls of Nicosia in Freedom Square above the old moat, the words fell new-minted, challenging and invigor-

41

ating. Like Old Testament psalms, Makarios's speeches relied on the incantatory force of repetition and balanced cadences. He delivered them without notes, after much rehearsal and in a well-modulated voice that he seldom needed to raise. The passion was always controlled and the speech the more compelling because of it.

In pursuit of Makarios's first objective – coordination on the home front – the Ethnarchy Council was again reorganised. Its members now included, apart from the bishops and abbots, most of the leading right-wing politicians, lawyers and journalists – categories that often overlapped. Some were less devoted to Makarios than others – in particular the Bishop of Kyrenia, Kyprianos, who never forgave the man who had stolen a march on him, and Dr Themistocles Dervis, the mayor of Nicosia, who resented the Archbishop's encroachment on his own authority. Nikos Kranidiotis now ran the Ethnarchy Bureau, but its work and the functioning of the 'consultative' Ethnarchy Council were strictly controlled by Makarios. Sometimes, as in April 1952 for the first time, he summoned a 'National Assembly' of representatives from all parts of the island, to emphasise the popular nature of his leadership or to launch some special effort. But this occasional 'Assembly' did little more than endorse the decisions of the Ethnarch.

In the meantime Makarios began to strengthen the Church's influence over other nationalist organisations. Among them were SEK, the smaller, breakaway confederation of the 'new' or right-wing trade unions, and the much more powerful PEK (Pan-agrarian Union of Cyprus), which had a club in almost every village. Control of SEK was achieved through its sycophantic secretary-general, Michael Pissas, who often acted as Makarios's mouthpiece. This enabled the Archbishop to establish contact with the trade union movement in Greece, which in the aftermath of the civil war was solidly right-wing and nationalistic. Even more importantly, in 1949, while Makarios was still Bishop of Kitium and in charge of the Church's propaganda machine, Socrates Loïzideses, a fervent Enotist, was installed as secretary-general of PEK. Like Grivas, he had become a Greek national and had served in the Greek army. In 1950 the colonial government deported Loïzides on the grounds that he had been using the farmers' organisation for subversive purposes. His successor paid more attention to agrarian matters, but in Makarios's eyes he was lukewarm about

Enosis and too ready to support the government's programme for rural development. The Archbishop had to be patient. In 1953 the government published two Bills designed to improve marketing arrangements and to give the farmers better prices for their produce. The wholesalers in the towns feared a cut in their profits and attacked the proposed measures as an attempt to lure the peasants away from the 'national cause'. Archbishop Makarios saw his opportunity and stepped in with the offer of a subsidy to the farmers. At the same time he secured the election of one of his own protégés, Andreas Azinas, to the post of secretary-general of PEK. The Bills were abandoned. Azinas, who had a diploma in agriculture from Reading University, was soon to become one of the founder-members of EOKA, the guerrilla organisation which Colonel Grivas set up in 1955.[1] Loïzides too was one of the original members; he had returned in secret with Grivas. There can be no doubt that Loïzides – and Azinas even more – found PEK invaluable for creating the rural 'sea' which – according to Mao Tse-tung's famous dictum – the guerrillas of a national liberation movement needed to 'swim' in.

But there was still something lacking: a youth movement. This would be all the more necessary if – as Makarios realised – it was likely to be a long struggle. In 1951, a few months after his enthronement as Archbishop, he founded the Pancyprian National Youth Organisation (PEON). It drew its members from the top classes of the Greek gymnasia and from young workers of the same age. Its mission was to inculcate pride in being Greek and to sharpen the desire for Enosis. At the same time it was to combat Communist influence. British government sources said later that Makarios had asked the advice of Grivas on organising PEON. It is true that Grivas went to Cyprus openly, and ostensibly for a holiday, early in July 1951 – his first return to his homeland in twenty years. He saw the Archbishop twice, soon after his arrival and again a month later. Grivas's main interest then was to assess the chances of waging a successful guerrilla war in the island. He recalls in his Memoirs that, in spite of the obvious difficulties, he was satisfied with what he found – apart from Makarios's attitude.[2] Makarios was not only reluctant to resort to violence; he had misgivings even then about the lengths to which the little colonel's fanaticism would carry him. Grivas's post-war *Khi* organisation in Greece had been notorious for the brutal, arrogant behaviour of its young adherents. Although the EOKA young were later to be corrupted by violence, they were on the whole different from the *Khites*. It is unlikely that Archbishop Makarios really looked to Grivas for help with the organisation of PEON – or was offered it from that quarter except in the most general way.

There was already in existence another organisation for the young, more religious than political. This was the Orthodox Christian Union of Youth (OHEN), which appealed particularly to young women. In June 1953 the colonial government refused to renew the registration of the PEON clubs, after some of them had been involved in anti-British demonstrations at the time of Queen Elizabeth II's coronation. PEON thereupon went underground, but many of its members joined OHEN, which subsequently took on a more militant character.

As Makarios strengthened the Church's leadership, he deliberately sought occasions for confrontation with the government. As early as December 1950, barely two months after his installation as Archbishop, the Ethnarchy denounced the government's Improvement Boards – a long-overdue scheme to develop backward rural areas – as mere bait for another constitutional offer. Those who were afraid of offending the Church or of seeming less patriotic than their neighbours wistfully withdrew their co-operation. In August 1952 the government offered to pay the salaries of secondary school teachers where the institutions concerned were prepared to let the government decide the curriculum and control the recruitment of staff. This rather crude attempt to check Enotist indoctrination in the Greek Cypriot gymnasia was immediately rebuffed as a move to 'dehellenise' secondary education and destroy the 'national conscience'. For all that, many Greek Cypriots were proud to be citizens of the British Commonwealth and saw nothing incompatible in that with their desire to be regarded as Greeks.

Throughout the early 1950s AKEL was quite unable to recover the initiative it had taken, and then lost to the Church, during the previous decade. Of necessity it found itself sharing the same political platform as the Ethnarchy, but it was always dangerously near the edge. From time to time AKEL approached the Church with a proposal that they should coordinate their efforts in the common struggle. Makarios always ignored their offers, not so much out of anti-Communism as because he was unwilling to share the leadership. He refrained from attacking the Communists as political opponents – knowing that he needed their support – and left the invective to his more bigoted bishops and the ultra-nationalistic laymen who upheld the Church.

The strategy imposed on AKEL at this time was clearly indicated by the so-called 'Free Greece' radio – a station run by KKE, the Greek Communist Party, from its sanctuary in the Balkans. Broadcasting in November 1951, the station argued that, in the circumstances then prevailing, the 'Enosis' slogan allowed the greatest mobilisation of the people against the forces of imperialism and the reactionaries in Cyprus and Greece. In practice this meant that, while the Nationalists said Britain could have whatever bases she wanted – after Enosis – the Greek and Greek Cypriot Communists proclaimed themselves against all foreign, i.e. Western, bases and looked principally to the Soviet Union for help in internationalising the Cyprus question. That made AKEL's support of Enosis even more suspect, since Moscow had no love of 'monarchofascist' Greece.

While AKEL and the Ethnarchy pursued their seemingly parallel campaigns on the home front, with the Church ever in the ascendant, Archbishop Makarios began to develop his strategy for internationalising the Cyprus question. The delegation led by the Bishop of Kyrenia, which had set out in May 1950 for Athens, London, New York and Paris with the results of the 'plebiscite', had returned in December virtually empty-handed. The British Foreign Secretary, Mr James Griffiths, had refused to see it. At the United Nations the delegates were politely told that only a member-government could raise a question. In Paris they did no more than leave a memorandum at the Quai d'Orsay. Earlier, in Athens, King Paul and his Prime Minister, General Plastiras, had received the delegation, but the Greek Government had shown great caution in answering the Cypriot appeal for action. General Plastiras gave the stock reply that his government would take the matter up with Britain 'within the framework of Anglo-Greek friendship' and when the time was ripe. (Bishop Makarios had already rejected this formula as treacherous evasion.) General Plastiras also pointed out that his government could not officially accept the results of the 'plebiscite', since that would be interpreted by Britain as an unfriendly act. After persistent lobbying of MPs, the delegation got the entire Greek parliament, with the exception of ministers, to sign a declaration recognising the desire of the Cypriot people. The General Confederation of Greek Workers, prompted by its colleagues in SEK, proposed the formation of a Panhellenic Committee for the Union of Cyprus with Greece, and the Primate of All Greece, Archbishop Spyridon of Athens, subsequently became its president. He said the Church of Greece had decided to shoulder its responsibilities where the government hesitated. During the summer the committee organised a number of pro-Enosis rallies in Athens and other cities. With these gratifying but insubstantial results, the Cypriot delegation eventually returned to Nicosia, where Makarios was now enthroned as Archbishop.

He decided he must take the next steps himself. He was encouraged by a statement from the new Greek Prime Minister, Mr Sophocles Venizelos. (General Plastiras had lasted only five months, and Greece was still going through a period of great instability, with weak governments following each other in quick succession.) In February 1951 the Minister of State at the Foreign Office, Mr Kenneth Younger, said the British Government had received no communication from Greece on the subject of Enosis. The following day – with more concern for his own position than for strict accuracy – Mr Venizelos told his indignant parliament that Greek governments had never stopped raising the question of Cyprus since 1915. He added that he was happy to say there and then that his own government demanded the union of Cyprus with Greece as the dearest wish of both their peoples.

Later, in a more sober mood, Venizelos told the British ambassador in Athens, Sir Clifford Norton, that he was not asking for immediate Enosis. What he envisaged was some kind of 'Balfour Declaration' whereby the British Government would promise to discuss the Cyprus question with Greece in order to reach a mutually satisfactory solution – more bases in return for a change of sovereignty – once the 'Cold War' was over. The ambassador was not encouraging, but Makarios arrived in Athens that same day.

He stayed a month, making many contacts. At his first meeting with Venizelos he urged him to put the matter squarely to the British Government and, if it still refused to discuss Cyprus, to appeal to the United Nations. Later, as they stood together on a balcony of the Grande-Bretagne Hotel, facing a crowd of demonstrating students – many of them Cypriots – in Constitution Square, Venizelos told them: 'I promise you we will take the issue wherever necessary... Be sure that official Greece will do its duty.' Subsequently Venizelos called a meeting of party leaders and it was agreed that any recourse to the United Nations, involving an open breach with Britain, was out of the question at that time. Greece – like Turkey – had been trying for months to be admitted to NATO, in the face of considerable doubt whether either would be a reliable member of the Western alliance. On his return to Cypprus Makarios reported to the Ethnarchy Council and criticised the Greek Government in no uncertain terms.

Later that year – in November – the leader of the Greek delegation to the United Nations, Mr John Politis, complained to the General Assembly that the UN Charter failed to impose on colonial powers the duty of leading their dependent territories to complete freedom. In the Fourth (Trusteeship) Committee Mr George Mavros deplored the fact that Britain had given no account of political evolution in Cyprus and had ignored the 'plebiscite'. Greece now had yet another government – a coalition under Plastiras and Venizelos – but its tentative effort to raise the question of Cyprus at the UN was more than nullified by Sir Anthony Eden's curt refusal to discuss Cyprus with the Greek Foreign Minister, Mr Evangelos Averoff, at a NATO meeting in Rome the same month. Averoff had offered Britain four bases in Greece as well as whatever defence facilities she needed in Cyprus, in return for Enosis. The British Government, which believed there was already a certain risk in admitting Greece to NATO, had no intention of hazarding Cyprus by entrusting it to a weak government in Athens, apart from the danger of upsetting Turkey, the other prospective member of NATO.

The following year – 1952 – Makarios tried a new tack. In April he called his first 'National Assembly' and declared he would make every effort to get the Greek Government to put the Cyprus question on the UN agenda that year. 'If we fail', he added, 'we have many other means at our disposal for carrying on the struggle.' The following month he indicated one new approach to the problem by visiting Egypt, Lebanon and Syria. Apart from making contact with the Greek and other Orthodox communities in those countries, Makarios began to lobby Arab politicians and journalists. King Farouk was to remain on his throne for another two months, but Britain was under great pressure in Egypt. She had abandoned her mandate in Palestine four years earlier in the face of Jewish terrorism. Makarios saw that, with the chronic weakness of Greek governments and the importance that the West attached to NATO, Arab nationalism might be a most useful ally. These were his first soundings of what was beginning to emerge as the 'Third World', that grouping of 'non-aligned' countries on which he afterwards came to rely so much for support.

In June 1952 Makarios went to Athens again and tried to put more pressure on Venizelos, who was then Acting Prime Minister, as Plastiras was sick and dying. Amongst other things the Archbishop hinted that he might ask Syria to take up the Cyprus cause at the United Nations. (It was just as well he did not carry out this threat because later, in a confused debate on Cyprus at the UN, Syria was to assert that, historically, *she* had claims to the island.) On 18 June Makarios said in a statement broadcast by Athens radio that there was only one course of action open to the Greek Government – an appeal to the UN. This brought a public rebuke from the Foreign Ministry, that the government would handle the issue 'within the framework of the general interests of the country'.

Throughout the summer, and especially during Makarios's visit, there were popular demonstrations in Greece in support of Enosis, largely organised by Archbishop Spyridon and the Greek trade unions. Apart from this, Makarios got little satisfaction, but before he left Athens he delivered a broadside. In a farewell message to the Greek people broadcast over Athens radio on 25 July, he told them that he knew their desire for an appeal to the United Nations on 'our national question'. He went on:

> However, your leaders are pursuing a devious, highly diplomatic course which creates fundamental fears that the question will not go straight to the UN. I must speak to you in the language of truth and denounce both the Government and the Opposition... They say the door is still open for friendly talks with Britain. In fact, friendly Britain has left no open door – not a crack – for such talks. She has shut every door and window tight in Greece's face with the crude answer that there is no Cyprus question to discuss... The [Greek] political leadership is fooling itself – even worse, it is fooling the Greek people, it is fooling the poor Cypriots, when it talks about an open door for friendly discussions. The doors and windows will open only when they are forced by the leverage of the United Nations... And there are other levers we can use... You have the power to make your political leaders comply with your demand and mandate, to bring the Cyprus question before the Assembly of

the international organisation. To you then I entrust the hand-ling of the sacred cause of Cyprus on the Greek side.[3]

This appeal to the people over the heads of the politicians marked an important stage in Makarios's campaign. He was sure now that he could put popular pressure on any Greek government, even if the present one was too weak to respond. These tactics were the result of long frustration in the face of Britain's refusal even to admit that a Cyprus question existed. It was a demonstration of Makarios's single-mindedness, but also a proof of his complete in-ability to appreciate Greece's problems or the international situ-ation in which she was enmeshed.

While he was in Athens this time Makarios presided over the first meeting – on 2 July – of a secret liberation committee got together by Grivas. It included George Stratos (a former War Minister), a retired general of Cypriot origin, another senior officer and ex-member of *Khi*, two university professors and Socrates Loï-zides, the deported PEK secretary-general and his brother Savvas. Grivas expressed the view that the liberation struggle should be based on the use of small guerrilla groups and sabotage squads. Makarios – who had presided over the meeting because the con-spirators needed him and because he could not afford to be igno-rant of their planning – told Grivas that he thought he would not find fifty Cypriots to follow him. Grivas disagreed; he claimed he knew his fellow-countrymen, and the ex-Minister of War, Stratos, declared: 'No one is born brave; he becomes brave, given the right leadership'.[4]

Makarios was worried about Grivas's intentions and believed it was only a question of time before the diplomatic pressures he himself preferred could be successfully applied. Grivas too was more confident than the situation warranted. After testing the strength of Enosis feeling in Cyprus through a scout as early as August 1950, he had turned to his former commanding officer, now General George Kosmas, chief of the general staff. Kosmas was close to Field-Marshal Alexander Papagos, the hero of the Greek stand against Italy in 1940 and the architect of victory in the Greek civil war. Papagos had entered politics and was building up support for a broadly-based Greek Rally, modelled on General de Gaulle's *Rassemblement*, in the hope that its success in elections would eventually end the long sequence of weak governments. Early in 1951 Grivas had asked Kosmas to try to get Papagos's backing for an armed struggle in Cyprus. In the summer of that year he made his first reconnaissance of the island, looking over the terrain in the two mountain areas and assuring himself that there would be sanctuary and logistical support in places like Kykko Monastery. He got little encouragement from Makarios. When he returned to Athens Kosmas told him that Papagos thought a liberation campaign would be 'premature' and – more to the point – that, as leader of the Greek parliamentary Opposition, hoping soon to form a government, he could not afford to be exposed as plotting against Britain. Papagos's excuse reflected the average Greek politician's continuing respect for British influence, and behind that for American power, particularly in NATO. Grivas thought it merely pusillanimous. But it was another year before he could get his liberation committee together for its first meeting, with Makarios in the chair throwing doubts on the possibility of an armed struggle. Another meeting three weeks later was as inconclusive as the first, apart from the decision to set up two more committees, one political and one military. Before Makarios left Athens he told Grivas not to return to Cyprus until he sent for him.

Shortly afterwards Stratos and the Greek Primate, Spyridon, encouraged Grivas to defy this ban, and early in October 1952 the little colonel arrived in Cyprus again, this time to remain for five months. He saw Makarios just before the Archbishop left for New York to follow the proceedings of the Seventh General Assembly of the United Nations and to study form. Grivas was told to keep in touch with the Bishop of Kitium, the tough and burly Anthimos. He spent most of the time surveying the Troodos mountains and the Kyrenia range for suitable hide-outs, looking for secret landing-places on the coast and recruiting young men to collect and store arms when they should be brought in. Here his main helpers were the leaders of the two Christian Youth organisations, Stavros Poskotis of PEON and Father Papastavros Papagathangelou of OHEN. He met for the first time Makarios's young protégé, Andreas Azinas, the future secretary-general of PEK. Together they selected a beach for the gun-running – a small, sandy bay near the village of Khlorakas, where Azinas's family lived, a few miles north of Paphos. Grivas organised a trial run with a caïque from Greece carrying a cargo of pottery. But the vessel behaved so suspiciously that the police at Paphos detained it for a time and interrogated its captain. As nothing was known against him, he was allowed to go. Grivas decided he must be more careful.

Meanwhile Makarios was attending United Nations debates in New York, lobbying delegations and giving press and radio interviews on the case for Enosis. Although there was barely any mention of Cyprus during the official proceedings, Makarios was greatly heartened by the General Assembly's resolution of 16 December 1952, which supported the principle of self-determination and urged all member-states to apply it to the peoples of non-self-governing territories under their control. The Archbishop also went to Washington and made contact again with the Greek American communities he had known in his student days; they were impressed by his new stature. He remained in the United States till the end of February 1953. Then after a brief stop in London, where the Colonial Office ignored him and only the *Daily Express* showed any interest in his campaign, he arrived once more in Athens. Grivas was also back from Cyprus.

The situation in Greece had changed. After the final collapse of the Plastiras-Venizelos coalition, Field-Marshal Papagos's Rally had won a resounding victory in the elections of November 1952, taking 239 out of the 300 seats in parliament. Greece at last had a strong government. But Papagos was not going to ruin his prospects by an incautious move over Cyprus that would antagonise Britain and upset NATO. Moreover, on the eve of Makarios's return, Greece had signed a 'treaty of friendship and cooperation' with Turkey and Yugoslavia. Papagos knew that any hint of official Greek backing for Enosis would revive Turkish hostility and kill the Balkan Pact stone dead. However, he assured Makarios that Greece would do her duty by the people of Cyprus, but he warned him that they must be patient.

Makarios met Grivas again and told him that he accepted the need for dynamic action, but he insisted that this should be limited to sabotage; there must be no armed revolt. They parted in disagreement. A few days later Grivas received a message from Papagos that he wanted to hear no more of his plans or to have any contact with his movement. Grivas recalls that he then began to receive a series of warnings from the Greek Government that he must abandon any idea of an armed struggle in Cyprus and leave it to diplomacy.

Makarios's attitude to the use of violence was still ambiguous. By nature and as a churchman he was against it, especially if it involved the taking of human life. Yet the whole history of the struggle for Greek independence had been written in blood – and the Archbishop was continuing that struggle. At the same time he knew the unwarlike temperament of the Greek Cypriots and the reluctance with which they would take up arms against the British. It might also lead to savage reprisals. The Archbishop was increasingly confident that he could step up the diplomatic pressures on Britain. But he saw they would need to be backed by some show of force. Sabotage at the right moment might do the trick – and Grivas was available. However, Makarios doubted whether he would be able to keep him under control. In this uncertainty he sent Azinas to Greece early in June with a message for Grivas, requesting the despatch of mines and hand-grenades for sabotage, but expressly ruling out the sending of rifles or automatics. There was also an order that nobody was to be infiltrated with the stores. Grivas took this as a personal affront.

Three weeks later Makarios's supporters organised a massive rally in and around the Church of Phaneromeni in the centre of Nicosia. AKEL was there in force. Addressing a crowd estimated (by Kranidiotis) at more than 15,000 strong, Makarios declared:

> Anglo-Greek friendship is unacceptable to the Greek people because it is one-sided and because the freedom of Cyprus is strangled in the name of that friendship ... The statements of the Greek Government on the Cyprus question, whether clear or confused, satisfy neither the Greeks who are free nor their enslaved brothers in Cyprus. The question will not be solved by statements, but by decisive measures, as national dignity demands.

Makarios called on the Greek Government again to take the matter up at the United Nations, invoking the General Assembly resolution of 16 December 1952 about self-determination. Then, suiting the action to the words, he went on: 'In our effort to win the freedom we desire we shall stretch out both our right hand and our left to take the help offered by East and West.' The oblique reference to the Soviet Union encouraged part of the congregation to strike up the Communist 'Internationale'.[5] Makarios ended by saying that, if Greece and the United Nations all failed her, Cyprus would still fight on the internal front in every possible way and with all the means available. Violence, he implied, was not excluded.

Outwardly Cyprus was still quiet, apart from occasional outbursts like PEON's orgy of stone-throwing in the Paphos area at the beginning of that month, as Queen Elizabeth II's coronation was being celebrated. Makarios continued to urge Greece to appeal to the United Nations General Assembly in the autumn. There were hints that otherwise Thailand might do so or, at AKEL's request, Czechoslovakia or Poland or even Guatemala! Papagos refused to be blackmailed by these appeals to Greek honour. He was still hoping to see the British Foreign Secretary, Sir Anthony Eden, whose projected visit to Athens in the spring had been cancelled because of his illness.

On 21 September the leader of the Greek delegation to the UN told the General Assembly that, while his Government sympathised with the Cypriot appeal, it had not asked for it to be put on the agenda because Greece still hoped the question could be solved by direct negotiations with Britain. Eden was already in Athens, on a private visit to convalesce after his operation, and Papagos had called on him once as a matter of courtesy. Eden had agreed to see the Prime Minister only on condition that there was no talk of politics. On the day after the Greek statement at the UN Papagos saw Eden again at the British Embassy. Worried, no doubt, by the pressures on him and the thought that another year must pass before an appeal could be lodged with the United Nations, Papagos tried to get some encouragement to think that the two governments could reach an agreement over Cyprus. Eden exploded. His illness had left him tetchy and bad-tempered – and he thought the Prime Minister had gone back on his word. With his own worries about the future of the British bases in Egypt, Eden said angrily that there was no Cyprus question to discuss, now or in the future. Why, he asked sarcastically, did the Greeks not ask for New York, or Alexandria, where there were so many of their fellow-countrymen? Papagos's sense of honour – his Greek *philotimo* – was deeply wounded. He replied stiffly that, in that case, his Government would reserve its freedom of action.[6]

That unfortunate encounter hardened Papagos's heart more than all Makarios's importunities. If Eden had only lied and said that Britain understood Greek feeling and would consider the possibilities when the international situation permitted, the politeness would have counted more than the insincerity and Papagos would probably have been patient, though his own health was to crack up during the next few months.

Events now began to move more quickly. In November the Greek Foreign Minister, Mr Stephanos Stephanopoulos,

announced that the Cyprus question was being handled personally by Field-Marshal Papagos. In February 1954 Makarios was
back again in Athens, confident that the time was ripe. Before he
left he said in a broadcast that he had received a categorical assurance from the Prime Minister that the question of Cyprus would be
brought before the United Nations in the following September, if
bilateral talks with Britain had not produced the desired solution.
Papagos declared that his Government's policy was unchanged,
that it took full account of the need for security in the south-east
Mediterranean, and that nothing would give it an anti-British
edge. Two days later there were anti-British riots in Rhodes, where
Makarios had stopped on his way home. He knew now that he had
the Greek Government on the run.

Some weeks later Papagos told an Italian journalist that Greece
did not expect the immediate cession of Cyprus. She would
propose the granting of a constitution for two or three years, at the
end of which time the Cypriots should decide their future by a plebiscite. Britain, he said, could have whatever bases she wanted,
either in Cyprus or in the rest of Greece.

On 23 July Archbishop Makarios addressed his second
'National Assembly' in Nicosia. He told the people that, as Britain
was being pushed out of Egypt, she was determined to keep Cyprus
as a substitute for Suez. Her bases in the island were being enlarged
in the name of defending freedom. In reality, Makarios said, the
freedom of Cyprus was being sacrificed on the altar of British
interests.

Hard upon this came the second disastrous *contretemps* that alienated even the most moderate Greek opinion. On 28 July the Churchill Government formally announced that British troops would
be evacuating their Suez base. On the same day the Minister of
State for Colonial Affairs, Mr Henry Hopkinson (later Lord
Colyton), told the House of Commons that, as the Cypriots had not
taken up the 1948 offer of a constitution, a modified version would
be introduced as the first step in associating the people of Cyprus
with the management of their own affairs. The minister repeated
the usual statement that no change of sovereignty was contemplated. It aroused no comment. It was only after some blundering
but persistent questioning from the deputy leader of the Opposition, Mr James Griffiths (Labour), as to whether the Cypriots
would eventually have the right to decide their own future and
reach Dominion status (not Enosis!) that Mr Hopkinson said: 'it

has always been understood and agreed that there are certain territories in the Commonwealth which, owing to their particular circumstances, can never expect to be fully independent'. There were cries of 'Oh!' The minister went on: 'I am not going as far as that this afternoon, but I have said that the question of the abrogation of British sovereignty cannot arise – that British sovereignty will remain.'

This was the notorious 'never' that infuriated the Greeks, split Government and Opposition in Britain after years of a bipartisan policy over Cyprus, and gave Archbishop Makarios just the extra leverage he needed. Hopkinson had been caught off balance. He had no reason to think that the Labour Party would suddenly repudiate (apparently) the views it had always maintained when in government. Even eighteen months later Lord Attlee, Mr Griffiths himself and Mr Aneurin Bevan, among other Socialists, agreed that, for Malta, the road to full self-government was blocked. Mr Hopkinson stopped short of applying the 'never' to Cyprus, but it was taken that he had done so, when he was merely trying to restate a general principle. Unfortunately, the timing was wrong. A number of MPs from all parties were concerned at the Government's flat refusal to talk to the friendly Greeks about Cyprus. Britain was soon going to be arraigned before the United Nations for refusing self-determination to a small people after she had granted India its freedom and begun to dismantle her Empire. She had made no attempt to justify her policy over Cyprus or to point to the dangers and misconceptions in the Enosis campaign. As Aneurin Bevan said in the heated exchanges that followed the Hopkinson statement:

> If we are leaving Egypt for the reasons that we all know about and if we are to take up residence in Cyprus, surely it is the duty of the Government so to adjust their policy as to produce as friendly an atmosphere as possible in Cyprus. Instead, what have they done? The Minister of State for Colonial Affairs bluntly tells the Cypriots that they can only get their own way by doing what the Egyptians have done.

Aneurin Bevan was unduly hard on Hopkinson. Makarios had already made up his mind. Five days before the announcement about Suez and the Hopkinson statement he had told his 'National Assembly' that, although the Cypriot struggle was a peaceful one, events in a neighbouring country pointed to the conclusion that the British could be made to understand only by the use of force.[7]

Hopkinson's 'never' was made even more offensive to the Greeks when the Secretary of State for the Colonies, Mr Oliver Lyttelton, intervened in the debate. He dwelt on the importance of Turkey to NATO and to the security of the eastern Mediterranean. Any support in Britain for Enosis, he said, might have grave repercussions on Turkish public opinion. Then, trampling even harder on the wreckage of Anglo-Greek relations, the Secretary of State declared: 'I cannot imagine any policy more disastrous for Cyprus than to hand it over to an unstable power, however friendly.'

There were angry demonstrations in Greece and Cyprus. Papagos had so lost control of the situation that the Greek Government issued a stamp which showed a page of Hansard (the official report of British parliamentary debates) obliterated by a large ink-blot. On 2 August the Cyprus government announced that the existing sedition laws would be strictly enforced, but little action was taken and Archbishop Makarios continued to deliver his fiery speeches. On 16 August Greece asked for the Cyprus question to be put on the agenda for the United Nations' Ninth General Assembly under the heading 'Application . . . of the principle of equal rights and self-determination of peoples in the case of the population of Cyprus'. The careless wording overlooked the fact that, chiefly as a result of Greek Cypriot propaganda, there were two 'peoples' in Cyprus – even if one was much larger than the other – and that the ethnic minority might equally claim the right of self-determination. (It had happened in India.) On 23 September the UN Steering Committee considered the appeal. Nine members – the Soviet Union among them – voted in favour of putting the question on the agenda; three voted against it and three, including the United States, abstained. The Steering Committee's recommendation then went to the General Assembly, where only half the membership at that time – thirty nations – voted in favour of debating the Cyprus question. Nineteen were opposed to discussing it, and eleven abstained. The representative of India refused to vote on the grounds that it was a territorial dispute between two countries and not a question of independence.

The Cyprus item was sent to the Political Committee, where the debate on it opened on 14 December. Few countries showed any knowledge of the subject. The Cypriot-born Greek delegate, Mr Alexis Kyrou, who had been a fanatical Enotist at least since his consulship in Nicosia at the time of the 1931 riots, said the issue was one of self-determination, not of a change of sovereignty; Greece made no claim to Cyprus. The Czechoslovak delegate thought the Greek Cypriots fulfilled all the requirements of nationhood – but failed to notice that his arguments applied equally to the Turkish Cypriots. The Yemeni delegate fell into the same trap. Turkey launched a violent attack on Greek chauvinism and questioned the competence of the UN to discuss Cyprus. Mr Henry Cabot Lodge, for the United States, urged an effort to reach a friendly solution by negotiation outside the United Nations. On the second day of an oddly muted debate a resolution that, 'for the time being' it did not seem appropriate to take a decision on the Cyprus question, was adopted by forty-nine votes, with none against it and nine abstentions. Even Mr Kyrou voted for it, describing the result as a Greek victory since the phrase 'for the time being' meant that the Cyprus question would remain on the UN books. (In fact, it failed to get on the agenda the following year.) The Political Committee's vote was endorsed by the General Assembly, and the Greek Government was relieved that it had fared no worse.

However, the popular reaction among Greeks and Greek Cypriots was one of anger and bewilderment, after all the windy hopes that had been raised. They could not believe that the United Nations had not immediately seen the justice of their claim, and they blamed the Americans for side-tracking the issue, though the United States in fact had recommended the direct negotiations which the Greeks themselves said they wanted. There were violent student demonstrations in Athens and Salonika, where British and American flags were burned. A general strike was proclaimed in Cyprus, the police were stoned, and in Limassol three youths were wounded when British troops opened fire to disperse a rioting crowd. Cyprus had its new martyrs.

Makarios, who had attended the debate at the United Nations, returned to an enthusiastic welcome in Cyprus early in the New Year. He showed no disappointment and proclaimed that the struggle would continue to the end.

By that time (January 1955) Grivas had been in the island for three months, with the Archbishop's approval; Makarios was now committed to 'dynamic action', but still wavering as to the form it should take. Early in June 1953 he had told Grivas that he wanted only sabotage – no arms and no fighters from Greece. Later that month, Grivas heard from his doctor brother in Nicosia that

Makarios had accepted his argument that a few sabotage incidents would achieve nothing. According to Grivas, it was then that Savvas Loïzides first received money from Makarios to buy arms. When the Archbishop arrived in Athens in February 1954, Grivas had a small shipload of arms ready for despatch. Makarios still hesitated and, to pin him down, Grivas says he got Admiral Sakellariou, the former commander-in-chief of the Greek Navy who was helping over the arms caïque, to urge the Archbishop to greater boldness. Makarios evidently weakened a little and sent for Azinas to give him instructions. On 2 March a cargo was loaded on to a caïque on a quiet beach in Attica, and later unloaded at Khlorakas and safely stowed away. It consisted of three Bren guns, three Italian Bredas (one in poor condition), four tommy-guns, some British and German automatics, seven revolvers, 47 rifles of various ages and origin, 20 kilos of explosive, nearly 300 hand-grenades and some 40,000 rounds of mixed ammunition. These were almost the only arms that Grivas had for nearly a year of his guerrilla activity, but the starting-date for that was still far off.

The Greek Government was well aware of what was going on, and in April 1954 it warned Grivas that recourse to violence would do 'incalculable harm' to the Cyprus question, which was making good progress diplomatically. Later Grivas got a hint that Papagos had taken steps in Cyprus to restrain him. He went ahead with his plans. In August he heard from his brother that Makarios was sending more money to buy arms and explosives. The new shipment was ready for despatch by October. As Makarios passed through Athens on his way to the United Nations, he reportedly told Grivas that both he and the Greek Foreign Minister, Mr Stephanopoulos, considered action was necessary before the debate, so as to warn the Americans that, if they adopted a hostile attitude, there could be serious trouble in Cyprus which might affect the Middle East. This was 'a new Makarios', says Grivas, though he adds that even at this stage the Archbishop 'dithered'. At one meeting he told Grivas to wait for a signal from him from the United States. At the next he told him to start action as soon as he arrived in Cyprus. Grivas left Athens on 26 October, going first to Rhodes by steamer and then by caïque, through a bad storm, to Khlorakas, where he landed with Socrates Loïzides on the night of 10 November. During the next fortnight he began to choose fighters from the young men of PEON and OHEN and to train them in the use of arms.

At the end of November Grivas moved to Nicosia to organise sabotage groups and a courier service. Makarios sent word through Kranidiotis that he was to wait for the signal, but Grivas was determined to choose his own time, when he was satisfied that he was ready; training his enthusiastic but undisciplined recruits was more difficult than he had expected. On 11 January, the day after Makarios's return from America, they met in the Larnaca bishopric. The Archbishop reported that Papagos was now in full agreement that they should go ahead. They discussed a starting-date. Makarios wanted 25 March, Greek Independence Day and the anniversary of the 1821 revolt against the Turks. Grivas thought that was too late; they might lose the element of surprise. In fact, they had almost lost it already.

Grivas knew, from a copy of a confidential police report shown to him at the beginning of January, that the British authorities were aware he had arrived in the island in November and stayed for a time in the Paphos area. The second cargo of arms and of even more essential explosives left Greece in the *Ayios Yeoryios* on 13 January. Two days later Archbishop Makarios told Grivas that someone had betrayed them; the British had got wind of the operation and were watching the western coasts. There were no means of warning the caïque. On the night of the 25/26 January a British destroyer intercepted the *Ayios Yeoryios* off Khlorakas. Its cargo was seized, and its crew and the beach reception party – Socrates Loïzides among them – were all arrested. They were later given terms of up to twelve years' imprisonment, mainly on the evidence of the cargo and a leaflet in the possession of Loïzides, which announced the existence of 'a strictly secret revolutionary organisation', fully armed and with Enosis as its only aim.

This was a bad setback for Grivas and disturbing for the Archbishop. Grivas at once suspended training and went into the hills. But as the British authorities appeared to think that the capture of the *Ayios Yeoryios* was the end of the affair, he presently returned to Nicosia and began to organise a supply of explosives from mines and quarries and even retrieved some TNT from old shells dumped in the sea at the end of the war. Apart from the risks and difficulties involved in making amateur bombs and grenades, Grivas had trouble with security and administration; there was even a dishonest liaison officer who embezzled the money intended for the grocer's bill. But by the middle of March Grivas was ready and had chosen his first targets for sabotage; Makarios still insisted there should be no use of arms and that every effort must be made to avoid casualties. He sent for Grivas to see him on 29 March and gave him his blessing. Zero hour was fixed for 0030 hours on 1 April.[8]

Grivas prepared his first proclamation. He had decided to call his movement 'The National Organisation of Cypriot Fighters' – from its Greek initials, EOKA. For himself he chose the pseudonym 'Dighenis', the name of the legendary Byzantine hero who had defended the boundaries of empire – including Cyprus – during the Arab raids between the seventh and tenth centuries of the Christian era. EOKA's first proclamation invoked the Spartans at Thermopylae, the Athenians at Marathon, the Greeks of 1821 and the 'Albanian epic' of 1940–1. It called on all Cypriots – Greek Cypriots, that is – to show the world that, if they were denied their freedom, they would win it with their blood.

In the early hours of 1 April a few dull explosions and one loud bang were heard in Nicosia. A four-man group had overpowered the night-watchman at the Cyprus Broadcasting Service and put a bomb in a transmitter; this did the most damage. Another group, led by Charalambos Mouskos, a cousin of the Archbishop, lobbed bombs through the windows of the unguarded Secretariat, one of the main government buildings. Other home-made devices exploded in the Education Office and behind the Wolseley barracks, where they destroyed some radio equipment. In Limassol and Larnaca, government offices and police stations suffered minor damage, and one bomb at Larnaca was placed in the house of a senior Turkish Cypriot official. The only casualty, apart from a Cypriot policeman injured by flying glass, was a thirty-one-year-old EOKA saboteur, who was electrocuted when he thew a rope wet from the dew over some high-tension cables at Famagusta in an attempt to cut the electricity supply. Four other EOKA men were arrested and one, Gregoris Afxentiou, who was later to become an EOKA hero and martyr, with statues in his honour and ballads about his exploits, found himself immediately on the run.

In his twice-edited Memoirs Grivas claims: 'The attack took the world by surprise.' In his day-to-day diary, found and published by the British, he complained that most of the operations produced insignificant results and that some had failed or never been started out of timidity.

In four and a half years Archbishop Makarios had achieved one of his main aims; he had internationalised the Cyprus question, though without realising how this would eventually boomerang. Through sheer persistence – and some demagogy – he had worn down successive Greek governments till one of them – ironically, the strongest for many years – took up the Greek Cypriot case at the United Nations, in what was to be the beginning of a long series of fruitless debates and unimplemented resolutions. Through British obstinacy and lack of imagination – not to mention poor diplomacy – the Archbishop had got the reluctant backing of the Papagos Government for a campaign of violence in Cyprus. In his other objective – to unite the home front – Makarios had been less successful. The gap between the Church and the Communist-led Left had widened, although both proclaimed they were aiming at the same goal. AKEL was quick to denounce EOKA's first bombs. The Greek Communist Party soon revealed the identity of 'Dighenis', although the British had already half-suspected it. As EOKA grew more efficient and more ruthless, unpolitical Greek Cypriots became afraid of not cooperating with it, even when British reprisals were at their worst. Yet before the 1959–60 independence agreements the number of Greek Cypriots killed by EOKA was to exceed the combined total of its British and Turkish Cypriot victims. The Archbishop had enchanted his people with a vision of national liberation, but the sorcerer's apprentice had got the powerful magic of bombs and guns in his own hands.

6 'By Force Alone'

All Fool's Day 1955 marked the beginning of a new phase of the
Cyprus problem, in which none of those involved were to show con-
spicuous wisdom. Although the British were not as 'stunned and
panic-stricken' as Grivas later claimed in the English version of his
memoirs, they appeared surprised. The knowledge that Grivas
had returned to the island, the capture of the *Ayios Yeoryios* with its
cargo of arms and explosives, all the inflammatory propaganda
from the pulpit and from Athens radio, the slogans on the walls and
the calls for sacrifice had not convinced the authorities that the
Greek Cypriots were serious or had the stomach for violence.
Hence the almost total lack of security precautions when EOKA
launched its campaign. There was even less sign of any contingency plan. For his part, Archbishop Makarios hoped that a brief
show of force would push the British into negotiations with Greece
before the next appeal to the United Nations in the autumn.
Grivas, with more understanding of the British, had no such expectations. He was disappointed with the meagre results of EOKA's
first action, apart from the easy success at the radio station. He saw
that his men would need much more training and discipline. He
was furious with AKEL when it denounced the explosions as the
work of right-wing fanatics who were playing into the hands of the
British. He was even more indignant with Athens radio which,
after months of exhorting the Greek Cypriots to throw off the yoke
of slavery, suddenly declared in its 'Voice of the Motherland'[1] programme beamed to Cyprus that freedom was not won by terrorism. Grivas complained bitterly to Makarios, who replied that he
too was grieved by the tone of the broadcasts. He said he was
sending an emissary immediately to Athens radio to put things
right. Makarios congratulated Grivas, wished him well and

added: 'The rulers realise we have entered upon a serious stage of the struggle.'

Yet the next day (4 April) Grivas received another letter from the Archbishop, asking him to stop his activities and reorganise. After some sporadic and fairly ineffectual bomb-throwing at British military vehicles and buildings Grivas called a halt. He also had to move from his carefully-prepared cellar hide-out in a suburb of Nicosia where many English service families lived. Several EOKA men had been captured and Grivas was afraid they might betray his whereabouts.

Two things only had impressed him – the response of the young to the stirring words of 'Dighenis' in EOKA's first proclamation, and the vulnerability of the police. On the morning after the first explosions schoolchildren had picked up copies of the proclamation scattered in the streets. Members of PEON and OHEN were only too eager to stick them up on walls, especially outside the Pancyprian Gymnasium opposite the archbishopric. Grivas decided that he must 'turn the youth of Cyprus into the seed-bed of EOKA'. That they were ready for action was clear. A fifteen-year old schoolboy was injured on 3 April when a grenade in his possession exploded. On the same day another fifteen-year-old was caught trying to smuggle blasting-powder into a petrol depot. These tiny cracks in the dam warned the Archbishop that there could be an uncontrollable flood of violence. They explain his instructions to Grivas to suspend activity in the towns.

However, early in May, when Makarios was out of the country, Grivas gave orders that boys and girls should be enrolled in his organisation to distribute leaflets, take part in demonstrations and keep a watch on the police and anybody suspected of being a British agent. The liveliest and bravest boys – and some girls – would later graduate to EOKA's combat units. All were required to swear 'in the name of the Holy Trinity' that they would carry out the organisation's instructions without questioning, even if it cost them their lives. Neither capture nor torture would make them reveal EOKA's secrets. If they broke their oaths – these children readily declared – they deserved the punishment of traitors and eternal shame.[2]

Grivas's second and more immediate aim was to demoralise the police. He saw that, if he could compel the authorities to use British troops rather than Cypriot policemen for security duties, the picture of brutal colonial repression would be made more convincing, especially if the troops had to tangle with schoolchildren. The Greek Cypriots among the police – nearly two-thirds of the force in 1954 – were obviously in a difficult position. If they were loyal to the government they could be branded as 'traitors'. If they stayed in their posts mainly for economic reasons, they were often obliged to become informers for EOKA. Either course was dangerous. As more and more Greek Cypriots were driven into leaving the force and their place was taken by Turkish Cypriots, the altered balance was made to show that the British were using Turks to crush the Greeks.

Although the secretary-general of the Greek Communist Party, Nikos Zachariades, deliberately revealed the identity of 'Dighenis' in a broadcast from an Iron Curtain country on 24 April, the British were not convinced for months that Grivas was the brains behind EOKA. AKEL and the mainland Greek Communists were much more alarmed. While they ridiculed the efforts of the saboteurs as mere 'fireworks' and the action of irresponsible 'adventurers', they took advantage of EOKA's poor showing at the start and the half-hearted British reaction to it to suggest that it was a device of Anglo-Aerican imperialism to justify repression of the Greek Cypriot Left. They urged the people not to fall into this trap – fearing that the Church had again taken the initiative. All Grivas's old anti-Communism flared up and he sent a warning to AKEL to keep out or face the consequences.

In spite of the Archbishop's misgivings about Grivas's intentions he turned his back on this scene and left Cyprus early in April to seek new friends. After stopping in Athens to confer with the Greek Government he flew to Bandung in Indonesia to attend the world's first Afro-Asian Conference, where he hoped to get support from that mainly anti-colonial grouping for the next Greek appeal to the United Nations. Makarios left for Bandung on Greek Good Friday, the most solemn day in the Orthodox Church calendar.[3] It showed how far political considerations had overridden the Archbishop's more spiritual concern for his people. He arrived when the conference was half over, but he met Nehru, Nasser, Sukarno and other leaders of the emerging 'Third World'. Makarios was already gaining international stature. The conference, however, achieved very little, because of its composition. Besides the 'non-aligned' members it included the Chinese People's Republic, still in partnership with the Soviet Union, as well as countries allied with the West through NATO or the newly-formed Baghdad Pact;

Turkey belonged to both. But Makarios was satisfied that he had publicised the Greek Cypriot case and got some support for it. He returned to Athens on 1 May.

Events were now moving rapidly. Two days earlier the leader of OHEN, Father Papastavros, had passed on written instructions from Makarios to Grivas that there should be no more EOKA activity until further notice because 'important national interests' were at stake. Apart from wanting to restrain Grivas, the Archbishop was encouraged not only by the support he had found in Bandung but also by the attitude of the British Labour Party – and there might soon be a change of government at Westminster. Churchill had stepped down on 5 April – some Greeks may have been persuaded that EOKA's defiance of the old imperialism was the last straw – and Eden had taken his place as Prime Minister. Elections were announced for 26 May – and the Labour Party Conference the previous year had voted to oppose Government stubbornness over Cyprus 'on all occasions'.

On 3 May the trial of those accused in the *Ayios Yioryios* case opened in Cyprus. Eleven out of the thirteen defendants pleaded guilty either to preparing armed force against the government or to unlawfully importing explosives. After a three-day hearing Socrates Loïzides was sentenced to twelve years imprisonment and the rest to terms ranging from one to six years. This treatment of 'heroes' was splendid recruiting propaganda for EOKA. Athens radio's 'Voice of the Motherland' declared: 'If the new (British) Government adopts the same policy, the Cypriots must take up arms and fight under the flag of "Dighenis".' Archbishop Makarios, now in Athens, preached in the Church of St Irene where he had once been deacon and told the Greeks:

Stand by your Cypriot brothers to the end. I give you assurance that the Cypriots have reached the decision – an irrevocable decision – to be free of foreign rule. We shall not be afraid, we shall not be intimidated, we shall not bow to illiberal laws, oppression, imprisonment, exile or even death. All for freedom! Long live freedom!

On the same day Makarios issued a statement in Athens, saying that he had repeatedly advised the Cypriots not to use force. In a reference to the colonial government's charge that he had failed to condemn or even to comment on 'a patently irreligious oath' taken by Greek Cypriot schoolboys contemplating violence, the Archbishop declared that, as *he* had not bound anyone by such an oath, he could not be expected to release them from it.

Makarios spent some time in Athens and then returned to Cyprus, oddly enough by way of Cairo. It is not clear whether he went to Egypt to clinch Colonel Nasser's political support or to check on the arms that Grivas was trying to get from a Cypriot in Suez. He arrived back unexpectedly in Nicosia on 27 May, to the disagreeable knowledge that Britain now had another Conservative Government – under Eden. On the 24th hundreds of boys and girls, mostly from the Pancyprian Gymnasium, had marched through Nicosia on Grivas's orders to protest against being given a holiday for 'Empire Day'. They stoned the police, and troops were called out.

Makarios, who had been away from Cyprus for more than six weeks, arranged for Grivas to meet him at the Kykko Metokhi in the suburbs of Nicosia early on the morning of 7 June.[4] Grivas got the impression that the Archbishop approved of the activity of the EOKA Youth but wanted to keep it, like everything else, under his own control. They agreed that Dr Spyridakis, the headmaster of the Pancryprian Gymnasium, was a cowardly little man, for all his Enotist sentiment. (He had reason to be. He was once beaten up by his own pupils when he tried to restrain them, and his deputy head, a science man, was one of the main sources of EOKA bombs.) Makarios made it clear that he did not expect – and did not want – arms from Egypt, but he approved of Grivas's plan to put a bomb in Government House on the Queen's Birthday, provided it caused no casualties. The attempt failed.

Grivas had prepared a report for the Archbishop in which he outlined his plan of action. There were to be three stages in the campaign: first, sabotage in the towns and attacks on police stations in remote areas to compel the enemy to disperse his forces; then, lightning raids by small combat groups on army units and police stations; finally, if all this went well, a general uprising of the population, led by the youth. Grivas hoped that the struggle could last at least until October, when he reckoned that the Cyprus question would be debated at the United Nations.

Makarios vetoed Grivas's idea of ambushing and killing the Commander-in-Chief of Middle East Land Forces, General Keightley, as he drove over one day from Kyrenia to Nicosia. However, Grivas launched a new offensive in mid-June and wrote in his diary on the 22nd:

> According to reports in the press, last night's dynamite explos-
> ions were a success. In Nicosia a time-bomb went off in the
> Central Police Station with one townsman dead and a lot of
> others wounded (policemen and civilians, especially Turks). A
> hand-grenade was thrown at the English in Varosha
> [Famagusta]. It was good work ... The situation is developing
> favourably.

There was a sharp warning from the Turkish Cypriot leadership
that another EOKA bomb in or near a Turkish quarter would lead
to bloody intercommunal strife. Grivas ignored it. He was more
concerned about the situation he described only two days later, in
an Order to his men dated 24 June:

> The results of our continued struggle, when we think of what we
> intended to do, are very poor. As I have repeatedly stressed, both
> orally and in writing, our main target is the execution of police
> traitors; the turn of the English soldiers will come after.

Already, within three months, killing Greeks and not caring how
many Turks got killed in the process was more immediately important to Grivas than attacking the colonial power itself.

Grivas records that at the end of June leaflets were picked up in
Limassol, calling on Turkish Cypriot youth to enrol in an organisation to fight EOKA and oppose Enosis. He also heard from a
police source that Turkish Cypriot policemen were training civilian members of their community in the use of arms. It was a
pointer to the years of intercommunal bloodshed that lay ahead.

Britain's feeble resistance to EOKA at the beginning was partly
because she did not take the movement seriously, partly because
for much of April and May people were preoccupied with a
General Election. As the new Eden Government settled in, it began
to appreciate the threat to Cyprus and to Britain's already eroded
position in the Middle East. It was decided to make a fresh attempt
to persuade the Cypriots to accept what Eden saw as 'a liberal
instalment of self-government' (defence, foreign affairs and internal security excluded) in order to lower the tension. Eden wrote
later in his memoirs: 'Even if we could not grant self-
determination, we ought to be able to show the Cypriots that the

self-government we offered was an important stage towards it.'[5] This was not only disingenuous; it was quite unrealistic. The Greek Cypriots were in no mood to consider such an offer, however much some of them wanted to run their own affairs. Eden was frankly Turcophile; he also believed that Turkey was now the hinge of Western defence arrangements in the Middle East and that any trouble in Cyprus which upset the Turks would be dangerous to British interests and commitments. Eden thought that he might get cooperation from the Cypriots if he could secure the support of Greece and Turkey for a limited constitution which would satisfy Greek honour and reassure the Turks. He also knew that he could count on Turkey backing Britain against any change in the *status quo.*

On 30 June the British Government invited Greece and Turkey to send representatives to London to discuss 'political and defence questions which affect the Eastern Mediterranean, including Cyprus.' There was no mention of EOKA terrorism or of the constitutional proposals. Turkey quickly accepted the invitation. As Greece hesitated, because Papagos was a sick man and his ministers could not easily agree on what to do, Archbishop Makarios denounced the British move as a trap. He called on the Greek Government to reject the invitation unless Britain first conceded the principle of self-determination and was willing to apply it at the beginning of the talks; he also insisted that Greece should renew her appeal to the United Nations before the conference began. A few days later the Papagos Government accepted Eden's invitation without conditions; it even wanted the conference to begin earlier than Britain found convenient. The Colonial Secretary, Lennox-Boyd, had first to go to South-East Asia, to discuss the future of Malaya and Singapore. Before he went, he paid a flying visit to Cyprus to give the Governor some idea of the £38 million development plan which was being hurriedly drawn up for the island and to see whether it was necessary to proclaim a state of emergency. Eden was reluctant to do so since this might prejudice the outcome of the London conference. As the situation seemed quieter after the British offer – only because Grivas left Nicosia on 6 July to train guerrilla groups on Troodos and to prepare for an offensive which would coincide with the Greek appeal to the United Nations – the Governor was authorised merely to enact a new Detention of Persons law to facilitate the holding of EOKA suspects. Lennox-Boyd had a brief meeting with Makarios and reported him as 'entirely non-committal'. On 11 July the Archbishop flew to Athens, after writing to Grivas: 'I congratulate you. EOKA has done vastly more for the Cyprus struggle than seventy-five years of a war on paper'.

In Athens Makarios again publicly called on the Greek Government to lodge its appeal with the United Nations before going to the London talks. Papagos told the Archbishop that, while this would not be politic, the appeal would be made before 20 August, if by then the London conference had not produced a satisfactory result. Makarios feared the worst. He realised now that, even if EOKA eventually compelled Britain to give up full sovereignty over Cyprus, the Eden Government was determined to give Turkey a say in its future that would choke all Greek and Greek Cypriot aspirations.

The start of the conference was delayed – no doubt deliberately, because of the Colonial Secretary's convenient absence – until 29 August, one day before the time-limit for submitting items for the UN General Assembly's agenda. In fact, the Greek application had been made more than a month before, but the British Government clearly hoped that the Tripartite Conference would persuade UN members that Britain was trying to find a solution. In the meantime arrests under the new Detention of Persons Act prompted EOKA to accuse the British of imposing a 'Hitlerite terror' and Athens radio was not slow to amplify this. By the end of August some eighty-three Greek Cypriots were under detention in the Central Prisons, Nicosia, and about a dozen Greek nationals – mostly school-teachers – had been deported.

Archbishop Makarios convened his third 'National Assembly' three days before the start of the London talks. He told the Greek Cypriots that Britain's security measures had created 'a callous police regime of tyranny and violence'. The 'Assembly' passed a resolution proclaiming that the people of Cyprus would accept no decision from the Tripartite Conference other than immediate self-determination. On the following day a Turkish Cypriot constable was injured when a bomb exploded in the Famagusta police head-quarters. Then on the very eve of the London talks EOKA carried out its first cold-blooded killing of a policeman. Michael Karaolis, the leader of a three-man 'execution squad', shot dead a Greek Cypriot Special Branch man, Michael Poullis, in Nicosia's busy Ledra Street. Grivas was appalled when AKEL called Karaolis a 'murderer'.

The Tripartite Conference opened at a leisurely pace with formal statements by the three Foreign Ministers. Mr Macmillan spoke soothingly of Britain's long friendship with Greece and respect for Turkey and set out his government's reasons for needing to retain sovereignty over Cyprus. Mr Stephanopoulos, who – according to Grivas – had urged EOKA to action, said Greece repudiated the use of violence and asked only that the Cypriot people should be allowed to exercise their right to self-determination after a short period of self-government; he added that the rights of the Turkish minority would be fully guaranteed. Mr Zorlu complained that the Orthodox Church had stirred up antagonism between the two communities. He rejected self-determination for Cyprus altogether, on the grounds that this would be tantamount to a revision of the Treaty of Lausanne, on which Greek-Turkish friendship depended.

After a restricted meeting on 2 September the conference adjourned until the 6th. By that time Lennox-Boyd had returned to London. The Greek and Turkish Foreign Ministers were deadlocked over the question of self-determination. This was the cue for Mr Macmillan to produce the British proposals for a constitution. They envisaged an assembly with an elected majority; the gradual transfer of all departments of government, apart from defence, foreign affairs and internal security, to Cypriot ministers; a quota of seats and ministerial portfolios for the Turkish community in proportion to its size; and a Chief Minister chosen by the assembly with the approval of the Governor. The Greek Foreign Minister said Britain was discriminating against the Cypriots by not allowing self-government to lead to self-determination. The Turkish Foreign Minister sought – and got – an assurance from Mr Macmillan that Britain did not regard the principle of self-determination as one of universal application and that there would be no change in the sovereignty of Cyprus.

It was an outcome that should have satisfied the Turks completely, but they were determined to teach the Greeks a lesson. On the day that the conference reached this carefully-engineered deadlock – in which, as Mr Macmillan said, the parties should take 'the practical and sensible course' and 'agree to differ' – anti-Greek riots broke out in Istanbul and Izmir. The night before, there had been an explosion in the garden of the Turkish consulate at Salonika. It broke several windows, including some in the house next door where Ataturk, the founder of modern Turkey had been born.

About seven o'clock on the evening of 6 September thousands poured on to the streets of Istanbul, carrying flags and portraits of Ataturk and shouting 'Cyprus is Turkish'. Many of the demonstrators were armed with iron bars which they found conveniently by the lorry-load in different parts of the city. They moved systematically, smashing up every shop, house or other property known to belong to a Greek. Goods and furniture were burnt or thrown into the street to be trampled on by the mob. All but a few of the eighty-odd Greek churches in the city were stripped and desecrated; many were set on fire. The rioters even invaded Greek cemeteries, broke open coffins and scattered their contents. The police took no action. Greek reports later spoke of massacre and rape, but these were not substantiated. It was an orgy of material destruction, releasing much of the pent-up Turkish hatred of a despised but prosperous minority. Probably not more than two or three Greeks out of the 100,000 in Istanbul lost their lives. The devastation stopped only towards midnight, when the Prime Minister, Mr Adnan Menderes, reached Istanbul, declared martial law and called out the troops. The riots were less serious in Izmir, where the mob confined itself mainly to burning down the Greek pavilion at the International Fair, attacking the Greek consulate and invading buildings occupied by Greek officers at the NATO headquarters.

There is no doubt that the riots were officially sanctioned but got out of hand. The explosion near Ataturk's house in Salonika was the work of *agents provocateurs* – the Turkish porter at the consulate and a Greek student of Turkish origin. Five years later, in 1960, when Menderes and his Foreign Minister, Zorlu, were on trial for their lives after the military *coup* against their Government, the public prosecutor accused them of having instigated the Salonika incident, but it was never proved. Some twenty Turkish rioters were killed before the troops restored order, and early in 1956 the Menderes Government agreed to pay the Greek community forty million Turkish pounds (about three million pounds sterling) as compensation.

Greeks everywhere were stunned by the savagery of the riots. The city of Constantine, the very centre of their Byzantine world, had again been 'sacked' by the barbarian Turks. Even the riots in Izmir (Smyrna) brought back memories to the older generation of how that city had burned in 1922 when the Greek expeditionary force which had marched up-country with such confidence of reclaiming lost territory was thrown back into the sea. For

Makarios it was an occasion of bitter grief and anger at the British for encouraging such Turkish insolence.

The Tripartite Conference broke up the next day – or rather, 'stood suspended' to await formal replies from the Greek and Turkish Governments to the British proposals. Ankara rejected self-government for Cyprus as impossible under existing conditions. Athens described the offer as inadequate for a people as highly developed and civilised as the Cypriots. Later the Greeks and Greek Cypriots were to accuse Britain of having devised the Tripartite Conference in order to bring in the Turks and internationalise the Cyprus question. But Archbishop Makarios had worked for five years to internationalise it *without* the Turks.

There was another blow for the Greeks a fortnight later. The British Government was afraid that the Greek appeal to the United Nations might get more sympathy this time because of the Turks' misbehaviour. So Eden approached Washington.[6]

We pointed out that it was the Greeks who had started the trouble, and that it would go on until their agitation stopped. One thing which would help to make them stop would be a rebuff by a clear majority at the United Nations. To secure this, we needed active American support.

On 21 September the Greek appeal was rejected in the Steering Committee by seven votes to four with four abstentions. Two days later the General Assembly decided by twenty-eight votes to twenty-two with ten abstentions to leave the Cyprus question to 'quiet diplomacy'.

It was a measure of Eden's failure to understand the Greek Cypriots that he thought a rebuff at the United Nations would damp down Enosis agitation. Archbishop Makarios at once proclaimed a policy of 'passive resistance' and called on those of his people who were in official positions to withdraw from the administration. This appeal had only limited success. But EOKA violence increased.

Eden had already decided that the situation was getting beyond the capacity of a civilian Governor. On 25 September it was announced that Sir Robert Armitage would be replaced by Field-Marshal Sir John Harding, chief of the imperial general staff, who had been on the point of retiring. Harding was chosen because of his diplomatic ability as well as for his military experience, but even before he arrived, Greek and Greek Cypriot propaganda described him as a 'war criminal', fresh from 'exterminating' colonial peoples in Malaya and Kenya and ordered now to crush the Cypriot struggle for liberty. In spite of this, Grivas was flattered by Sir John's appointment. He wrote later in his Memoirs: 'no higher compliment could have been paid us than to send against our tiny forces a man with so great a reputation and so brilliant a career.'

There were changes too in Greece. Field-Marshal Papagos died, old and disillusioned, at the beginning of October. He was succeeded as Prime Minister by his Minister of Works, Mr Constantine Karamanlis. This was a surprise appointment, but the best possible in the light of later developments.

Before Sir John Harding's arrival in Cyprus, Archbishop Makarios indicated that he was ready to meet the new Governor. Sir John, for his part, made it clear that, while his first duty was to restore order, he was prepared to talk to the Archbishop as 'man to man'. This was an important, if very belated, recognition of the Ethnarch's moral and political authority; no Governor had ever before considered negotiating with the Archbishop. The first meeting between Makarios and Harding took place within twenty-four hours, in the neutral territory of the Ledra Palace Hotel; it was followed by two other meetings within the week. The Governor urged the Archbishop to leave the question of self-determination to one side for the time being and to see the problem in the context of the struggle between the free world and the Soviet *bloc*; he appealed to him, as a Christian leader, to appreciate the Communist danger. Sir John assured Makarios that, if he would condemn violence and cooperate in the plans for constitutional development, Britain would be ready to discuss self-determination, once self-government was working. These were instructions from Downing Street, but Harding, with his customary frankness and honesty, felt bound to emphasise Turkey's interest in the island.

Makarios took his stand on three points: Britain must first recognise that the Cypriots' right to self-determination was the only basis for a solution; once this was done, he would be prepared to cooperate in the arrangements for self-government; Britain must then discuss the date for self-determination with the elected representatives of the people of Cyprus. Makarios completely rejected Turkey's claim to have a say in the matter and implied that he would prefer Greece to be kept out of it too. With some reluctance the Archbishop said he would use his influence to discourage acts of violence while his talks with the Governor continued.

But the violence did not stop. There were more attacks on police stations, and from these and raids on a military store and a mine EOKA acquired a considerable stock of arms and explosives. It is unlikely that Makarios could have prevented it; Grivas was in no mood to take orders from the Archbishop. But even he was not fully in control of what he had started, especially in the towns. Makarios too was under some pressure. When he met the Ethnarchy Council on 10 October to report on his talks with the Governor, his old rival, the fanatical Bishop of Kyrenia, Kyprianos, accused him of weakening in that he was ready to consider even a short period of self-government. AKEL warned the people against 'secret negotiations ... behind closed doors' and denounced any compromise with the colonial power. In the Ethnarchy Council Makarios defended his 'three points' as a tactical manoeuvre.

Makarios believed – with some reason – that the British were now being forced into concessions, and he wanted the talks to continue, in spite of the deadlock over the right to self-determination. Harding reported back to Eden and Lennox-Boyd that he was faced with a sharp choice of alternatives: either he must find a 'formula' for an understanding with the Archbishop or he would have to mount a large-scale operation to crush EOKA. There was, in fact, no such choice. Even if he had won over Makarios, he would have had to deal with Grivas. However, Eden thought that Makarios was ready to compromise, and, after Sir John had returned to London for consultations, a 'formula' was agreed that stated the views of Her Majesty's ministers with a sophistry that must have appealed to the Archbishop. It began:

> It is not their position that the principle of self-determination can never be applicable to Cyprus. It is their position that it is not now a practical proposition both on account of the present strategic importance of the island and on account of the consequences on relations between NATO powers in the eastern Mediterranean.

This changed the Hopkinson 'never' into 'some time', but it was also meant to reassure the Turks that they still had a veto. Macmillan used the occasion of a Baghdad Pact meeting to convey a soothing message to the Turkish Prime Minister. It was not until 21 November that the 'formula', devised a whole month before, was communicated to the Archbishop. In the meantime he had been to Athens to discover the intentions of the new Greek Government. With the prospect of general elections early in 1956 and popular feeling on Cyprus running high, Mr Karamanlis decided to be careful, much as he wished to be rid of the Cyprus problem. Makarios received assurances that Greece would appeal again to the United Nations, but he was urged to show restraint and keep a dialogue going with the Governor, if he returned from London with new proposals.

The 'formula' repeated the British offer of talks with elected Cypriots when self-government was working and 'capable of safeguarding the interests of all elements of the people of Cyprus'. It added that Greece and Turkey should be associated with these discussions. That was totally unacceptable to Makarios and he rejected the 'formula' outright. The British ambassador in Athens, Sir Charles Peake, reported this to the new Greek Foreign Minister, Mr Spyros Theotokis, who was apparently 'very shaken' by the news; he said his Government had thought the British 'formula' constructive. Eden tried to get Karamanlis to put pressure on Makarios, but the Greek Government was paralysed by the thought of the elections and its fear of the Archbishop. After consulting with Kranidiotis, the Ethnarchy secretary, and with the Greek consul-general in Cyprus, it suggested that Britain should modify the 'formula' where it referred to conditions which must be satisfied before the right of self-determination could be exercised. The United States consul in Nicosia, Mr Raymond Courtney, had told the Archbishop that his Government strongly felt the 'formula' should be accepted. Now he began to think that Makarios was a prisoner of the extremists and took the Greek view that the 'formula' should be amended to make things easier for the Archbishop. On 5 December the Greek Government asked Britain to leave out references to treaty obligations – in other words, the need not to upset Turkey because of NATO – and to agree to hold talks with the Cypriots about a date for self-determination after 'a reasonable period' of self-government, which should be specified. Two days later the Ethnarchy called for the exercise of self-determination to be 'easy and quick'. Sir John Harding reported to London that the Archbishop had 'raised his sights'. He did not believe that Makarios was anybody's prisoner and thought he could carry the great majority of Greek Cypriots with him in any settlement he might accept. Sir John added: 'I suspect that he knows this very well and admits it to himself. But he will not hesitate to use pressure from the extremists to justify intransigence on his own part and to frighten the Greek Government.'[7]

Meanwhile the British Government had tried to respond to the appeal from Athens. On 9 December it sent Theotokis an amended 'formula'. This dropped the reference to associating Greece and Turkey, as NATO powers, with future discussions on self-determination, and said: 'If the people of Cyprus will now participate in the constitutional development, it is the intention of Her Majesty's Government to work for a final solution consistent with the treaty obligations and strategic interests of Her Majesty's Government and its allies, which will satisfy the wishes of the people of Cyprus.' There was nothing in this to suggest that the British Government contemplated eventual Enosis.

Athens was still unhappy with this formulation and asked for more changes. The British ambassador in Ankara gave a warning that any further juggling with the proposed statement would cause an explosion in Turkey. However, on Christmas Eve Theotokis sent a senior diplomat to Nicosia and, as the year ended, it was announced that the Governor and the Archbishop would shortly resume their talks. Makarios said he thought the problem of Cyprus was going to be solved, and there was a sudden feeling of relief in Athens and Nicosia.

The situation in Cyprus had very much worsened during the previous three months. Harding had immediately asked for – and got – police reinforcements from Britain to make good the Greek Cypriot resignations. As the bomb-throwing continued, night-curfews began to be imposed in the towns. Tension grew with the approach of 28 October – '*Ochi* Day' – the anniversary of Greece's defiance of Mussolini and her entry into the Second World War. Greek flags were run up everywhere; as fast as they were taken down by the security forces, others appeared. The Governor decided to ban all meetings and demonstrations on the 28th and explained in a broadcast that it was to prevent 'hooliganism' – an unfortunate word. On the 27th the first British soldier was killed, in an ambush in the Paphos area. On the 'National Day' itself – by some extraordinary mischance, though the Greeks thought it deliberate – Michael Karaolis was sentenced to death by a Nicosia court for the murder of a Greek Cypriot policeman. Athens radio claimed that he was a 'pure patriot' who had struck a blow for freedom and, simultaneously, that he had had nothing to do with the shooting.

By 18 November Grivas had organised his combat groups sufficiently to launch a new offensive. He claimed that more than fifty
bombs were exploded that first day. Some went off in army camps,
where Greek Cypriot civilians still moved freely. Other targets
were the bars frequented by British servicemen and the homes of
officers and their families. In the first week three NCOs and one
private were killed in separate attacks. A Greek Cypriot woman
died in a bomb explosion. A number of civilians, British and
Cypriot, received injuries. On 26 November Sir John Harding
declared a state of emergency, which allowed the authorities to
detain without trial and to impose the death penalty for possessing
arms or explosives. By now education was completely disrupted,
as schoolchildren abandoned their classes to demonstrate or fight
for EOKA. On 3 December the post office at Lefkoniko was burnt
down by a mob of youngsters. Harding imposed a collective fine of
£2000 on this small township. The people paid up promptly, but
resentment grew. EOKA leaflets were distributed in the secondary
schools, urging the pupils to kill British soldiers.

In mid-December Grivas had nearly thirty guerrillas operating
from his headquarters in the mountains of Troodos. It was too big a
concentration and he was almost caught when British troops
began a sweep. He and his men were saved only by the bad weather
– mist and rain – and their knowledge of the ground.

By now the British had nine battalions on the island which, with
auxiliaries and the police, raised the strength of the security forces
to about 15,000. But direct contact with EOKA was always difficult. The first real clash took place on 15 December when Major
Brian Coombe and his driver were ambushed by four EOKA men
on the north-western coast-road near Soli. The driver was killed
outright, but the Major, after grabbing the wheel and steering his
Land-Rover into a ditch, returned the fire. He killed one man,
Charalambos Mouskos, a cousin of the Archbishop's, and captured two others; the fourth, the already legendary Markos
Drakos, escaped with a head-wound. Makarios conducted the
funeral service for his cousin and the Greek Cypriots celebrated
'the battle of Soli'. Athens radio attributed the routing of EOKA,
when the odds in its favour were four to one, to the otherwise unre-
ported arrival of 'strong military forces'; Grivas merely claimed
that the automatics had jammed.

In his New Year message for 1956 Sir John Harding unwisely

said that the days of EOKA were numbered. The violence increased. A Turkish Cypriot police sergeant was shot and fatally wounded in Paphos – the first Turk to be killed deliberately. His death was followed by Turkish Cypriot riots in which a number of Greek Cypriot premises were damaged. Archbishop Makarios made no attempt to intervene.

At the end of January, after Harding had been back to London for talks, he had another meeting with Makarios. The Archbishop asked more questions about the proposed constitution. The Governor said he could not add to the statements already made by British Ministers and that details of the constitution were 'a matter for discussion with representatives of all sections of the community at the appropriate time'. The British 'formula' had again been slightly modified by dropping the reference to 'relations between NATO powers in the Eastern Mediterranean', which had implied a Turkish veto. Harding invited the Archbishop to make a statement saying that he found the British 'formula' acceptable as a basis for cooperation and that he would use all his influence to bring an end to violent and lawless acts so that constitutional government could be introduced in an orderly manner.

Makarios replied to Harding's formal confirmation of his proposals five days later. He said the offer of self-determination was too vague for him to accept in the form of a bilateral agreement, but that if it were made simply as a statement of British policy, he was prepared to make every effort to reduce the tension in Cyprus, while maintaining his reservations about the 'formula' and still demanding the early application of self-determination. On these terms Makarios said he was ready to cooperate with the British Government and with representatives of the Turkish Cypriot minority in the framing of a transitional constitution.

The Archbishop then went on to define what he said was 'the only reasonable and acceptable interpretation' of the term ' a wide measure of self-government'. In his view, all legislative, executive and judicial powers should be exercised by the people of Cyprus through their elected representatives, apart from the responsibility for defence and foreign affairs. This would have taken away the Governor's control of internal security, which – as Britain saw it – it was essential to maintain because of EOKA violence and in the interests of Greek and Turkish Cypriots who might be victimised through the access to confidential files. Makarios expressly rejected the idea of the Governor's reserve right to veto legislation and demanded machinery for an impartial settlement of any constitutional dispute between the Governor and the government or the elected assembly. He also insisted that there should be 'equality of all citizens' with everybody 'eligible to any public office'. That would have ruled out any special provision for the Turkish Cypriot minority, except in matters of religion and education. Finally the Archbishop called for an end to the state of emergency and an amnesty for all political offences as a prerequisite for his cooperation.

Those terms would have been unacceptable at that time even if the Archbishop's aim had been to make and keep Cyprus independent within the Commonwealth. Since his declared intention was to achieve the union of Cyprus with Greece at the earliest opportunity as the 'will' of the Greek Cypriot majority, in the face of Turkish and Turkish Cypriot opposition, the British Government's first inclination was to regard the talks as ended. However, the dialogue continued, mainly thanks to the intervention of Mr Francis Noel-Baker, the Labour MP for Swindon, whose family had long connections with Greece and owned property there. Noel-Baker undertook – with the Conservative Government's approval – a private mission of mediation between the Governor and the Archbishop. He persuaded Harding that Makarios would be more flexible if, in spite of Eden's original decision, details of the constitution could be discussed with the Archbishop before he was required to accept the 'formula'. Noel-Baker tried to get Makarios to see Britain's point of view about the need to retain control of security and the difficulty of granting an amnesty before violence had ended. On 14 February the Governor informed the Archbishop that London had agreed there could be private discussions as well as formal consultations about the constitution. It was conceded that internal security would be reserved to the Governor only 'as long as he deems necessary'. Harding said he intended to repeal some of the emergency regulations as soon as there was evidence of a genuine response to the Archbishop's appeal against violence. A few days later the Governor's office answered specific queries raised by Kranidiotis for the Ethnarchy. It was pointed out to him that the Archbishop was not asked to commit himself in advance on the form of self-government and that there was no reason to expect any delay in the transfer of powers. On 25 February Makarios noted these points but repeated his earlier demands, adding that he had made 'every possible concession'.

Meanwhile Grivas had informed the Archbishop that he would lay down arms only on condition that there was a complete amnesty for EOKA, that British troops and police brought in since the start of the struggle left, and that internal security, including control of the police, was not left in British hands during any interim period of self-government. Grivas later claimed that on 15 February he had ordered a suspension of all EOKA operations, so that no one could accuse him of being an obstacle to peace. The violence did not stop, but there were no major incidents for some days.

Towards the end of February Harding told London that it would help him if the Colonial Secretary could come to Cyprus. The Government agreed and Lennox-Boyd flew out on the 26th. Eden thought that Britain had gone as far as she could towards meeting Makarios's demands without antagonising the Turks and that it was time the world knew of this. Yet at one point it seems he was even prepared to go to Cyprus himself if it was likely he could clinch an agreement.

Lennox-Boyd had little of Harding's patience or of his understanding of the Archbishop. But his meeting with Makarios on the evening of 29 February – after two days of discussions with the Governor and his staff and with Noel-Baker – was not helped by Grivas's decision to explode nineteen bombs in Nicosia an hour beforehand as a show of strength. Grivas said that he 'decided to go against Makarios's wishes' because he had little belief in British sincerity and scant hopes that the Archbishop's terms would be accepted. It was a deliberate attempt to sabotage any discussion of self-government but the Archbishop missed the opportunity it gave him to condemn the violence.

There were some points of contact at the meeting. Makarios did not press the question of an amnesty for the four EOKA men already under sentence of death, but took it that there would be a stay of execution and a review of their cases by Cypriot ministers. Lennox-Boyd agreed that incitement to violence and bomb-attacks on unoccupied buildings were offences that could be covered by the amnesty. But he insisted that there could be no amnesty for those found guilty of violence against persons or of being illegally in possession of arms and explosives. This last exclusion meant no amnesty for EOKA or for an increasing number of Cypriots, who were often arming in self-defence. Makarios could not accept it. There was complete deadlock over the question of public security and no agreement as to what was meant by 'an elected majority' in the assembly. Lennox-Boyd argued disingenuously that the British Government could not tie the hands of the constitutional commissioner by committing itself in advance to the principle of a Greek Cypriot majority.

The talks lasted for more than two hours and, when the two men parted, Lennox-Boyd at least had decided that there was no point in continuing. On his return to London he told Eden he had little doubt that Makarios had not wanted to reach agreement. The full correspondence between the Governor and the Archbishop was published in a White Paper, and on 5 March the Colonial Secretary made a statement on Cyprus in the House of Commons. He said that five months of painstaking negotiations had ended in deadlock. Lennox-Boyd went on: 'We have made a series of concessions to the Archbishop's point of view. I must confess with distress, that as soon as one obstacle is out of the way, another one, unheard of until a week or two before, rears its head.' That was hardly a fair criticism. The Archbishop had never shifted his ground; he had merely tackled the obstacles one at a time, like any good tactician. The British, for all their concessions, had never committed themselves to anything that might make Enosis possible.

On the day after the House of Commons statement the British Government authorised the deportation of the Archbishop. Harding already had authority to deport persons responsible for disorder or disaffection, but Eden had asked him to take no action against Makarios or his bishops without consulting London. Now he decided, with Harding's agreement, that Makarios should be sent to some remote spot where he could no longer influence events. On 9 March the Archbishop was arrested as he was about to leave by plane for Athens. Three others were deported with him: Makarios's old adversary, the Bishop of Kyrenia, whose company was to be one of the greater torments of his exile; Polykarpos Ioannides, the bishop's equally fanatical secretary; and Father Papastavros Papagathangelou, the organiser of OHEN, the Christian youth movement. The four men were flown to Mombasa in an RAF plane and then taken by destroyer to Mahé, the principal island in Seychelles, far out in the Indian Ocean.

In a statement to the House of Commons on 14 March Eden justified the deportation of the Archbishop on the grounds that order could not be restored while Makarios was still in Cyprus. By that time the British Government had sufficient evidence of

Makarios's involvement in EOKA as its spiritual leader. That he had condoned violence and even encouraged it, while in general – and genuinely – professing himself to be against it was apparent from his sermons and speeches. It was known that Makarios had supplied funds for the purchase of arms and explosives to be used in Cyprus. But it was not true – as the British Government claimed – that Makarios had used terrorism to improve his bargaining position in the negotiations; that was Grivas's responsibility. Makarios was accused of acting in bad faith and of not wanting an agreement. Yet on 6 March, after Lennox-Boyd had broken off the negotiations and the Government had decided to exile the Archbishop, Charles Foley, the editor of The *Times of Cyprus*, saw Makarios and told him that the constitutional commissioner, Lord Radcliffe, whose appointment had just been announced, could not fail to produce a liberal constitution with an elected Greek majority. Makarios was sceptical but expressed his willingness to meet the man who would be drawing up a constitution.[8]

Still, Makarios had refused to condemn the violence he found repugnant, because to have done so would have brought him no obvious political advantage and would have led to accusations that he was weakening. His ambivalent attitude was never more clearly displayed than shortly before his deportation. On 11 February the Abbot of Chrysorroyiatissa was shot dead in his room by two masked men wearing the black robes of the clergy. He was killed on the orders of the local EOKA leader because of false information that the Abbot had betrayed two members of the organisation; he was also known for his friendliness towards the British. Archbishop Makarios conducted the funeral of the Abbot just along the road from his own village, Ano Panayia, honouring the supposed 'traitor' but never by a word condemning the men responsible for his murder. EOKA was above criticism[9]

The deportation of Makarios shocked the Greek world, delighted the Turks and gave critics of Britain everwhere – and the Opposition at home – an unfair opportunity to castigate the Government for using the old methods of repression against a people only wanting its freedom. There was a sharp increase in EOKA violence, and strikes and demonstrations throughout the island. In Greece the riots were bad enough to make the Archbishop of Athens cancel a mass protest meeting for fear of its being exploited by terrorists. The more serious consequences were that Britain now had no one to negotiate with or even to consult about a constitution, and Grivas all too gladly took over the political leadership. To hope that moderate opinion would emerge after the removal of the Archbishop showed great ignorance of the national character; the Greek Cypriots could contemplate no solution without their leader. The deportation of Makarios was a major blunder that only prolonged the agony of Cyprus and exposed the British Government and British troops to further humiliation.

7 Seychelles Interlude

Makarios was not altogether surprised by his deportation. Two bishops had been exiled in 1931 for a much less vigorous pursuit of Enosis and after far less violence. Yet his own international stature had increased to the point where he felt that Britain perhaps could not afford to alienate world opinion by deporting him. However, Lennox-Boyd's manner at their final meeting gave Makarios a shrewd idea that Eden was determined not to let Britain's position in the eastern Mediterranean crumble any further. The Archbishop had a warning from a contact in the government that his arrest was imminent, but he told Kranidiotis, with more self-confidence than was justified, that it was a thousand-to-one chance against. Still, as a precaution, he slipped some extra clothes and vestments and an Anglo-Greek dictionary into his suitcase before setting out on his intended journey to Athens.[1]

Makarios's sister, Maria, had been unwell and was going with him on the same plane to see a specialist. They were driven by their brother, Yiacovos, the Archbishop's usual chauffeur, to Nicosia airport with an Ethnarchy escort following. Presently they were overtaken by a car full of police. At the airport Makarios was politely separated from the rest of his party and driven to a remote section reserved for the RAF. He was ushered aboard a large plane and the deportation order was read to him. He listened in silence, without comment. Presently a very worried-looking Father Papastavros arrived, evidently – from the luggage he carried – not to say 'good-bye' but to share in the Archbishop's exile. After an interval the rotund figure of the Bishop of Kyrenia emerged from another car – a much less welcome sight. He was followed by yet a fourth car containing the bishop's secretary, Polykarpos Ioannides, who was excited and angry. The deportation order was read

84

each time. Eventually the plane took off. Makarios could only tell from the position of the sun that they were flying south-east. Later, before it was dark, he saw that they were over the Suez Canal area.

They reached Mombasa the next morning and after a twenty-four hours stop there were transferred to a destroyer, HMS *Loch Fada*. Although they were treated with great courtesy they were told nothing about their destination. Makarios remembered his geography and stories of other political deportations in that area. 'How long will it take us to get to Seychelles?', he asked a naval officer casually. 'About three days' was the answer. Makarios was satisfied.

It had been arranged that the four political prisoners should be accommodated at Sans Souci Lodge, the country retreat of the Governor of Seychelles, Sir William Addis. The Lodge stands some 800 feet above Port Victoria, on Mahé, with magnificent views of other islands in the group. A former Indian Army officer and ex-colonial official Captain P. S. Le Geyt, who had retired to Seychelles, agreed to become Controller of the Household and look after the unusual quartet. He and his wife, Margaret, a very conventional English couple, have left an entertaining account of living at close quarters with the Archbishop and his fellow-exiles.[2]

Captain Le Geyt had been told to make the internees 'as happy and comfortable as possible, subject to the necessary restrictions'. Since the Governor used the Lodge only for occasional week-ends and brought almost everything with him, the Le Geyts had to furnish the house. They spent £500 buying such things as carpets and refrigerators, Dunlopillo mattresses and bed-linen, glass and cutlery, and cane chairs for the verandah and the lawn – everything 'of good quality but in no way luxurious'.

When the 'guests' arrived Le Geyt found their appearance 'both ancient and oriental'. Makarios, in his black silk robes and with a large coloured enamel medallion hanging by a gold neck-chain, looked tall and dignified beside the stout and very short Bishop of Kyrenia and the almost as portly Father Papastavros. Ioannides, the only civilian in the party, was tall and very thin and wore a dark grey suit without a tie. Makarios was smiling and gracious and showed pleasure at his surroundings; the others were rather sullen.

They were given tea on the verandah and then shown around. Le Geyt had allotted the larger of two single bedrooms to the Archbishop and put Papastavros and Ioannides in a double room, leaving a smaller single for the Bishop of Kyrenia. Subsequently

Makarios claimed the double room on the grounds that he wanted to be able to study there; he was more anxious to get away from the snores of the bishop next door, which kept him awake.

The garage had been converted into a guard-room, but the two NCOs and six men who manned it were not armed. The internees were told that they must not leave the Lodge grounds without an escort or communicate with anybody outside. There was a domestic staff of five, apart from the gardeners. Poor Le Geyt had to live in a tent until a small house had been built for him.

He was very anxious to see that his charges got the food they liked and were kept pleasantly occupied. They told him they were very partial to salads with lots of garlic and raw onion, and that they ate a good deal of fruit. This presented no problem; there was even a new pleasure in store. Among the bougainvillaeas and the frangipani in the grounds of the Lodge there were some huge mango trees and the Cypriots enjoyed collecting basketsful of fallen fruit. They liked sitting about in the garden, talking among themselves or looking at the view, but it was difficult to find any more specific occupation for them. Mrs Le Geyt tried to interest them in sketching and bought them materials, but there was no response. Her husband asked his superiors for a croquet set – 'just the job', he thought, 'for the lawn' – but the request was refused. The mind conjures up a picture of the stout Kyprianos and the elegant Makarios 'croqueting' through the hoops in full canonicals.

They obviously needed some informal clothing suitable for the tropics. Le Geyt got a local tailor to make them – at their request – some dark-blue open-necked shirts to be worn over black trousers. The Bishop of Kyrenia was found to have a 54″ waist.

Makarios was keen on keeping fit. He and Father Papastavros did regular exercises on the lawn. Sometimes they ran races. Although the Archbishop could always beat the priest, the tubby little cleric showed an unusual turn of speed. At other times he would act as the drill-sergeant, making Makarios march up and down to sharp words of command. Makarios asked for a skipping-rope, but, it seems, none was available.

Le Geyt was concerned to see that his charges had some entertainment. He lent them his gramophone and collection of records – mostly musical comedy and songs from the First World War. What they thought of them is not recorded. They had more than enough music of their own. Papastavros had a very powerful baritone and used to walk up the hill behind the Lodge at sunset and sing to the sea. The Brothers in the Catholic College said they could hear him 800 feet below. Makarios complained about the noise, but only half in earnest.

Gradually some social life was provided for the internees – carefully vetted by the chief of police. The most obviously suitable visitors were the local clergy – Archdeacon Preece and Canon Dymond from the Anglican church in Port Victoria and the Roman Catholic Bishop of Seychelles, Monseigneur Maradan. They would come to tea and discuss theology or compare notes about their respective Churches.

The internees were given an allowance by the Cyprus government – £150 a month for the Archbishop, £100 for the bishop and £50 each for the other two. They refused to accept the money except as remittances to be sent to their families.

They waited eagerly for letters from Cyprus and were despondent or angry when some arrived and were sent back because they had not been censored. Ioannides, the bishop's secretary, was caught smuggling out letters through the servants; two of them were dismissed, but no action was taken against the internees.

Indeed, they were given greater freedom. In exchange for their parole and a promise that they would not try to escape or issue political statements, they were allowed to leave the grounds, without an escort, by day or night.[3] This greatly pleased Makarios who was able to resume his old habit of taking long solitary walks or climbing the hills.

It also gave him an opportunity to indulge his interest in nature study. Makarios expressed great delight in the exotic fauna and flora of Seychelles – though Cyprus has a much greater variety of wild life – and he was allowed to buy a pair of binoculars and a camera for his excursions. Even when he was sitting in his room working he would keep an observant eye on some insect activity. There were many mason flies about the place – creatures like elongated black-and-red wasps which collected mud to build little pottery nests on the edges of cupboards and picture-frames. Makarios told Mrs Le Geyt, who shared his interest in the small things around him, how he had timed the whole process from start to finish.

Sometimes there were joint expeditions to places of interest. On one occasion Makarios expressed a desire to climb the highest peak in Mahé – Morne Seychellois, which rises nearly 3000 feet above the sea. A date was fixed, Father Papastavros gamely decided to join in, and a Mr du Buissons from the Department of Agriculture went with them as a guide, taking two porters to carry the lunch and panga-knives for hacking through the undergrowth. They reached the summit – all but Father Papastavros, who could not quite make it – in three hours. Makarios carved the letter 'M' on a tree near the top and then climbed the tree itself so that he could say with a teasing smile that he had been higher than anyone else. Earlier they had found a little trickle of a mountain stream where it ran through crevices among the rocks. They were very hot and thirsty but the water was out of reach. If only they had a tin and a piece of string, du Buissons lamented. Makarios was not to be put off. 'Come on', he said, 'hold on to my ankles'. And down he went head first with du Buissons grimly holding on to the Archbishop's legs while he scooped up the water with his hands.

Captain Le Geyt's comment on this incident was: 'It is difficult to understand why a man with such a sporting nature has not condemned the unsporting tactics of the EOKA terrorists'.

The internees had been provided with a radio on which they listened avidly to BBC news bulletins relayed by Radio Seychelles and, whenever they could, to short-wave broadcasts from Athens. They were aware that Makarios's deportation had created a profound shock among Greek Cypriots and a surge of EOKA anger against the British and anyone who was thought to collaborate with them. An English police sergeant was shot dead in Nicosia. A Greek Cypriot was deliberately gunned down by masked men who entered a church during a service to get him. Schoolgirls attacked a Turkish village. A week after the internees had settled in at Sans Souci a time-bomb was placed in Field-Marshal Sir John Harding's bed by one of his own servants. Harding put a reward of £10,000 on the head of Grivas. Grivas proclaimed that the man who killed the Governor would be a 'national hero' and have his name 'written in letters of gold'.

Feelings were further exacerbated when, in Easter week, the British hanged Michael Karaolis and Andreas Dimitriou, two members of EOKA's execution squads. Grivas responded by executing two British soldiers, Corporal Hill and Private Shilton, who had been taken as hostages.

News of this kind appeared to depress Makarios who realised he had completely lost control of events in Cyprus. Yet when he heard a suggestion on the radio that he might be sent to London he showed a noticeable reluctance for some days to be separated from his companions for a walk or a drive. He was apparently worried that he might be spirited away by the British to have pressure put on him.

In the spring of 1956 British troops began to concentrate their efforts against EOKA's small combat units operating in the forested area of Troodos around Kykko Monastery. They were not long in suspecting that the monastery itself was regularly used as a guerrilla supply centre. On one occasion during a search they found a quantity of ammunition, an EOKA duplicating machine and a locked safe. The monks said the key had been lost; when the safe was taken away and opened it was found to contain dynamite. Athens radio reported the incident as the 'pillaging' of historic spiritual treasures from the 'most sacred ark' of the Cypriots.

Harding ordered a major sweep through the mountains, using Kykko Monastery as a base. More than once Grivas was pinned down and nearly captured. A dozen of his men were taken prisoner but – as Grivas himself said – Harding was 'using a tank to catch field-mice'. The worst disaster was a forest fire which raged for six days; at least nineteen soldiers died in the flames. Grivas accused the British of starting the fire deliberately in order to trap him. They said *he* had done it to enable him to escape.

In spite of Grivas's contempt for the British military, the Troodos operation forced him to change his plan of campaign. Escaping down to Limassol he set up headquarters in a suburban house belonging to a young bank-clerk and his family, which remained his base for almost the next three years, until near the end of the Emergency. A special hide-out was constructed for him and his lieutenant, Antonis Yeoryiadis, underneath the kitchen floor and a hen-run in the garden. From here Grivas began to reorganise his scattered combat groups. To give himself time and to see whether he could exploit the situation politically he declared a truce in mid-August 1956 and demanded that the British should resume negotiations with Makarios. Harding, knowing EOKA's disarray but misjudging Grivas's spirit, called on EOKA to surrender. He offered its members the choice between a safe-conduct to Greece and staying in Cyprus with a liability to be put on trial for any specific crimes. This produced from Grivas the defiant cry of the Spartans at Thermopylae: 'Come and get us!' The young EOKA turned a donkey loose in the streets of Nicosia, loaded with toy guns and carrying a placard which said: 'Field-marshal, I surrender'. While the Cypriots were laughing over their disappointed hopes of peace, Grivas ordered his men to be prepared for a long struggle.

At this point the British Government published extracts from some of Grivas's diaries and correspondence which had fallen into its hands. Grivas was a compulsive writer who always felt the need to justify himself on paper when he could not convince others of the rightness of his views. Just before the start of EOKA's operations in April 1955 Grivas entrusted some of his archives to two brothers who buried them, on his instructions, in glass bottles in a field near Lysi, a village on the way to Famagusta. The only other person who knew about this – according to Grivas – was his Nicosia landlord of the time, who afterwards turned informer and betrayed the hidden papers to the British. Parts of Grivas's diary written later also came to light, and the lengthy extracts published by the British covered the period from October 1954 to June 1956. They substantiated the statement made by the Government immediately after Makarios's deportation, that there was a large volume of evidence to show that the Archbishop was deeply implicated in EOKA's terrorist campaign. The statement – reproduced in the Seychelles 'Government Bulletin' – caused considerable indignation among three of the internees, more because of the use of the word 'terrorism' than because they questioned any of the allegations. Makarios alone was outwardly calm, though the news must have increased his apprehensions about Grivas's activities, now that he was under no restraint.

The publication of extracts from the Grivas diaries plunged the whole party into gloom. Here were details of EOKA's organisation and all its early difficulties with the names and code-names of those involved.[4]

19 November 1954: Papastavros also sent three men for training.

5 January 1955: Papagos [the Greek Prime Minister] is in favour of action and has asked why we have not yet started. The Archbishop also.

The Archbishop offered money for a caïque and for purchasing of more arms and ammunition. . . .

Later in the diary Makarios was referred to as Genikos or Gen or G (indicating his 'general' or overall leadership).

4 June 1955: The Gen has fixed a meeting with me in the Met [the Kykko Metokhi] on 7th inst. at 1830 hours.

Grivas's all-too-candid diaries revealed his disappointment with EOKA and with the general Greek Cypriot response to its activities. They also showed the reluctance with which Makarios had accepted the armed struggle. However, Grivas guessed that the British Government had published the diaries in order to discredit the Archbishop still further and so avoid negotiations with him at a moment when EOKA had been seriously weakened. Realising the damage this would do to Greek Cypriot morale, Grivas decided on wholesale, if unconvincing denial. He confided to the current volume of his diary:

I have put out leaflets saying that the whole story of my journal has been fabricated by the British in order to distract world attention from the situation in Cyprus which they themselves have created.

Sir John Harding used the publication of the diaries to put Anthimos, the Bishop of Kitium, and Kranidiotis, the Ethnarchy secretary, under house arrest; both had been incriminated. Grivas decided he must take over the full political direction of the struggle himself.

Captain Le Geyt had always considered it his duty to ignore the reasons for his charges' internment; whatever his private feelings were, he did not let the Grivas diaries change his attitude to the Greek Cypriots, with whom he was now on very good terms. (Only a fortnight before he had had a special cake made for Makarios's birthday.) Another ex-colonial official was much less tolerant. Soon after his arrival in Seychelles Makarios had asked if he could have lessons to improve his English, which then was poorer than might have been expected of someone who had spent a year and a half in the United States. Le Geyt accordingly produced an elderly Welshman, a retired district commissioner from Tanganyika named Stanley Jones – 'one of the best of the "Old School"', according to Le Geyt – who undertook to give English lessons to the Archbishop and his companions.

All went well for the next four months or so, in spite of the fact that Le Geyt offered Makarios as a first text-book a copy of his own pamphlet, '101 Pillars and Planks of Bridge', more to improve Mr Jones's contract bridge than to make the Archbishop's English more idiomatic. However, when details of the Grivas diaries reached Seychelles, Mr Jones decided on grounds of conscience that he could no longer give lessons to the Archbishop or the Bishop of Kyrenia.

Otherwise life at Sans Souci continued uneventfully, though it was observed that Makarios had begun to show signs of strain. He looked pale and worried and his increasing baldness gave his bare head a moon-like appearance as he sat in the shade of a mango tree and wrote letters or recorded his thoughts. For a time the Cypriots discontinued their evening walks and Ioannides gave up his gardening. They had long conferences, followed by even longer silences, and then the typewriters provided for them would be clicking far into the night.

In mid-September Makarios was admitted to the hospital in Port Victoria with a suspected duodenal ulcer. However, it proved a false alarm and after a few days he was back again in Sans Souci, calm and contemplative and often preferring solitude to the company of the others. He was given a tent in a remote corner of the garden to use as an office.

During the summer of 1956 the British Government sounded out Turkey about fixing a date for talks with representatives of the Cypriot people on the question of self-determination, to be allowed perhaps after ten years of self-government. It also raised the question of conceding an elected Greek Cypriot majority in a future assembly with built-in safeguards for the Turkish Cypriots. Ankara's attitude was completely negative. However, in July Britain sent the eminent jurist, Lord Radcliffe, to Cyprus to study the situation for himself, unrestricted by any terms of reference. Lord Radcliffe, who had had much experience in advising on post-colonial constitutions, went quietly to work and talked to many Greek and Turkish Cypriots. His mission was much overshadowed by President Nasser's nationalisation of the Suez Canal in the same month and by the Anglo-French landings in Egypt in October. When British and French troops poured into Cyprus as their jumping-off ground for the intervention at Suez, Grivas saw this as an opportunity to step up his attacks on the occupation authorities. EOKA violence reached a new peak during October and November. It was countered by the wholesale arrest and detention of suspects, day-time curfews and collective fines which, together with EOKA's intimidation, drove the majority of Greek Cypriots into a sullen obstinacy.

After the failure of the Suez intervention, Harding had more troops at his disposal and by the end of the year he had begun to make life difficult again for EOKA in the countryside. But Grivas was now concentrating on his urban execution squads whose targets were more often Greeks than British or Turks. He claimed in his Memoirs[5] that between August 1956 and January 1957 the Nicosia team alone was responsible for more than twenty killings, mostly in the crowded shopping-streets of the old city. The leader of the team was a young free-lance photographer named Nikos Sampson, who was later to acquire his greatest notoriety as the puppet-President installed by the Greek 'Colonels' in 1974 after their *coup* against Makarios. The young Sampson drew attention to himself by the frequency with which he offered newspapers the first picture of someone shot dead in a Nicosia street – not surprising when he or one of his team had made the killing and tossed the gun to some innocent-looking girl or other bystander who quickly disappeared.

Just before Christmas 1956 the Colonial Secretary, Lennox-Boyd, announced that the British Government was offering Cyprus a new constitution drawn up by Lord Radcliffe. After studying the demographic character of Cyprus during two visits, Lord Radcliffe reported that he could not accept the Turkish Cypriots' demand for equal representation with the Greek Cypriots, although he appreciated their anxieties. To divide political power equally between 18 and 80 per cent of the population was, he said, to admit that there was no way of protecting the minority from oppression except by a federal system. Could Cyprus be organised as a federation? Lord Ratcliffe answered his own question in these memorable words: 'There is no pattern of territorial separation between the two communities'.

His aim therefore was to give the Turkish Cypriots such unshakeable guarantees of their security and civil rights that Britain could throw all her liberal and democratic sympathies on the side of the Greek Cypriot majority. By his terms of reference, published in September, Lord Radcliffe was required to reserve external affairs, defence and internal security to the Governor, since no change of sovereignty was contemplated. Outside these limitations Lord Radcliffe decided to reject the earlier British idea of a phased transfer of power on the grounds that the Cypriots were a mature people. Within the prescribed sphere of self-government the Greek Cypriot majority was to have immediate and full control, except that legislation exclusively affecting the Turkish Cypriots was to need the approval of at least two-thirds of their elected members in the assembly. There were to be fundamental guarantees that no law or official action could interfere with the rights of either community in matters of language, religion, education and cultural activities.

The proposed Radcliffe constitution was the best ever offered to Cyprus – and many Greeks and Greek Cypriots have since acknowledged this. It had 'the jewelled precision of a fine watch, yet was sturdy and sensible enough for everyday use'.[6] It was true there was no mention of self-determination at some future date, and when Lennox-Boyd presented the proposals to the House of Commons on 19 December he was unwise enough – or malicious enough, as some people thought – to do so in terms which enraged the Greeks and delighted the Turks. He said that, when the time came to ascertain the political wishes of the people of Cyprus, the views of the Turkish Cypriots would have to be sought if there was a desire for a change of sovereignty. Yet even Archbishop Makarios had once said, in an unguarded moment (20 October 1954 in London) that he believed in self-determination for the Turks of Cyprus as well as for the Greeks.

The Greek Government rejected the Radcliffe proposals totally and immediately on the day they were announced, although Lennox-Boyd had been to Athens a week before to explain them. The Turkish Government welcomed them as a 'reasonable' basis for discussion, but said it would expect equal representation for the two communities in the assembly (which would have made nonsense of the majority principle). However, on 28 December Prime Minister Menderes, noting the Greek Government's rejection of the proposals and Lennox-Boyd's broad hint of an ultimate Turkish veto, said that partition was the only solution since Turkey needed an outpost in Cyprus for her own security. It was a claim that was to be advanced with more and more determination.

Grivas had denounced the constitutional proposals, even before they were announced, as an Anglo-Turk conspiracy. Many Greek Cypriots would have liked to study them, but EOKA gave them no chance. Leaflets were showered on the streets saying 'Bring back Makarios! Down with the Constitution'. The Ethnarchy, or what was left of it, wanted to consult Makarios, but when Harding suggested sending Kranidiotis and the elected mayors of Cyprus to Seychelles to discuss the Radcliffe proposals, it objected that it was not for Britain to choose his advisers. Dr Dervis, the mayor of Nicosia, said he was ready to get Makarios's views if the meeting could be in London. The Greek Government made a similar offer, provided Makarios was allowed to go to Athens. Eden and Lennox-Boyd were in no mood to make concessions to the Archbishop but they quietly sent Lord Radcliffe's secretary, Mr D. L. Pearson, and the attorney-general of Cyprus, Mr Criton Tornaritis (then seconded to the Colonial Office), to Seychelles with a copy of the constitutional proposals and authority to answer questions about them.

They arrived on 21 December and had long consultations with Makarios, interrupted only by the Christmas and New Year festivities. The atmosphere was unusually cheerful. Tornaritis had a fund of good stories and kept the party amused. He even teased Ioannides by reminding him that he had once sent him to prison for sedition and was prepared to do so again. Ioannides, discomfited for a moment, then joined in the general laughter.

There was much expectation on Mahé that the internees would be leaving by the next boat with Pearson and Tornaritis. Arrangements were made for them to go on an excursion to some of the other islands which they had not yet seen and did not want to miss. Father Papastavros and Ioannides began buying souvenirs. But on 13 January – again that significant number, and the anniversary of Makarios's ordination as deacon – the mail-boat left with the two government envoys but without the internees. Tornaritis had had a last walk and talk with the Archbishop that morning.

Makarios took a firm stand that he would not discuss the future of Cyprus while he was interned, and the British Government had no intention of releasing him unless he condemned terrorism. Concerned as he was about the effects of Grivas's erratic campaign of violence, Makarios still believed what he had told the Archbishop of Canterbury eighteen months before, that to condemn EOKA would expose him unprofitably. He would be accused of abandoning the struggle for Enosis, and the leadership would pass to others.

Makarios admitted later that he had been worried during his banishment in case the people should forget him;[7] his predecessor at Kitium, the bishop who had led the revolt in 1931, had died obscurely in exile. For all that Makarios was prepared to play the British at their own waiting game.

The volume of his correspondence had greatly increased and, after his lessons with Mr Jones had stopped, the Archbishop found the English side of it more difficult. The chief of police, who had to vet such appointments, tried to find a suitable replacement but without success. Eventually Le Geyt suggested that his wife might coach the Archbishop – without payment, of course, since they did not want to take financial advantage of Mr Jones's scruples. So, immediately after Christmas, Margaret Le Geyt began to give Makarios six hours' practice a week in reading, writing and conversing in English. Her later account of these sessions was charmingly naïve but it revealed a side of Makarios's character that was not widely known.

On the first occasion he produced answers to three letters which he had already drafted in a mixture of Greek and English. With the help of Roget's Thesaurus and a student's English dictionary Margaret licked them into shape. Two were addressed to young mothers, and in one of them Makarios wrote: 'Please convey to your small son my apologies for having inadvertently cast a slur upon his manhood when I last wrote. I had heard that the baby was a girl!'

With the letters out of the way Makarios astonished Mrs Le Geyt by asking for a lesson on English table manners. Such things, he said, were different in every country. Once he had not found his table-napkin until the maid took away the plate. Were you allowed to put your elbows on the table in England? Only at the dessert stage, Margaret thought, after some hesitation. Her husband, more strict, told her later that she should have said: 'Never when ladies are present'.

Makarios was intrigued by English metaphors and proverbial phrases, especially when they involved animals. 'How does he know that secret?', Margaret once asked as a test question. The Archbishop smiled broadly and answered: 'Someone has let the cat out of the bag.' Then he added: 'Once I let one small cat out of the bag', without elaborating further.

To gain fluency in speaking English Makarios told his tutor

about his early life in Cyprus – in the village and at Kykko Monastery, which he was delighted to find Mrs Le Geyt had visited
many years before during a holiday in the island. He also told her
about some of his experiences in Athens and in the United States.
Reading aloud was more of a problem because of the shortage of
suitable books. Soon after his arrival Makarios had bought a copy
of *The Five Hundred Best Letters in the English Language* down in Port
Victoria, but this was rather heavy going stylistically. He liked
reading from Oscar Wilde's *De Profundis*, which he had once had to
study at college, and he also enjoyed Pearl Buck's autobiography.

It occurred to Mrs Le Geyt that the best way for the Archbishop
to get practice in good conversational English would be to read a
play together. She thought of *Outward Bound*, that somewhat moral
tale in which the passengers on a ship eventually realise they are all
bound for heaven or hell – but there was no copy in the public
library. Of the plays available she rejected Restoration comedy
('not very suitable'), plays in dialect – for obvious reasons – and
thrillers ('too many tough guys'). A volume lent by a friend of Margaret's yielded some good scenes from John Drinkwater's *Abraham
Lincoln* – the American President was evidently a hero of the Archbishop's[8] – and from Terence Rattigan's *The Winslow Boy* – the
story of an Osborne cadet cleared of a false accusation of theft by a
brilliant QC. 'The Archbishop', Margaret recalls, 'made quite a
good impersonation of the terrifying interlocutor of the shivering
small boy'.

Makarios reached the peak of his performances in James
Bridie's charming re-working of a story from the Apocrypha –
Tobias and the Angel. He and Margaret read the whole play together,
dividing the characters between them. At one moment Makarios
was the timid young man, wrestling with the giant mud-fish that
attacked him when he went to bathe in the Tigris ('Ough! I've got
him. By gum, he is strong!'). Then he was the Archangel Raphael,
first disguised as the porter who accompanies and protects Tobias
on his dangerous journey, afterwards resplendent in golden
armour and rolling out the sonorous cadences of the Hebrew
chronicler. Between times – to his great delight – the Archbishop
had to double as the foul-smelling Demon Asmoday. ('Don't you
know me, Stinker? Don't you remember the College of Cherubim?
Look at me, Asmoday.')

Makarios, as usual, had great hopes of the now annual Greek

appeal to the United Nations on the question of Cyprus, especially as, this time, Britain was smarting from her humiliation over Suez, which had exposed her – in many countries' eyes – as unrepentantly imperialist. The Anglo-French fiasco in Egypt and the more successful Soviet military intervention in Hungary held up the work of the Eleventh General Assembly, so that the Cyprus question did not come before the Political Committee until February 1957. Before the debate the Greek Foreign Minister, Averoff, warned Grivas that the outcome might be unfavourable since the United States thought the Radcliffe proposals were a good basis for negotiation. Grivas refused to consider Averoff's appeal for a cease-fire to improve the atmosphere, but he said he would scale down his operations. (He needed to do so because several of his best men had recently been killed or captured; one of those caught was Nikos Sampson.)

During the UN debate the Indian delegate, Mr Krishna Menon, argued that, although his country saw the issue as one of Cypriot nationalism, the fact that many Cypriots spoke Greek did not make them Greek any more than the use of English made the United States British; he advised the Cypriots to opt for independence as the only solution. Eventually the Political Committee adopted, by seventy-six votes to nil with two abstentions, a vague resolution tabled by India which called for 'a peaceful, democratic and just solution' of the Cyprus problem through negotiation. The General Assembly endorsed it, and all the governments directly concerned hailed it as a victory. Averoff said the resolution clearly called for talks between Britain and the Cypriots. Menderes, the Turkish Prime Minister, told the National Assembly that Greece had been rebuffed on the issue of self-determination and that the vote was plainly in favour of negotiations between all the interested parties. The United Kingdom delegate to the UN, Commander Noble, said there was recognition of the fact that Britain, Greece and Turkey all had an interest in a solution and could start talks again when there was no violence or intimidation.

On 14 March Grivas, who was now hard-pressed, offered to suspend EOKA's operations if Makarios was released to negotiate with Britain as the only representative of the Cypriot people. There was great excitement in Mahé as the news came through. Father Papastavros sang jubilantly in the moonlight. The next day Makarios told Le Geyt he saw no obstacle in the way of talks.

But there was an obstacle; indeed, more than one. Harold Macmillan, who had succeeded Eden as Prime Minister in the wake of the Suez crisis, was more pragmatic, less doctrinaire than his predecessor. He had immediately, in January, begun.a reappraisal of Britain's position in the Middle East and the eastern Mediterranean. In this context he began to wonder whether there could not be some disengagement in Cyprus – whether Britain, in fact, needed more than an airfield there or 'a sort of Gibraltar'.

Then came Grivas's offer to suspend hostilities if Makarios were set free for talks. This almost coincided with a suggestion from Lord Ismay, the secretary-general of NATO, that he might use his good offices to try to mediate between Greece and Turkey. There was general agreement in the Government that Lord Ismay's offer should be accepted. Grivas's proposal however presented a dilemma. Most ministers acknowledged that Makarios could not be kept in Seychelles indefinitely, and Sir John Harding, with closer knowledge of Greek Cypriot feeling, argued strongly that the Archbishop should be released for talks even before EOKA was defeated. The Government had little doubt that Grivas's offer to 'suspend', not to 'cease' operations was simply a device to buy time to reorganise, and it feared that Makarios's release at that moment might prevent wider negotiations. However, Harding's view seemed to prevail when Macmillan went off with the Foreign Minister, Selwyn Lloyd, to meet President Eisenhower in Bermuda. The following day, after more discussion in the Cabinet, Lennox-Boyd, the Colonial Secretary, told the Commons that the Government could not accept a temporary suspension of hostilities but that Makarios would be released from internment if he would call for an end to violence. He was not asked to condemn terrorism, but Lennox-Boyd said there was no question of the Archbishop's return to Cyprus at the moment and he made no reference to any future negotiations with Makarios. He went further, and let it be understood that there would be no discussion of the internal government of Cyprus before Lord Ismay had had a chance to reconcile the conflicting views of Greece and Turkey.

A week after Grivas's offer the Governor of Seychelles, Sir William Addis, called on Makarios for the first time during his internment and conveyed a message from Lennox-Boyd. The next day the Archbishop looked pale and anxious. He told Le Geyt that he had had a sleepless night thinking out his reply to the British Government. He said it was difficult for him to take a decision on such a crucial matter without the advice of various sections of opinion in Cyprus. He spent most of the day drafting and re-drafting his reply, which was finally handed to the chief of police in the evening. The Governor came up again the next day for a further meeting with Makarios. Another five days passed before the outcome was known. On 28 March it was announced from London that the internees were free to go anywhere in the world – except, for the time being, to Cyprus. Makarios had parried with an offer to call on EOKA to stop all violence, if the British Government lifted the emergency regulations in Cyprus. He rejected the idea that his own freedom could be the subject of bargaining. The British Government decided, on balance, that it was better to let the Arch-bishop go, so long as he was kept out of Cyprus. The Lord President of the Council, Lord Salisbury, resigned from the Government in protest.

He – like others in Britain – believed there had been no change of heart in Makarios during his year of exile. Yet it was naïve to think that the Archbishop could have condemned EOKA or even ap-pealed to Grivas to stop operations while Harding was making every effort to capture him and crush his organisation. The British Government, which had made the mistake of exiling Makarios in the first place and then fumbled over his release, had only increased the Archbishop's stature. It was now letting him free to conduct the campaign for Enosis anywhere outside Cyprus, although – in spite of all his correspondence with people in the island – he was out of touch with popular feeling there about EOKA. Had the British Government been shrewder and paid more attention to the evidence from the Grivas diaries of the Arch-bishop's reluctance to condone terrorism, it might have devised a formula, whereby Makarios could have been allowed to praise EOKA for its 'heroic' struggle, while proclaiming that its goal had been achieved with the UN call for negotiations and his own release. Makarios might even have thought of this for himself. By dissociating himself from any *future* action by EOKA he could have emphasised the need for a political solution to which he must be a party. It was another lost opportunity for both sides.

The news that Makarios had been freed was greeted in Cyprus with the ringing of church bells and wild demonstrations of joy among the Greek community. People poured into the streets, '*zito*'-ing the Archbishop, EOKA, Enosis – and the British. English sol-diers who met with little but sullen looks in the last twelve months were suddenly embraced or carried shoulder-high. The Turkish Cypriots looked on in gloom and foreboding at the stupidity of the British.

The day after the news of his release Makarios gave a press conference and handled it adequately in English without an interpreter. Both here and in answering the questions cabled to him by foreign newspapers the Archbishop was blandly evasive:

Q. Do you regret the violence in Cyprus?
A. Nobody would be pleased by the suffering caused by an anomalous situation.

Q. Do you look on your release as a hopeful gesture towards a settlement of the Cyprus question?
A. I understand my release to be a sign of the British Government's realisation of its wrong policy and I hope they will take further steps towards pacification. I hope that with the goodwill and understanding of the British Government a peaceful solution will be found.

There were suddenly many visitors to Sans Souci – among them Mr Stanley Jones who told the Archbishop why he had felt obliged to stop giving him English lessons. 'You should never mix people with politics', was Makarios's benign comment.

As the Cypriots prepared for their departure Makarios told Le Geyt of the farewell parties he wished to give at his own expense. There was to be a reception for the officials with whom he had come in contact and for all the clergy, Anglicans and Catholics, who had called on him socially to discuss theology or compare notes about their respective Churches. There was to be a tea-party for the five members of a committee who would have the job of nominating a boy and a girl in Seychelles to be educated on scholarships provided out of a £1000 investment fund endowed by the Archbishop.[9] But the party that proved most successful was the one on the last night in the garden for past and present members of the Lodge's domestic staff.

The servants and their families – about forty persons altogether – were dressed in their best suits and frocks, and some of them had brought flowers or small pieces of local handwork to give the Archbishop. He stood in line with the other Cypriots and they shook hands with everybody. Makarios had been that day for a strenuous excursion to Praslin Island and had had to hurry back, not only for the party but because a Greek tanker belonging to Onassis, *Olympic Thunder*, was expected that night to pick up the former internees. The Cypriots were all in good form – even the Bishop of Kyrenia and the dour Ioannides – and Makarios was indefatigable in attending to his guests. Margaret Le Geyt remembers the Archbishop 'rushing to and fro with trays of food, fetching extra chairs, serving drinks, and listening with a beaming smile to the music and singing, till about 11 p.m.'. Afterwards he finished a letter to the local paper in which he thanked everybody for their kindness and praised the beauty of the islands.

He bore no grudges.

The *Olympic Thunder* came with a blaze of lights at midnight, and the next morning Makarios and his companions said their 'goodbyes' and went aboard.

8 Manoeuvring for a Solution

As Makarios travelled towards Greece he gave a series of press conferences that showed he had lost none of his fighting spirit in the enervating atmosphere of the tropics. At Tamatave in Madagascar, where he landed from the tanker, he attributed his release to the influence of the United Nations and was quoted as saying that he thought the Greek Cypriots would soon achieve Enosis. A few miles further on, at Tananarive, he called on the British Government to show the same goodwill as EOKA and said he would later go to London to contact public opinion there and particularly to meet members of the Labour Party. The Archbishop had evidently been impressed by demands from such Labour leaders as Hugh Gaitskell and James Callaghan that the Government should resume talks with him. (In this context it is interesting to note that an opinion poll sponsored by the *News Chronicle* on the question 'Do you think that the Government was right to release Archbishop Makarios?' found the British public evenly divided between 'Yes', and 'No' and 'Don't know'. Oddly enough, 42 per cent of Conservatives said 'Yes'; only 32 per cent of the Labour voters consulted thought the Government had done the right thing.) At Nairobi the Archbishop declared he would not negotiate until he was allowed to return to Cyprus. He ruled out NATO mediation and talks with the Turkish Cypriot minority, but he said he would give it guarantees – though no veto, except on matters solely affecting that community.

The plethora of statements by the Archbishop – whether he was always correctly reported or not – caused some concern in London. Grivas had also threatened to begin operations again if the emergency regulations were not lifted completely. (Harding had eased them even before the Archbishop left Seychelles, but the army continued its pursuit of EOKA.) In a House of Lords debate on 12 April the Archbishop of Canterbury, Dr Fisher, hoped that his fellow prelate would restrain himself until he had had time to consult his friends and advisers in Greece and elsewhere. He thought that, unless Makarios declared himself in favour of a solution based on the Radcliffe proposals and one that considered the interests of NATO, the worst would happen: there would be partition, which would solve nothing.

The Greek Government was also uneasy about Makarios's statements and the coming visitation. The Archbishop arrived by air on the morning of 17 April and was given a tumultuous popular welcome. He drove through cheering crowds to the centre of Athens among banners proclaiming: 'Makarios must return to Cyprus' and 'Negotiations only with Makarios'. In Constitution Square he denounced the 'tortures' and the 'concentration camps' of the British and declared, to frenzied shouts of approval, that the Cypriots would continue their struggle. The official welcome was more reserved. The Foreign Minister, Mr Averoff, two other members of the Cabinet, Archbishop Dorotheos and senior officers of the army, navy and air force were among the reception party. But it was significant that the Prime Minister, Mr Karamanlis, did not go to the airport and first spoke to Makarios only on the telephone. The Archbishop was not invited to lay a wreath on the tomb of the Unknown Soldier, and his speech in the Square was not broadcast by Athens radio. In this way the Government tried to play down the occasion so as not to provoke Turkey, which had already been angered by the Archbishop's intransigent pronouncements and might well have unleashed the mob again against the Greeks of Istanbul.

Yet, after these first rhetorical, if ill-judged gestures, Archbishop Makarios showed himself much more cautious, and his tactics were very close to those of the Greek Government. Both wanted to get Grivas out of Cyprus, or at least to ensure that EOKA abandoned violence. A fortnight before the Archbishop's arrival, the Greek consul in Nicosia had passed on a message to Grivas, saying that the Foreign Ministry would have no objection if an end to operations were announced on the day that Makarios reached Athens; the Archbishop would then be consulted about a date for Grivas's departure. The little man was furious; he replied that he had no intention of laying down his arms or of leaving Cyprus until the outcome of the struggle was assured. He was in no way mollified when, after further exchanges with the consul, he got what he described as an 'unctuous' letter from Averoff, expressing anxiety for Grivas's personal safety: 'I am deeply worried about you ... Your loss would be a grievous blow'.

A few days later Grivas received a letter from Makarios which said:

> I am proud of your superb fight which has given me complete satisfaction ... I can only say you have become a legend and a symbol ... The truce you have declared is a very good idea ... I think that, after the UN resolution, a peaceful climate must be created for bilateral talks ... In view of the situation today, in Cyprus and on the international scene, is it expedient to continue the armed struggle? I sincerely believe we must find a way of ending operations without it reflecting at all on your prestige ... I would like to have your views.[1]

To this polite but forceful hint Grivas replied in a long, rambling letter that the Greek Government had failed to exploit the EOKA campaign, that a definite cease-fire would be a colossal mistake because the British would be inflexible, that the people of Cyprus would curse their leaders for abandoning them after they had made such sacrifices, and that AKEL would take over the struggle in the interests of international Communism. The argument continued until the middle of May when the Archbishop and Averoff agreed – because they could do no other – that Grivas should stay in Cyprus but refrain from action, at least until the next appeal to the United Nations in the autumn. Grivas says he found out much later, after his return to Greece in 1959, that Makarios had stopped a senior army officer from sending any more arms to Cyprus as soon as he arrived from Seychelles. Grivas's respect for the Archbishop's judgment was badly dented, but he largely observed an undeclared unilateral 'cease-fire' from March to September, although the British continued their drive against EOKA.

As Makarios began to appreciate the new situation – from sources which Grivas regarded as defeatist or hostile – he showed himself less intransigent. He maintained that his objective was still self-determination, but now after a fixed period of self-government under a constitution more liberal than the Radcliffe proposals. He said he would agree to the Turkish Cypriots taking part in the negotiations, but only in so far as they concerned safeguards for the rights of the minority; for these he was prepared to accept international guarantees. The American ambassador in Athens, Mr George Allen, and the philhellene Labour MP, Mr Francis Noel-Baker, both urged Makarios to go to London for talks, but the Archbishop insisted that he must return to Cyprus before he could negotiate. A Greek Cypriot newspaper, *Phileleftheros*, was evidently 'inspired' to point out that, if Grivas left Cyprus, the Archbishop could go back and Harding would be replaced because his job as military governor would have been completed. This had no effect on Grivas, and the failure of Makarios – and of the Greek Government – to dislodge him meant that, although the violence had temporarily ceased, there could be no political dialogue with the Cypriots.

Towards the end of April the Minister of Defence, Mr Duncan Sandys, paid a brief visit to Cyprus to try to judge what role the island would have to play in future in support of NATO and the Baghdad Pact and to honour Britain's few remaining commitments in the Middle East. His report confirmed the growing view of the Macmillan Government that Britain needed only 'a base in Cyprus, not Cyprus as a base'. At the beginning of May the Foreign Office hinted to Greece that, as Britain did not want to keep 20,000 men tied up in Cyprus, she might – if the deadlock continued – withdraw into her bases and leave the rest of the island to be partitioned. Makarios thought the British were simply bluffing – and, indeed, it was no more than an attempt to put pressure on Athens. Makarios was still waiting for an invitation to London, but it did not come. At the end of May he wrote to Macmillan, expressing his readiness to negotiate with the British Government 'in the name of Cyprus' on the application of the principle of self-determination; and he again demanded an end to the emergency regulations. Macmillan replied through the British ambassador in Athens that his Government could not negotiate with the Archbishop while he refused to condemn terrorism or negotiate with him alone because of the 'larger interests' involved.

Ankara would certainly have reacted strongly if Britain had begun talks with Makarios – and Turkey was vital to the Baghdad Pact as well as to NATO. During the spring and summer of 1957 the attitude of the Menderes Government became tougher and even threatening, as it failed to cope with mounting inflation and popular discontent.[2] Turkey was also worried by the growth of Soviet influence in Syria. For the Menderes Government an aggressive policy over Cyprus, towards Britain now as much as towards Greece, was partly a way of relieving the internal pressures on it, but also partly due to Turkey's genuine fears that Cyprus might one day be used as a base against her, if it fell into the wrong hands. She began to insist that partition was the only solution.

There were many attempts to break the deadlock. In June NATO's new secretary-general, M. Paul-Henri Spaak of Belgium, suggested that Cyprus should become independent for a fixed period and have its status protected by international guarantees, in the way that Austria was independent but debarred from uniting with Germany. The Menderes Government immediately rejected this on the grounds that Turkey had made enough concessions already in proposing partition(!). At the end of July Mr Macmillan suggested another Tripartite Conference, but this time with an open agenda and the freedom to consider any solution. The British ambassador in Athens indicated that his Government was prepared to give up sovereignty over Cyprus, except for the retention of a military base, and that it would try to persuade Turkey to be more 'reasonable'. Averoff saw some progress here, but Karamanlis rejected the idea of talks in which Turkey would again put forward her unacceptable demand for partition. Makarios agreed with that decision.

By this time Grivas had received a letter from the Greek consul-general in Nicosia, which said that Makarios's thoughts were now turning in the direction of 'independence' as a solution, provided Enosis was not permanently ruled out. The Turks were against this, the letter added, because they realised that 'once such a solution is achieved, no international guarantee, no international arrangement can prevent the natural progress from independence to Enosis'. Grivas was astonished, and refused to believe that Britain would ever give the Cypriots genuine independence. At the end of August Averoff wrote to him to say that the situation had now changed considerably in that 'most of the Allies have been convinced – and they say this – that a solution must be sought on the basis of creating an independent state of Cyprus, *without any guarantee that independence will be for ever*'. Grivas was still not impressed. He replied with a long letter to Averoff, demanding that Greece should stick to the claim for self-determination.

In an interview published in the Greek Cypriot newspaper *Eleftheria* on 21 July, Makarios said that he was ready to discuss 'real independence' for Cyprus that would not exclude self-determination. Grivas's comment later in his Memoirs was that this statement marked the first official step in the Archbishop's retreat – a step which had not been authorised by the Cypriot 'National Assembly'.

Makarios was now living in a suburban villa near Athens,[3] where his drawing-room displayed two souvenirs of his stay in Seychelles – the smooth, polished shell of a giant tortoise and a less innocent-looking *coco-de-mer*, that tropical nut whose hairy exterior recalls the more intimate parts of the female anatomy. Here the Archbishop received many visitors from Cyprus, while he waited patiently for the next appeal to the United Nations. Makarios showed great concern at the reports that detainees were being subjected to systematic torture and ill-treatment by the British. On 19 June he told the press he had in his possession 317 signed statements by Greek Cypriots about atrocities. He read extracts, professing shame at having to describe some things in detail. There was much emphasis on the indignities offered to priests and young girls, but very little concrete evidence. However, these and similar reports disturbed British public opinion. The Governor admitted there had been some rough handling during arrests, and five members of the security forces had been convicted of assaults against Cypriots. On the whole however British troops had shown great forbearance in Cyprus under much provocation. The Greek Government found itself obliged by the pressures from Makarios and Greek public opinion to bring 49 specific charges of brutality by British troops before the European Commission on Human Rights. By May 1959 it was known that, after a full enquiry, the Commission had cleared the British troops on most counts, but the findings were not published because by then a settlement had been reached. The Army took it philosophically.

One of the cases that received most publicity was that of Nikos Sampson, who was tried at the end of May 1957 for the alleged murder of a British policeman. The prosecution produced a signed confession in which Sampson, at the time of his arrest, admitted he had killed not one but two policemen. Counsel for the defence said the confession had been extracted by force, and there was medical evidence that Sampson had had a finger-nail torn off and that his body was covered in bruises at the time. Mr Justice Shaw described this as 'scandalous' and said that more force had been used in the arrest than was necessary. He rejected the confession and Sampson was acquitted, only to be immediately re-arrested, tried and sentenced to death by another judge for carrying a firearm. The sentence was later commuted to life imprisonment, but Sampson was freed in 1959, after the independence agreements. Subsequently he boasted in his newspaper *Makhi* that he had indeed killed the two policemen and several others.

Makarios's indictment of the British for their brutality served only to muddy the waters for a little: it contributed nothing towards a solution. In his concentration on the 'atrocity' stories he failed to see the dangers building up from the way in which the Turkish Cypriots were arming themselves for what they saw as the inevitable confrontation with EOKA. The underground Turkish Cypriot organisation *Volkan*, which originally had been mainly a propaganda unit run by a lawyer, Mr Rauf Denktash, turned more and more to violence. A bomb was exploded at the offices of the English-language *Times of Cyprus* because of that newspaper's sympathy towards EOKA and Makarios. There were attempts to kill Turkish Cypriots known to be hostile towards the demand for 'partition'. Later in the year, after the killing of a Turkish Cypriot police inspector and shortly before the Cyprus debate at the United Nations, leaflets announced the setting-up of a 'Turkish Defence Organisation', which became known from its initials as TMT.

The fourth Greek appeal to the United Nations, calling for self-determination for Cyprus and a condemnation of British brutality, was accepted for the agenda in September 1957, but only under the neutral heading of 'the Cyprus question'. The United States had tried to prevent what it foresaw as another sterile and embarrassing debate, and the Greek Government was pessimistic about the outcome. But Archbishop Makarios was already in New York, lobbying delegations, giving television interviews and using all his charm and persuasiveness in an effort to convince the world of the justice of the Greek Cypriot case. While he waited for the debate at the British Labour Party's annual conference, held at Brighton in October, Mrs Barbara Castle MP, speaking on behalf of the national executive, had said that the Party would try, within the lifetime of the next Labour Government, to achieve self-determination for Cyprus, without partition. To many Greeks and Greek Cypriots this was virtually a promise of Enosis by 1965, since they had no doubt that Labour would win the next elections in Britain because of Conservative policy over Suez and Cyprus.[4] Although Mrs Castle later explained that the national executive's statement had been intended 'to pave the way for negotiations', Makarios was even less inclined to come to terms with a Conservative government. On the other hand Turkey, which was already in the throes of an embittered general election, was even more determined to make a quick bid for partition.

Greek hopes and Turkish fears that Britain was weakening were further increased by the announcement that Field-Marshal Sir John Harding had asked to be relieved of his post as Governor and that London had 'reluctantly agreed'. (Sir John had done two years in Cyprus, beyond his intended retirement date.) A fortnight later a civilian, Sir Hugh Foot, a man known for his liberal outlook, who was familiar with Cyprus from having served there in the administration between 1943 and 1945, was named as Harding's successor.

Grivas was determined to show that EOKA was not finished, especially as he feared that Makarios and the Greek Government were yielding to pressure. Although the 'execution' of Greek Cypriot 'traitors' had continued – often a cover for striking at AKEL – Grivas had avoided action against the British for six months. Now, in October, after the killing of two more EOKA men by the security forces and the surrender of a third, time-bombs were planted at the government broadcasting station and in an RAF camp in Nicosia; they did considerable damage. Later a British cargo vessel was holed by a magnetic mine, at Karavostasi on the north-west coast. But EOKA's most spectacular achievement was an explosion in a hangar at the RAF base at Akrotiri; five planes were destroyed. The seventeen-year-old electrician responsible for the sabotage went on working at the base for another two months.

These demonstrations of strength were meant to impress the United Nations; they did nothing to reassure Makarios or the Greek Government that they would help the cause. The debate in the Political Committee began on 9 December and turned mainly on the question whether self-determination was applicable in all cases, regardless of other considerations. Turkey emphasised the existence of two 'peoples' in Cyprus and again accused Greece of trying to annex the island. Britain spoke of the need to consult both communities, and to get the agreement of Greece and Turkey to any solution. Many of the delegates had little interest in Cyprus, but there was considerable sympathy for the Greek argument for self-determination, as presented by Mr Averoff. On the third day of the debate the Indian delegate, Mr Krishna Menon, suggested a compromise that would get the support of the United States. The Indian resolution called for the Cypriots to have the chance of achieving their freedom and preserving it. This was acceptable to Averoff and all the Greek delegation with the exception of the Cypriot-born Savvas Loïzides, who had been one of the founder-members of EOKA. Makarios also opposed any departure from the demand for self-determination originally put forward by Averoff; he went hurriedly to the United Nations building when he heard of what sounded like Greek backsliding towards the idea of independence for Cyprus with Enosis ruled out. Averoff was forced to toe the Greek Cypriot line. Eventually after four days of tortuous and often confusing debate, thirty-three countries voted in favour of an amended Greek resolution which called for negotiations leading to self-determination, and twenty countries voted against it. There were twenty-five abstentions, but since only a simple majority is required in the Political Committee, this was a Greek victory – the first real one at the United Nations. However, the triumph was short-lived. When the resolution came for endorsement by the General Assembly, where a two-thirds majority is needed, it received only thirty-one votes – two less than in the Political Committee – and three more countries voted against it. Nevertheless the Greeks claimed they had won a 'moral victory', though the only UN verdict which stood was the one recorded ten months before, that there should be further negotiations – of a kind unspecified – towards finding 'a peaceful, democratic and just solution' of the Cyprus problem.

Sir Hugh Foot arrived in Cyprus on 3 December, just before the UN debate, to take up his duties as Governor. Macmillan had offered him the appointment because he believed that Foot's 'idealism' and inherent sympathy for colonial peoples would help towards a solution, although he made it clear to him that there was to be no fundamental change in British policy. Grivas saw that Foot, whom he described as a 'two-faced Janus', could be more dangerous than Harding, and he warned the mayors of Cyprus not to be drawn into any negotiations with him but to insist on the return of Makarios. Foot wanted to get rid of the whole paraphernalia of repression – searches, detention, curfews and collective punishment – as quickly as possible but he insisted that there must also be an end to 'violence' – and this displeased Grivas. However, when Foot appealed for 'a credit of time', Grivas grudgingly consented. In spite of the clashes during the UN debate, when Greek Cypriot demonstrators tangled with the police and troops, and the Turkish Cypriots went on the rampage, Foot began to present a new image of the Governor, touring the villages on horseback, dropping into a coffee-shop for a chat and lighting a candle in a Greek Orthodox church. Just before Christmas Foot released a hundred detainees and lifted the restrictions on the movements of six hundred other persons. There were wild scenes of rejoicing in the Greek Cypriot community. Many British were doubtful about the wisdom of such a step. The Turkish Cypriots, in spite of their misgivings, showed restraint.

However, the better atmosphere did not last for long. 1958 was to be the worst year of the emergency, with intercommunal clashes bringing the island almost to civil war and the Greek Cypriots divided against themselves, EOKA against AKEL, Grivas against Makarios.

Foot returned to London on New Year's Eve, convinced that what was needed was a period of self-government for perhaps five or seven years before there was a final decision on the island's future. The form of self-government, he thought, must be agreed with the leaders of the two communities after the state of emergency had been lifted and Makarios had been allowed to return to Cyprus; the ultimate status of the island would have to be acceptable both to Greeks and Turks. This was moving rather fast for the British Government: Lennox-Boyd, in particular, was still opposed to Makarios's return unless he condemned violence unequivocally. Harding, in his retirement, also thought that Foot had unwisely given Grivas a chance to resume action. At the end of January Foot went with Selwyn Lloyd to Ankara, where there was a meeting of the Baghdad Pact countries. During the conference they talked to Menderes and his Foreign Minister, Zorlu – both confirmed in office by the recent elections – about the new plan for Cyprus. They found them totally uncompromising – angered at Harding's replacement by Foot, furious with the British Labour Party, and rejecting everything except partition. To drive home their point the Turkish Cypriots were encouraged to hold massive anti-British demonstrations, which quickly turned into riots worse than anything organised by EOKA. In the clashes with the security forces seven Turkish Cypriots were killed and many more injured. The British were aghast. Menderes called off the rioters, but the leader of the Turkish Cypriot community, the mild Dr

Kuchuk who had been in Ankara during the talks, expressed confidence that half of Cyprus would soon become a province of Turkey.

In February Selwyn Lloyd and Foot went to Athens for talks with the Greek Government, but Turkey had already killed the new proposals stone dead. Foot sought and readily obtained an interview with Makarios. But the Governor had nothing to offer and even asked for a further 'credit of time'. He gave a warning that, if the Greek Cypriot nationalists persisted too strongly in their demands, it would lead to partition. The Archbishop took this as a threat and complained that Britain attached too much importance to Turkey.

So the new diplomatic initiative launched by Sir Hugh Foot came to an abrupt end. Nothing could be expected from the Turks, and the Greeks were soon preoccupied with a general election campaign. Karamanlis had resigned because of a revolt in his Government over his proposed electoral reform. Grivas again began to call the tune.

He no longer had the combat units for attacking the British. He therefore decided, at the beginning of March 1958, to put into action a plan of 'passive resistance' which he had long had in mind. It was to take the form of widespread minor sabotage backed by an economic boycott of everything British. The explosions were no problem; what proved more difficult was to get Greek Cypriots to respond to EOKA's week-by-week lists of goods they must not buy. First it was alcoholic drinks, confectionery and shoes from Britain. Then the ban extended to cigarettes, soap, clothing, cars, cosmetics, furniture, tinned food – and finally the football pools, which Grivas said had been taking £50,000 every month out of Cyprus. Later Grivas applied the boycott to British advertisements and the employment of British girls as secretaries in Greek Cypriot companies. All this was highly unpopular. Although the boycott was only partially successful, Cypriot businessmen appealed to the Bishop of Kitium and the Greek consul-general, and finally put pressure on Makarios. The Archbishop told Grivas in April that this campaign could damage the Cyprus economy without having any effect on Britain. Grivas's puritanical nature was shocked at the unpatriotic greed of the Cypriot businessman and the fact the Archbishop seemed to condone it, but he was also angry that Makarios had not warned him earlier. He complained of the Archbishop's lack of frankness and told him: 'There is a parting of the ways ahead and I must choose which way to follow.'

Grivas was even more indignant over what he saw as Makarios's failure to appreciate the new danger from the 'Communists'. He says in his Memoirs:

> I warned Makarios ... that they were very active politically; if we persisted in ignoring them they would reap the benefits of the harvest sown by our fighters. This warning went unheeded, and when I went on to execute a few Left-wing traitors, the Communist Mayors rushed to Athens to protest to Makarios ... I learned that the Archbishop had shown sympathy towards the Mayors.

But if Makarios realised the strength of AKEL and knew that he needed the support of the whole Greek community, his attitude towards the Turkish Cypriots at this time showed complete unawareness of the extent to which they had been armed. Grivas quotes from a letter which he says the Archbishop wrote to him early in March, advising him not to provoke the Turks, but also not to show weakness. If they gathered in the Greek sector, the letter went on, 'I think we should throw a grenade or two among them from a roof-top, so they will be taught a lesson and will not dare to congregate in mobs in future.'

The Archbishop apparently gave the same advice again in mid-April after an intercommunal clash in Limassol in which a Greek Cypriot was killed. Grivas was appalled that Makarios should try to tell him how to cope with the Turks, and the rift between them widened.

Grivas was now determined to assert his own political leadership and pursue a strategy regardless of the views of Makarios or the Greek Government. There were many bomb explosions during April as EOKA entered its fourth year of activity. Foot, worried in case the sabotage should lead to full-scale terrorist attacks again, took the unorthodox step of writing secretly to Grivas, offering to meet him anywhere, at any time, alone and unarmed if this would help to save the people of Cyprus from the disaster which was so near. Grivas admired the Governor's daring but decided that the offer was a trap.

It became known in May that a new 'Macmillan plan' for Cyprus was almost ready. Announcement of the details was unaccountably postponed for several weeks, partly perhaps because the army hoped to capture Grivas in the meantime and so remove one obstacle to the plan's acceptance. The intention now was not to seek the approval of Greece and Turkey but merely to inform their Governments about the plan a few days beforehand. In Greece Mr Karamanlis had only just returned to office after the two-month hiatus of a 'caretaker' Government and general elections. Turkey, which had kept quiet since her rejection of the 'Foot plan', now moved again, like a python getting a better grip with its jaws on its prospective dinner. The Turkish Cypriot leader, Dr Kuchuk, saw Prime Minister Menderes on 3 June and after their meeting accused Britain of trying to impose a solution on Cyprus that was against the interests of his community. On 6 June Mr Denktash made an inflammatory speech at Larnaca. The following night a small bomb exploded outside Turkey's information office in Nicosia. Like the bomb in the Turkish consulate at Salonika which had preceded the anti-Greek riots in Istanbul and Izmir in September 1955, this was the work of an *agent provocateur.* It was the signal for hundreds of Turkish Cypriots to pour into the streets, attacking Greek property, burning, looting and killing. The violence quickly spread to the villages and EOKA soon went over to the counter-attack, putting into operation Grivas's contingency plans T-P and T-Ch for dealing with the Turks in towns (*Poleis*) and villages (*Choria*) respectively. For a time the security forces seemed to be giving the Turks their head, to teach EOKA a lesson. But soon they were fully occupied trying to stamp out the flames of civil war and protect the innocent of both communities. When the intercommunal clashes eventually subsided two months later, more than fifty people had been killed on either side and many more injured or, in the mixed villages, forced to leave their homes.

When the 'Macmillan plan' was announced on 19 June, during a temporary lull in the violence, it was already doomed to failure. Labelled, with incredible optimism if not naïvety, 'an adventure in partnership', it offered a seven-year period of self-government, after which Britain would be prepared to share sovereignty over Cyprus with Greece and Turkey, provided she had assured bases and military facilities in the island. There was the further suggestion that Greek and Turkish Cypriots might be offered the appropriate dual nationality. Archbishop Makarios, after summoning the Cypriot mayors to Athens for consultation, rejected the idea of partnership as 'wholly unacceptable' because it ran counter to the fundamental right of the people of Cyprus to self-determination and destroyed their unity. The Greek Government, faced by a clamorous Opposition, with one newspaper even calling for Archbishop Makarios to become Prime Minister, then had no choice but to reject the 'Macmillan plan' too. It did so on the somewhat inadequate grounds that it violated the Treaty of Lausanne, was undemocratic, and was founded on the 'artificial' tension created between Greek and Turkish Cypriots during the past few months. But Mr Karamanlis offered to discuss the problem with the British Government, with a view to establishing temporary self-government under British sovereignty, leaving the issue of self-determination to a more appropriate time. This had the approval of Makarios: a major concession. Both men would probably have settled now for something like the Radcliffe proposals which they had rejected out of hand in 1956. But Turkey was bent on getting partition or at least an equal share in the island. She formally rejected the 'Macmillan plan', but later Mr Zorlu agreed that it was not incompatible with Turkish aims. This confirmed the worst fears of the Greeks.

The violence in Cyprus increased and tension grew between Greece and Turkey; Greek officers had already been withdrawn from the joint NATO headquarters in Izmir. Then, on 4 August, after appeals from Karamanlis, Menderes, Macmillan and Makarios for an end to the intercommunal fighting, Grivas ordered an EOKA cease-fire. TMT did the same two days later. Macmillan flew out to Athens, Ankara and Nicosia, determined to sell his plan as the only way of buying time. Modifications were made in it to answer some of the objections of the Greeks and Greek Cypriots. The Turks were appeased with a massive aid programme from the United States, the International Monetary Fund and the Organisation for European Economic Cooperation (OEEC). A start was to be made by setting up separate municipalities for the two communities in Cyprus which were already divided by barbed wire in Nicosia and other towns; the Turkish Cypriots in fact were beginning to run their own municipal services. Back in London Mr Macmillan announced his amended plan on 15 August. Makarios angrily rejected it as being unchanged in essentials and accused the British Government of setting one community against the other. The Karamanlis Government said it could not cooperate in the British plan so long as it was unacceptable to the Greek Cypriots. Ankara declared it was ready to accept 'partnership'.

Grivas was determined to frustrate what he saw as an Anglo-

Turkish conspiracy. Averoff tried hard to get him to see the likely consequences if EOKA resumed action. Turkey, he argued, now had a real interest in Cyprus, however artificially it had been created. The whole Greek nation would be in danger, and particularly the Greeks of Constantinople (Istanbul). Greece's position in the Western alliance would be threatened since, if it came to a choice between them, the West, unfortunately, would side with Turkey rather than with Greece, because of Turkey's greater importance for the safeguarding of Middle East oil. These arguments fell on deaf ears; Grivas was convinced it was Turkey's toughness, not her strategic position that gave her rewards.[5] Makarios, like Averoff, was aware of the dangers, but he had rejected Foot's suggestion that he should get Grivas out of Cyprus as the only prerequisite for his own return. The Archbishop knew that Grivas would not obey him, but he also feared that without EOKA's threat of action he would be powerless in negotiation. Yet if he had called unequivocally for an end to all Greek Cypriot attacks on the British and the Turks and had been disobeyed, the British Government would probably have been ready to talk to him.

On 21 August Grivas launched a leaflet-proclamation which declared that Britain would impose the 'Macmillan plan' only over the bodies of 450,000 Cypriots. (Makarios unwisely echoed this phrase in a sermon he preached in Athens.) A few days earlier the leaders of all the trade union organisations in Cyprus – left-wing, right-wing, Turkish and independent – had issued a joint appeal for peace, and a spokesman had said this could be regarded as a pledge that the truce would not be broken. The army's harassment of EOKA continued and Grivas stepped up the urban killings.

Foot flew to London for consultations and it was decided that he should start to implement the 'Macmillan plan' on 1 October. In the meantime there was an important development. Makarios and the Greek Government were both concerned to prevent the arrival in Cyprus of the Turkish commissioner provided for in the 'Macmillan plan' to give Ankara a say in its implementation; he was due in Nicosia at the end of September. On 5 September the Greek Government discussed the way it should handle the annual appeal to the United Nations. Makarios was consulted, and on 7 September he told the Government he would be prepared to accept *independence for Cyprus under UN auspices* after a period of self-government. That the idea of asking for 'independence' rather than 'self-determination' originally came from the Greek Government is indicated by Averoff's hint to Grivas in a letter dated 23 August. In it he spoke of 'another good way' to a solution which the Greek Government intended to use in its appeal to the United Nations, but he did not want to say more about it because it was hoped to take them by surprise. (Averoff hesitated to mention the word 'independence' to Grivas because he knew what the reaction would be.) On 19 September Karamanlis had a meeting with Makarios and told him of the Greek Government's efforts to frustrate the 'Macmillan plan' by appealing to NATO. Makarios was unimpressed; he argued that Greece should threaten to withdraw from NATO and even do so temporarily, if need be, as a way of putting pressure on Britain. Karamanlis rejected such tactics as far too dangerous for Greece, and a new coolness sprang up between the two men. However, Makarios confirmed his willingness to accept 'unconditional independence' for Cyprus, and apparently mentioned that he had already discussed this with Mrs Barbara Castle, vice-chairman of the Labour Party's national executive, a few days before, as she passed through Athens on her way to Cyprus.

Mrs Castle's three days' investigation in the island led to her passing strictures on the conduct of British troops which infuriated the Government and greatly embarrassed the Parliamentary Labour Party, even after she had partly retracted. On her way home she again saw Makarios, who authorised publication of an interview he gave her on 21 September. In it he accused Britain of trying to complicate the situation by wanting to give the Turks sovereign rights in Cyprus. He suggested that the best way to take both Greece and Turkey out of the dispute was for Cyprus to become independent, after a period of self-government, with its status not to be changed by Enosis or partition or in any other way except with the consent of the United Nations. There would be also full safeguards for the Turkish Cypriot minority. The Archbishop sent his formal proposals to Mr Macmillan a few days later.

The Labour Party welcomed them as offering new hopes of a solution, but they were treated with great scepticism by the British Government which could not believe that Makarios would long be satisfied with independence or that Turkey would accept it. Ankara's attitude was completely hostile: an independent Cyprus would mean oppression of the Turkish Cypriot community and lead inevitably to Enosis, unless this were ruled out contractually. The Greek Government endorsed Makarios's proposals, but

Karamanlis was obviously annoyed that the Archbishop had made them unofficially through Barbara Castle; he said later, in December, that they had not been presented in the best way or at the right time. The Greek Cypriot mayors applauded the call for independence but the Bishop of Kyrenia – like Makarios, still banned from Cyprus – protested vehemently against the abandonment of Enosis.

On the day after his interview with Barbara Castle, the Archbishop wrote to Grivas to explain what he had done:

> Although this new line could be described as a retreat, it is a matter of tactics imposed by the present situation and a cool appraisement of realities ... British public opinion has turned strongly against us ... America has fully aligned her policy with Britain ... Our chances at the United Nations are very limited; we would not even have last year's success if we ask for self-determination ... Barbara Castle and others in the Labour Party said they could not oppose the British plan unless the Archbishop offered something new ... In that event, they said, they would be ready to approach the Prime Minister and to push the Archbishop's views during their (Party) conference and in the press ... We had to face the situation boldly and realistically and take decisions before there was a *fait accompli*. The imposition of the British plan – no matter how bravely and resolutely the Greek Cypriot people had resisted it – would inevitably have led to partition or at least created a situation and given the Turks rights which it would have been impossible to get rid of later, even if the international situation changed.[6]

Grivas was shocked and upset by this letter. He replied immediately with an attack on the 'feebleness' of the Greek Government and on Makarios's arbitrary change of direction, though as usual he referred to him in the third person:

> Of course, the Greek Government has a right to direct Greece's foreign policy, but we also have an inalienable right to say *it is making a mistake* and to censure it for handling the Cyprus question in a lamentable way ... As for the Archbishop's new proposals about independence, I do not know what their real purpose is. If the aim is to overcome British intransigence through the so-called pressure of the British Labourites, after

Greek policy has proved bankrupt, I am afraid we shall fall into a new British trap... What we need is *a man who can back* ONE PLAN *and follow it through to the end until our opponents accept it.* We can be flexible about its details but not about its basic principles.... At any rate, I declare that I am definitely opposed to the general policy being followed over the Cyprus question. I will not let this take any specific outward form so it may not be thought that I want to exploit the situation for political aims – since I have none – or that I am putting obstacles in the way of a new political attempt at a settlement....[7]

Those reassuring phrases were immediately belied by Grivas's next words: 'and I shall remain a soldier'. He had already ordered a new EOKA offensive against the British and begun to intensify it as the date for the 'Macmillan plan' – 1 October – came nearer. In theory there were to be 'controlled attacks' against 'manned and unmanned targets', and no action against the Turks unless they deliberately provoked it. On 18 September an RAF man was shot and wounded while he was walking with his wife and two children, one of them a baby in a perambulator. The same evening there was a murderous attack on the American vice-consul in Nicosia, and two Turkish Cypriots were shot as they sat outside a coffee-shop; one of them died later. On 26 September the GOC, Major-General Kendrew, narrowly escaped being blown up as his car passed over a mine while he was on his way to Government House. He was a more legitimate target than the army sergeant's wife, Mrs Catherine Cutliffe, who, a week later, was killed with five bullets in the back as she was shopping in Famagusta; her companion, another sergeant's wife, was wounded. Within the hour British troops went on the rampage, and hundreds of Greek Cypriots were rounded up and many brutally manhandled; three died, one at least of heart failure. EOKA disclaimed responsibility for the murder of Mrs Cutliffe, the Greek Foreign Ministry lamely suggested it was a *crime passionel*, and Archbishop Makarios condemned both the killing of the woman and the fury of the British troops.[8] Yet EOKA had justified the killing of civilians in a leaflet issued in mid-September, and it had never scrupled about attacking women. On the very day of the murder in Famagusta Makarios had called upon the Greek Cypriots in a broadcast from Athens to 'fight as one man for the defence of their threatened hearths and homes'. His ambiguous words did not advocate violence, but when that was the result he held the British responsible.

In spite of Makarios's belief that the Greek Government was submitting to pressure from NATO, that organisation had considerable sympathy for Greece's efforts to frustrate the 'Macmillan plan' or at least delay it. As its members were not unanimous – the United States, in particular, backing Britain – NATO's secretary-general, M. Paul-Henri Spaak, decided to try to mediate by himself. He arrived in Athens on the day following the publication of Makarios's interview with Barbara Castle. After talks with Karamanlis, Spaak returned to Paris to propose to the NATO Council – with the secret agreement of the Greek Government and of Makarios – that there should be an immediate conference of Britain, Greece, Turkey and representatives of the two communities in Cyprus to discuss a 'Spaak plan' for an interim solution which would not prejudice the final outcome. Spaak's proposals mainly followed the lines of the 'Macmillan plan', but differed from it in two important respects. He suggested there should be a *joint* Cypriot assembly in addition to the two communal chambers and that the Governor should be assisted by the presidents of these chambers instead of being 'advised' by representatives from Greece and Turkey.

The majority of NATO members welcomed this as a brilliant move to break the deadlock, but Britain was embarrassed and Turkey hostile. The secretary-general's proposals clearly favoured the Greeks in keeping the Turkish Government out of Cyprus and counteracting the divisive elements in the 'Macmillan plan'. Turkey accused Spaak of partiality, rejected a conference and insisted that the 'Macmillan plan' be implemented as it stood. Britain, after playing for time, and consulting the Americans, said she could not abandon her plan but was ready to discuss amendments within its framework. At the beginning of October there were three days of intensive talks between Makarios and the Greek Government as to whether they should accept a conference on the British terms. Makarios, who at first had wanted no discussion of the island's eventual status, now insisted that his own proposals for independence should be on the agenda as well as the 'Macmillan plan' and the Spaak amendments.

Britain and Turkey reluctantly agreed to discuss the Archbishop's independence proposals – with him taking part – and to have M. Spaak and an American representative at the conference table. The talks dragged on in semi-secret for nearly a month, with rumour chasing rumour. They were still arguing in Paris over the question of admitting one more NATO country to the conference when, on 24 October, Makarios saw Averoff and said he thought it preferable not to have the conference. The Archbishop was convinced that the conference would be loaded against the Greek Cypriots unless Britain and Turkey were ready to rule out partition beforehand. The Greek Government knew it could not get the assurances that Makarios wanted, since neither Britain nor Turkey had any faith in the Archbishop's switch from Enosis to independence. In fact, a few days before, the Greek parliamentary Opposition under George Papandreou had mischievously – to embarrass the Government – challenged Makarios's right to renounce Enosis – which, of course, he had not done. To defend himself, Makarios had explained that his proposal would leave the future of an independent Cyprus entirely in the hands of its own people.

Averoff, who had never been optimistic about the outcome of a conference, warned the Archbishop that he must accept responsibility for rejecting it, because Greece could not afford to be denounced by NATO countries at the United Nations for being unjustifiably intransigent. Makarios willingly accepted the responsibility. His sights were now on the UN General Assembly, where he was confident that his demand for independence would fall on sympathetic ears. On the following day the Greek Government announced, with obvious embarrassment, that it could not attend the proposed conference unless there were guarantees that it would be 'constructive'. Later it made an unconvincing defence of its position before the NATO Council, without blaming Makarios, though everyone was aware it was the Archbishop who had torpedoed the conference.

October 1958 – the month of the NATO talks – was one of the blackest and bloodiest for Cyprus since the start of the EOKA campaign. According to British sources more than forty people were killed and nearly four hundred injured. The dead included six British civilians and ten members of the armed forces. A dozen Greek Cypriots were killed by EOKA and three Turks lost their lives. Halfway through the month Foot reintroduced emergency measures which had been rescinded and imposed new ones. The mutual slaughter continued during November and December but on a reduced scale.

Before Averoff and Makarios left to attend the United Nations both appealed to Grivas to help the Greek case by declaring a cease-fire. Grivas replied that he could not offer another truce that would be one-sided, but he promised to scale down EOKA's operations and later ordered his men not to initiate any action. The fifth UN debate on Cyprus opened in the Political Committee in late November. It was the longest, the most complicated and the most serious one yet, but none of the resolutions looked like commanding a majority. Eventually – to the surprise of the outside world – the General Assembly adopted, unanimously and without discussion or even a formal vote, a Mexican resolution which expressed *confidence* that the parties would continue their efforts to reach 'a peaceful, democratic and just solution'.

Something had happened that began to change the whole situation. At the end of the Political Committee's debate – on 4 December – while a dejected Averoff was talking to reporters, the usually aggressive Zorlu came up and congratulated him on his fine fight. When Averoff realised that the Turkish Foreign Minister was not being ironic or condescending, he responded with a similar compliment. As they talked, they agreed that their Governments were spending a disproportionate amount of time and energy on the Cyprus problem and making no real attempt to solve it while neglecting dangers that threatened them both. (Khrushchev had just precipitated another crisis over Berlin.) Even during the debate Zorlu had been more conciliatory, as Averoff had publicly acknowledged; he had said that the rights and aspirations of the Greek and Turkish Cypriots were not irreconcilable and had played down the theme of partition. Averoff had said Greece would welcome the demilitarisation of Cyprus and international safeguards for the Turkish Cypriots if the island became independent.

Averoff and Zorlu agreed to meet for informal talks and, as this became known, it was not difficult for the United States and Britain to get a new and optimistic formula for rounding-off the debate. In their exchange of views on 6 December Zorlu said Turkey was not thinking of territorial partition but rather of a federal system for an independent Cyprus. He also suggested that Greece and Turkey should have sovereign bases in the island. Averoff rejected this, but welcomed Zorlu's proposal that in certain areas of government the Greek Cypriots should have majority rights.

Averoff said nothing of these private exchanges in his report to the Greek parliament but he spoke of a more relaxed and conciliatory Turkish attitude to which he thought Greece should respond. There were more talks between Averoff and Zorlu when they attended the NATO ministerial meeting in Paris between 16 and 18 December. They asked Britain's Foreign Secretary, Mr Selwyn Lloyd, whether his government would agree to an independent Cyprus with some communal autonomy and sovereign British bases, the status of the new republic to be guaranteed by the three interested powers. In view of the virtual impossibility of going ahead with the 'Macmillan plan', the British Government guardedly agreed that Greece and Turkey should continue their negotiations over the internal regime of an independent Cyprus. The so-called 'Paris sketch', outlined in secret by Zorlu and Averoff before Christmas, had in it many of the elements ultimately incorporated in the Zürich and London agreements of the following year[9].

It has never been adequately explained why Turkey suddenly adopted a more conciliatory attitude. It is true she was worried by the weakening of the Baghdad Pact when the Iraqi monarchy was overthrown in July 1958 and the new regime turned 'neutralist'. But these military considerations – as later events showed – were not sufficient to bring about a reconciliation with Greece through concessions. It is more likely that Turkey realised she had effectively staked out her claim to a share of Cyprus when the British would eventually leave; she needed only to get the title-deeds from Greece.

The Greek Government had been much exhausted by the Cyprus campaign, and it had no real desire to become responsible for the island. It consulted Makarios as far as it thought necessary over the Turkish proposals, but Karamanlis was determined to get rid of the problem so long as he could avoid partition. Grivas was kept completely in the dark about these developments, except that Averoff told him there was now a chance of Turkey's accepting Makarios's demand for independence, provided there were guaranteed privileges for the minority. Makarios had already tried to convince Grivas that the Turks now realised time was not on their side. Both he and Averoff urged Grivas to keep EOKA activity to a minimum to help the atmosphere of *détente*. Grivas proclaimed a sort of truce for the fourth time on Christmas Eve. British troops kept up their harassment of EOKA but the Governor continued to commute death penalties.

Makarios and Grivas were now, each in his own way, isolated.

Grivas could not be controlled and had not been eliminated, and the problem of getting him out of Cyprus after a settlement still had to be found. But he no longer had the support of any but a handful of fanatics like the Bishop of Kyrenia who still believed that Enosis could be achieved by force. Makarios on the other hand had been circumvented by the Greek Government's direct negotiations with Turkey. The Archbishop's rejection of a NATO conference had lost him a vital bargaining position.

9 'Foundation for a Final Settlement'

The Greek-Turkish negotiations were not allowed to lose their momentum. Between Christmas 1958 and the end of January 1959 Zorlu had three rounds of talks with the Greek ambassador in Ankara, who was closely briefed by Averoff, and the two Foreign Ministers met again in Paris. Yet for a time there appeared to be an unbridgeable gap between their positions, though little was known publicly about the way the talks were going.[1]

Zorlu began by asserting that, if Cyprus was to bring their two countries together instead of dividing them, it was desirable that both should acquire strong military bases on the island and set up a combined military headquarters there, in addition to the bases that Britain would keep. The Greeks reacted sharply at the prospect of a Turkish military enclave in Cyprus, but came round to the idea of a joint headquarters, provided the Greek element was the larger. Zorlu also argued that, if Turkey gave up partition, public opinion in the country would accept nothing less than a federal state in Cyprus which should fly the flags of Greece and Turkey. The Greek Government flatly rejected federation and – with a new regard for the separate identity of the Cypriots – maintained that the Republic which should arise from the will of its people, Greeks and Turks, must have its own flag. Zorlu agreed to this so long as the other two flags were flown on holidays and ceremonial occasions, and this was acceptable to Greece.

Ankara then wanted a 50:50 ratio between the communities in the island's own security forces. Athens rejected this on the grounds that in many areas the Greek Cypriot majority would find themselves policed by Turkish Cypriots. Greece was prepared to accept a 70:30 ratio for the police force, as she had already done for the civil service – though here she complained that, while it might

126

work in the upper grades, enforcing it all the way down could be prejudicial to good government, since the Turkish Cypriots would not have enough qualified candidates. Ankara rejected this argument. Meanwhile Karamanlis had proposed that the President, Vice-President and members of the House of Representatives should be elected by the people as a whole, not separately by the communities, as the 'Paris sketch' had suggested. Turkey said this was totally unacceptable.

Makarios was kept informed of the negotiations while he was still in New York. He returned to Athens on 15 January, having cancelled a proposed trip to the Far East. On the 29th, after the Turks had demanded an early summit meeting to clinch a settlement, Karamanlis had a meeting with the Archbishop and the Acting Ethnarch, the Bishop of Kitium, in the presence of Averoff and a Greek Foreign Ministry official. Karamanlis reported that Turkey still insisted on having a military base in Cyprus which, he said, Greece had just as vigorously opposed. Makarios signified his approval of the Greek stand but raised no objection to Zorlu's idea of a Greek-Turkish headquarters on the island, which Karamanlis thought was worth considering. The Greek Prime Minister pointed out that, if Cyprus became a member of NATO, it would not matter whose troops manned the bases. Makarios – surprisingly, in view of his later attitude – is reported to have said that it would be entirely in the interests of an independent Cyprus to become part of the NATO alliance.

There was common ground now that Cyprus should be a Presidential Republic on the United States model and that the President should be a Greek Cypriot and the Vice-President a Turkish Cypriot. There would be a mixed House of Representatives on a 70:30 ratio and two Communal Chambers. Karamanlis said that Greece had raised no basic objection to Turkey's demand that the Vice-President should have the right of veto in matters of foreign policy and defence. Makarios accepted this but argued that there must be other well-defined areas in which there would be no Turkish Cypriot veto.

Makarios readily conceded that the Turkish Cypriot Communal Chamber should have sole authority in matters affecting the religion, education and personal status of members of the minority. Ankara also wanted the Turkish Cypriot community's economic development to be in the hands of its Communal Chamber. The Greek Government had expressed strong reservations about this, evidently because it might lead to a Turkish Cypriot claim for a larger share of the Republic's revenues. Makarios thought that further powers for the Communal Chambers should be strictly limited, but he had no objection to the Turkish Cypriots controlling their own banks. One issue which was later to create so much friction – the question of separate Greek and Turkish Cypriot municipalities – caused no trouble at this stage. Averoff said he had always opposed this idea as a divisive element in any constitution. However, Makarios and the Bishop of Kitium both thought that, if the spectre of partition had disappeared, separate municipalities might not be a bad thing. The Greek Cypriots would then be relieved of responsibility for improving conditions in the Turkish quarters of the towns, which lacked many of the amenities of the Greek side. It was an ungenerous attitude that could only have increased the existing divisions in the island.

The Archbishop's general view was that enough progress had been made to justify further negotiations between Athens and Ankara, provided the basic objections on the Greek and Greek Cypriot side were maintained. In fact, his chief fear seems to have been that Britain might still try to prevent agreement between Greece and Turkey for an independent Cyprus. Karamanlis thought the British Government was divided on the matter. He may have been influenced by the fact that Britain refused to cancel arrangements for implementing the 'Macmillan plan', but this was little more than a way of putting pressure on Greece to come to terms with Turkey.

A week later, on 6 February 1959, the Prime Ministers of Greece and Turkey, their Foreign Ministers and two teams of diplomats met on neutral territory, in the Grand Hotel at Dolder, a suburb of Zürich. After five days of intensive secret talks, at which no official minutes were kept, Karamanlis and Menderes signed a protocol which announced their agreement on four documents. The first set out the basic constitutional framework for the proposed new State of Cyprus. The second was the draft text of a Treaty of Guarantee between the Republic of Cyprus on the one hand and Greece, Turkey and Britain on the other. The third was a proposed Treaty of Alliance between Cyprus, Greece and Turkey. These three documents were published after the London Conference on Cyprus which took place the following week. The fourth document was never published: it included apparently a 'gentlemen's agreement' that Greece and Turkey would support the idea of NATO membership for Cyprus and that they would intervene respectively with the President and Vice-President to see that Communist activities in the island were suppressed. However, the 'gentlemen's agreement' also provided for a general amnesty and the lifting of all emergency measures after the necessary treaties had been signed and Cyprus had become independent.

In these negotiations the Turks did not get their base on Cyprus but accepted with alacrity a desperate Greek counter-proposal that Athens and Ankara should establish a token military presence in the island. The Greeks suggested fifty officers and men from each country. The Turks wanted a joint force of several thousand: Zorlu reportedly said that the military would kill him if they were not satisfied on this score. Eventually the two sides reached a compromise on 950 officers and men from Greece and 650 from Turkey, to be stationed at the Tripartite Headquarters which would be set up under the Treaty of Alliance. Greece pointed out – what she later forgot – that larger contingents were unnecessary since, if Turkey ever wanted to intervene in Cyprus under the Treaty of Guarantee, she was close enough to do so without difficulty.

The Turks also failed to get any suggestion in the constitution that the regime would have a federal character. None the less a separatist thread ran right through it. Karamanlis tried again to get agreement that the President, Vice-President and members of the House of Representatives should be chosen by the whole electorate and not on a community basis, but the Turks were adamant. They also got their way on the establishment of separate municipalities in the five largest towns, which Karamanlis would have opposed as the thin end of partition if Makarios had not already consented to it. There was agreement on a 70:30 ratio in the House of Representatives, the civil service and the police and gendarmerie, and the Turks finally accepted a 60:40 ratio in the proposed army of 2000. The constitution provided for seven Greek Cypriot and three Turkish Cypriot ministries, with either foreign affairs, defence or finance reserved for the minority. The Turks refused to set any limit on the presidential and vice-presidential right of veto, and the Greeks had to accept this. For Karamanlis and Averoff the main satisfaction was that the basic structure of the Republic gave some majority power to the Greek Cypriots and explicitly ruled out the partition of Cyprus into two separate states, though the cost of this was a constitutional ban on Enosis, reinforced by Turkish rights under the Treaty of Guarantee.

While Averoff and Zorlu went off to London to inform the British Government of the agreements, Karamanlis returned to Athens and invited Makarios round to his home the next day. The Archbishop had already congratulated the Prime Minister and publicly welcomed the Greek-Turkish *rapprochement*. After looking at the Zürich texts Makarios expressed his full agreement with them. Karamanlis told him that the British Government was already proposing a five-party round-table conference in London which would include representatives of the two communities in Cyprus, but it wanted to be sure beforehand that they approved of the Zürich agreements and would not wish to discuss them. Makarios promised not to query the agreements at the conference table, but said he would like to raise certain points with the Turkish Cypriot leadership where changes might be made by mutual consent. The Archbishop insisted it was important not to give the impression that the Cypriots had been invited to the conference simply to be told what had been decided for them.

Karamanlis and the British Government were understandably nervous about the Archbishop's ability to upset the apple-cart; they had no reason to fear that the Turkish Cypriots would question what Ankara had won for them. However, the Archbishop repeated his acceptance of the agreements, and then mentioned – almost casually – that, if there were a conference, he would invite the Bishop of Kitium and the mayors of the five main towns to go to London with him.

On the following day Karamanlis learnt that, after re-reading the texts, Makarios had been troubled by doubts. Two senior Foreign Ministry officials were sent to stiffen his resolve, but the Ethnarch maintained that he would have difficulty in putting his name to the agreements without first consulting representatives of the Cypriot people. For someone who had always been so sure of his popular mandate it was an unconvincing argument, even though Makarios had been out of Cyprus for nearly three years. Bitsios, a future Foreign Minister, pointed out that, if Makarios sought other approval, he would be undermining his own authority. He gave a warning that Karamanlis was determined to publish the Zürich agreements to show that Greece had done everything possible to help the Cypriots; if the London conference failed, the only alternative would be the Macmillan plan. The Bishop of Kitium and Makarios's old mentor, Abbot Chrysostomos of Kykko, were both present at this meeting. They urged the Archbishop to accept the agreements, which they assured him the people of Cyprus would welcome after so much suffering. Later in the day Karamanlis asked Makarios to explain his doubts, and the Archbishop pointed particularly to the Treaty of Guarantee which gave Turkey, like Greece and Britain, the right to intervene in Cyprus. Karamanlis replied that such intervention could take place only if Makarios failed to honour the agreements. The next day the Archbishop told Karamanlis that he would go to the London conference and definitely accept the Zürich agreements after merely 'consulting' the Greek Cypriots who went with him. But he asked the Greek Government to publish nothing about the bases to be retained by Britain, so that the Greek Cypriots could negotiate this matter themselves.

The Archbishop's hesitation can hardly have been due to the reading of any 'small print' in the documents. The agreements conformed to the basic line he had already accepted before the Zürich meeting. The Treaty of Guarantee was brief and to the point; it gave the three guarantor states the right to intervene only if the agreements were breached, and then only to restore the *status quo ante*. (Turkey abused her right of intervention when she invaded Cyprus in 1974, but by that time the agreements had been in shreds for years.) Makarios believed – and continued to believe – that a vote in the United Nations General Assembly supporting the unfettered right of the Greek Cypriot majority to self-determination would be stronger than any contractual obligations forced upon it, but he may have suddenly realised that the agreements gave him little room to manoeuvre. He may also have been troubled by appearing to go back on the oath he had taken at his enthronement as Archbishop that he would pursue 'Enosis and only Enosis'. He was not too worried about Grivas's predictable reaction or the expected fulminations from the Bishop of Kyrenia. He was probably more influenced by the certainty that AKEL would be hostile to a settlement which, while it gave Cyprus independence rather than Enosis, nevertheless saddled it with British bases and the troops of three NATO countries. Yet in first accepting, then rejecting, then again promising to accept the Zürich agreements – all within forty-eight hours – Makarios showed something of that irresolution which so often appeared from under his calm, confident exterior at moments of crisis.[2]

Grivas was profoundly worried when he heard on the radio that Karamanlis and Menderes were flying to a summit meeting in

Zürich. The speed with which the agreements were reached strengthened all his suspicions that EOKA's struggle had been betrayed and that Makarios was a party to it. He moved up from Limassol to a new hide-out in Nicosia to follow events more closely. On the day after the initialling of the agreements he received two notes – one from the Bishop of Kitium, the other from Frydas, the Greek consul in Nicosia. Both emphasised the need for EOKA and 'the Cypriot people' to give the Archbishop their full support. Grivas replied quickly and coldly that EOKA would make no comment on the little that was known about the agreements; it would gain more by silence. He said he had no intention of splitting the people but gave a warning that the Cypriot leadership as well as the Greek Government would have to account for the way they had handled the Cyprus question. If it were true, he said, that Turkish troops were going to be stationed in Cyprus, then he would have to reconsider his responsibilities.

On 13 February Grivas received a letter from Makarios. The Archbishop described the agreements as 'on the whole satisfactory' and the best that could be obtained in the circumstances. The goal had been Enosis, but it would be unrealistic to think that the policy of 'Enosis and only Enosis' was certain to lead to it: the Turkish element created by the British would still be an insurmountable obstacle, even if Labour came to power in Britain. The Zürich agreements at least laid the foundations of an independent and sovereign Cypriot state. Makarios played down the importance of the Turkish Cypriot veto and said that the only matter on which there might be reservations was the Treaty of Alliance which provided for a joint Greek-Turkish-Cypriot military headquarters in the island; but that, he added, would automatically disappear if Cyprus became a member of NATO. Makarios said they would probably succeed in improving some of the terms if there was a conference in London; but in any case he was 'rather pleased' with the outcome. He thought it would be a good idea if Grivas issued a proclamation saying he would agree to a solution acceptable to the political leadership. The Archbishop ended the letter: 'With much love' and his usual pseudonym, 'Haris'.

On the day after he received this letter Grivas heard on the radio that Makarios had invited some two dozen representative Greek Cypriots to join him immediately in London as an advisory body; there was no mention of including 'Dighenis'. Grivas was all the more indignant because Makarios's letter to him had expressed the hope that they would soon be able to meet to exchange views and take decisions together.

The London conference on Cyprus opened in Lancaster House on 17 February. Makarios had met his 'advisory body' the previous day, when the overwhelming majority of its members voted to reject the agreements. The Archbishop was not entirely displeased. He told them that the final decision must rest with him as the elected leader of his people, but the attitude of his 'advisers' had given him valuable ammunition. He reported to Averoff that he would not be able to accept the agreements.

At the opening session of the conference the three Foreign Ministers expressed their satisfaction with the compromise reached at Zürich. Then Makarios spoke. He too welcomed the new spirit of cooperation between Greece and Turkey and the generous response of the British Government. He said he had some reservations, but he thought the Zürich agreements were a good basis for the solution of the Cyprus problem, given goodwill between the two communities. Rauf Denktash also made a brief statement, on behalf of Dr Kuchuk, expressing Turkish Cypriot acceptance of the agreements.

Karamanlis flew into London later that day and, although he was running a high temperature, went straight to the Greek Embassy to confront Makarios. He had been told by Averoff that the Archbishop had again gone back on his word. Karamanlis tackled him bluntly, expressing astonishment that he was ready to throw away this unique opportunity of achieving independence for Cyprus. Makarios, unperturbed, said he could still accept the basic constitution – subject to certain modifications to be agreed with the Turkish Cypriots – but he would not sign the Treaty of Alliance or accept certain articles in the Treaty of Guarantee. He was prepared to abdicate first. Karamanlis declared that *he* would sign the agreements to protect the name of Greece; Makarios could continue the struggle alone if he wished. That was the end of the discussion. But before Makarios left the embassy that evening he had modified his position to the extent of accepting the Treaty of Alliance, provided it was not for a longer period than ten years.

Turkey's Prime Minister had also flown to London that day but the drama was further heightened when his plane crashed near Gatwick airport in thick fog. Half its occupants were killed and Menderes was rushed to hospital with what proved, after all, to be only minor injuries. The conference stood adjourned for most of the next day, less because of the accident to Menderes and the death of members of his entourage than because of the need to circumvent the Archbishop. The 'advisory body' of Greek Cypriots met in the afternoon and after a long argument voted in favour of giving Makarios full authority to decide whether or not to accept the agreements; they were apparently influenced by erroneous reports that Britain wanted the conference to break down. When it reassembled in the evening Makarios again gave a general welcome to the agreements, and then went into detail about his reservations. He foresaw trouble in the constitution's requirement of separate Greek Cypriot and Turkish Cypriot majorities in the House of Representatives for finance bills, especially in the matter of taxation. He wanted the Turkish Cypriot Vice-President's right of veto in foreign affairs to be limited, and he objected to the 30 per cent quota for Turkish Cypriots in the public service. As for the Treaty of Alliance, Makarios said it should be concluded by sovereign states and not be built into the constitution. He objected also to the right of any guarantor state to intervene *separately* in what he described as the internal affairs of Cyprus.

Makarios argued with all the persuasiveness at his command. Dr Kuchuk, who had met the Archbishop the previous day at Makarios's request, said that the Turkish Cypriots could not accept any reopening of negotiations on the agreements: these represented the ultimate in compromise and recognised the existence of two peoples in Cyprus. Averoff and Zorlu both appealed for trust and understanding and urged Makarios to consider his responsibilities. As the discussion became more and more confused, with Makarios and Averoff holding rapid exchanges in Greek, Selwyn Lloyd repeatedly asked the Archbishop to say plainly whether he accepted the documents before the conference as the foundation for a final settlement. Not as they stood, Makarios countered – 'without a single word being changed'. Selwyn Lloyd saw a crack in the stone wall and began to enlarge it. Of course there could be changes in detail and additions, but did the Archbishop accept the *essence* of the agreements? Makarios still played for time. Could he answer tomorrow? he asked; otherwise he must say No. After a brief adjournment to cool the air Selwyn Lloyd announced that Makarios had promised to give him a definite answer the next morning, and on it would depend whether the conference was reconvened.

That night Karamanlis and Averoff threw in everything against

Makarios. They warned him that he would bear full responsibility for the consequences if the conference collapsed. Macmillan was about to leave for his historic visit to Moscow and had decided that, if Makarios's answer was No, Britain would announce full agreement with Greece and Turkey and proceed to implement the Zürich plan. Makarios was isolated. Later mythology said that he spent much of the night in prayer at his Park Lane hotel. There was one reported intervention: a telephone call from Queen Frederika in Athens who is said to have urged the Archbishop to accept the agreements for the sake of Greece. The Greek Embassy certainly worked hard on the Greek Cypriot 'advisory body'. When it met early on the morning of 19 February there were twenty-seven votes to eight in favour of accepting the agreements. Those who voted against them included the five Communist (AKEL) representatives, the future Socialist leader, Dr Vasos Lyssarides, who became Makarios's personal physician, and Tasos Papadopoulos, who years later was to succeed Glafkos Clerides as the Greek Cypriot negotiator in the intercommunal talks. Papadopoulos was a member of PEKA (the so-called political wing of EOKA) and he had been nervous about accepting Makarios's invitation without first getting Grivas's approval; he realised he was being exploited but he was also ambitious.

At about half-past-nine on the morning of 19 February Makarios telephoned the Foreign Office and said he accepted the agreements. Selwyn Lloyd convened the last session of the conference for the afternoon and in a warm gush of mutual praise and congratulation the Zürich and Lancaster House documents were signed or initialled and the final statements were made. Afterwards Macmillan and Karamanlis went to the London Clinic to get Menderes to add his signature.

Averoff recalls that, later on that memorable day, when he was alone with Karamanlis and Makarios, the Archbishop asked teasingly: 'Did you really believe I would not sign the agreements?'

'Then why did you make all that turmoil for two days?' was Karamanlis's rejoinder.

'I had my reasons', Makarios replied.[3]

There can be little doubt that Makarios had always intended to sign. Even with the divisive elements in the constitution, the excessive and unusual privileges for the minority and the Turkish toehold on the island, the agreements were far better than the prospect of partition which Makarios thought was otherwise inevitable. He manoeuvred as much as he could to get some improvement on the terms; when the deadline arrived he gave in and postponed the struggle to a later date.

The immediate problem was to present the outcome simultaneously as both a defeat and a victory; the cold silence of EOKA and the general lack of enthusiasm in Cyprus required skilful handling. Here the initial rejection of the agreements by Makarios's 'advisory body' was helpful; it emphasised that the settlement was being forced upon him. At the final meeting with his 'advisers', when the majority had swung round to accepting the agreements, the Archbishop absolved them from all responsibility; the decision, he said, must be his alone. That left him a loophole for subsequently arguing that the agreements had not been endorsed by the people. Makarios never attempted to hold a referendum on the agreements, since this would probably have revealed that a majority of Greek Cypriots were in favour of them.

On the day after the London conference ended Makarios wrote to Grivas justifying his decision. The agreements, he said, put an immediate end to British sovereignty over Cyprus and created 'a little Greece in this part of the Eastern Mediterranean'. Cyprus would be an independent state and the rights granted to the Turkish minority were only to safeguard its interests, which the Greeks had always been ready to guarantee; the administration and the legislature would be indisputably in the hands of the Greek majority. As for the international obligations accepted by the State of Cyprus, they simply aimed at preventing any future link with countries of the Communist *bloc*. Neither this rosy interpretation of the agreements nor Makarios's fulsome tribute to EOKA's contribution to the struggle gave Grivas any pleasure; and he was especially indignant later because Makarios made no mention of the British sovereign bases.

The Zürich and London agreements were debated almost immediately in the Greek parliament and more leisurely by Turkey's Grand National Assembly and the British House of Commons. The Greek debate was long and stormy. The Liberal and Communist Opposition attacked the agreements for sounding the death-knell of Enosis, leaving Cyprus neither free nor independent but instead putting it under a triple occupation and, worst of all, bringing Turkey back into the island. The Turkish Opposition, more out of duty than conviction, protested that the safeguards for the Turkish Cypriot community were inadequate. At Westminster the

Labour Opposition – forgetting its own record in office – argued that the solution now reached could have been achieved years before at much less cost to Britain; and there were Tories who lamented the Government's weakness in giving up the island. All three debates ended with a comfortable government majority.

Meanwhile the deportation orders were cancelled and Makarios returned to Cyprus in triumph on 1 March. The huge Greek Cypriot crowds that gathered in Nicosia were there – as Grivas records – to welcome the charismatic figure of their Ethnarch and Archbishop who had been so long in exile, not to acclaim the agreements. There was still silence from EOKA, which took no part in the official reception. When newspaper reporters pressed the Archbishop for information about Grivas's whereabouts and his plans, Makarios parried the questions with a request for patience. On 3 March Grivas received a note from Makarios suggesting they should meet. He replied by sending his lieutenant Yeoryiadis to learn more about the agreements. Yeoryiadis reported the Archbishop as saying that he and Karamanlis had agreed the general framework before Zürich but that Karamanlis had then gone beyond it. When Yeoryiadis asked why 'Dighenis' had not been kept informed or invited to send EOKA representatives to London, Makarios said there had been no time.

Grivas was now faced with the most difficult decision of his career. Should he accept the settlement – and the frustration of all his endeavour – or continue the armed struggle? He claimed afterwards that he had still been in a position to go on fighting the British and the Turks, but that he was uncertain how much political support he would have inside and outside the island. Grivas decided that the odds were heavily against him – something which the Archbishop had failed to realise much earlier and to exploit politically.

Grivas rejected Foot's offer of an amnesty by stages and demanded that it should be total and immediate. Foot gave way, only insisting that the EOKA men in gaol in Britain – they included Nikos Sampson – must stay out of Cyprus until the Republic was proclaimed. (Most of them spent the intervening period in Rhodes, the nearest Greek island.) There was agreement, through Makarios's intervention, that EOKA's arms should be handed in at specified collecting-points – usually churches or monasteries – under the supervision of Greek Cypriot policemen and nobody else, to be kept in safe custody until they were delivered to the Republic's own security forces. Grivas demanded – and got – permission to leave the island carrying his revolver.

There was such anxiety to get him out of Cyprus that the Karamanlis Government was ready to send a fleet of Dakota aircraft or a warship to carry Grivas and his men to Athens, since he had refused a British safe-conduct. Averoff wrote to say that the King and Queen, the Government and the whole Greek people – except perhaps the Communists – wanted to honour Grivas; amongst other things he would be recalled to active service, promoted to the rank of lieutenant-general, and awarded a Grand Cross. Grivas replied that he was not interested in honours, but the prospect offered some balm to his soul.

On 9 March Grivas issued a leaflet ordering a general cease-fire – his first public reaction to the agreements. He had sent the proposed text to Makarios who – apparently without much trouble – got him to delete certain phrases on the grounds that they would undermine the people's confidence in the settlement. In his proclamation Grivas said that the aim of the hard four-year struggle he had led, with the full support of the Greek Cypriot people, had been the liberation of Cyprus. Now, after the agreements ratified in London by Ethnarch Makarios – Grivas had wanted to add 'and by those appointed by him as representatives of the Cypriot people' – he was 'obliged' to order an end to the struggle. Anyone who refused to accept the agreements and tried to fight on would divide not only the Cypriots but probably the whole Greek nation. The outcome would be infinitely more 'destructive' than the divisions which some people thought would result from the present solution. (Grivas had originally written: ' "compromise" solution which certainly does not satisfy our desires'.) He went on to say that he was now issuing a call for love and unity so that the new Republic could be built on the ashes of the Cypriot epic. He had decided not to become involved in public or political life, either in Cyprus or in Greece, but would share the joys and sorrows of his much-suffering homeland from afar. . . .[4]

Grivas met Makarios in Nicosia a few hours after he had issued his call; it was their first face-to-face encounter in nearly four years. No record exists of what passed between them, except that – according to Grivas – Makarios was at pains to emphasise the pressures that had been put upon him. Grivas went away with a heavy heart to prepare for his departure from Cyprus, bitterly aware that the Archbishop was now about to enjoy the political rewards of the struggle for which EOKA had made such sacrifices. (It was three years to the day since Makarios had gone to his comfortable exile in the Seychelles, leaving the rigours of the field and the political responsibility to 'Dighenis'.) Some evenings later, at the homes of two prominent businessmen in Nicosia, Grivas met his group leaders and a number of EOKA's rank and file; many of them had never seen him before. He was moved to tears by their devotion.

On the morning of 17 March 'Dighenis' was allowed to make his first – and what Makarios hoped would be his last – public appearance in Cyprus. He and his lieutenant Yeoryiadis drove with the Greek consul to a villa on the outskirts of Nicosia near Government House. There they met the Archbishop, the Bishop of Kitium, other prominent Greek Cypriots and a group of journalists. Grivas, looking small and emaciated but still fit and jaunty in his knee-breeches and calf-length boots, was photographed, embraced, questioned. Then, as a crowd began to collect outside the house, he was whisked away to the airport – Makarios following – before there was time for a popular demonstration. Two Royal Hellenic Air Force planes arrived, bringing four of Grivas's former fellow-officers – one of them now a general – to act as an escort of honour. Makarios's relief must have been immense as he watched the planes take off again with Grivas and his party – discreetly shadowed by two RAF fighters to see that they really did leave the island. As Grivas flew over Rhodes he talked by radio-telephone to some of the EOKA men who had just arrived there from British gaols. At Ellenikon Airport he was welcomed by a reception committee headed by the Foreign Minister, Averoff. The Archbishop of Athens crowned him with a silver laurel wreath, hailing Grivas as 'the worthy son of glorious and immortal Greece'. Then the EOKA leader drove in a convoy of hooting cars through cheering crowds to the centre of Athens, where he laid a wreath on the tomb of the Unknown Soldier and was greeted by Karamanlis. During the week that followed Grivas was overwhelmed with honours. Parliament conferred on him the rank of lieutenant-general with full pay for life. King Paul awarded him the Grand Cross of the Order of George I with Swords. Societies, clubs and organisations of every kind vied with one another to have him as their patron or president. The political Opposition – particularly the Left – was torn between a desire to honour the hero of a cause so shamefully 'betrayed' by the Government – and its own memories of the little fascist colonel, the leader of *Khi*. The Government encouraged the fever of adulation to burn itself out quickly. Only a week after Grivas's arrival he was conspicuously absent from the official celebrations of Greek Independence Day.

Meanwhile EOKA had handed in its arms – or those it chose to surrender. There can be little doubt that some of its best weapons were stowed away for future use. Then, as soon as Grivas was out of the island, the EOKA men came down from the hills or just appeared on the streets of Nicosia. In a carefully-orchestrated operation some 280 of them were taken in buses to the archiepiscopal palace where they kissed Makarios's hand and symbolically became his men. The crowds welcomed them as long-lost sons rather than as the liberators of Cyprus or the architects of a new era. It was easy to forget that these young men had been responsible for the deaths of more Greek Cypriots than of Turks and British together.

The London agreements had provided for the setting-up of three mixed bodies to arrange for the transfer of sovereignty within a year – that is, by February 1960 at the latest.[5] There was to be a Joint Commission in Nicosia, charged with the responsibility of putting flesh on the constitutional skeleton created at Zürich. There was also to be a Transitional Committee in Cyprus which would, in effect, reorganise the governmental machinery in preparation for the hand-over; its chief members would be the Archbishop, the British Governor and the Turkish Cypriot leader, Dr Kuchuk. Finally, a Joint Committee in London, made up of representatives of the two Cypriot communities and of the three guarantor Powers, was given the task of drawing up the international treaties which would cover, amongst other things, Britain's retention of two sovereign base areas and her right to certain facilities in the Republic.

The Joint (Constitutional) Commission got down to work on 13 April. Greece, Turkey and the two communities in Cyprus each provided a legal team, and there was also a neutral adviser, a former rector of the University of Lausanne, Professor Marcel Bridel. The commission's work was kept out of the news as much as possible, but it was soon common knowledge that almost every step was being contested. The Greek and Greek Cypriot members were not always in agreement but generally their efforts were directed towards eliminating the more divisive elements in the constitution. The Turks and Turkish Cypriots were equally determined not to give up any of the rights they had secured. Glafkos Clerides and Rauf Denktash, who were later to spend so many years trying to re-negotiate a Cyprus settlement, found themselves already at variance in interpreting the Zürich agreement.

The main area of conflict was the question of executive power. The Greeks insisted that power should derive from the people. The Turks wanted the word 'people' to be plural. The Greeks would have liked to describe the new Republic as 'democratic', but, as the neutral adviser, M. Bridel, pointed out that 'democratic' implied majority rule, the Turks managed to get this word deleted. There was still the question of whether the President and Vice-President were to have equal power, since each would have the same right of veto. It was never really solved. Some executive power went to the Council of Ministers – which gave the Greeks an advantage since the ratio here was seven to three – but certain executive functions were reserved to the Communal Chambers – which strengthened the Turkish side, since the Greeks had no real need of a Communal Chamber.

During these long-drawn-out constitutional manoeuvrings relations between the two communities were surprisingly harmonious in view of what had happened during the previous four years. There were mixed parties and receptions, the Greek navy paid a courtesy visit to Cyprus, and Turkey sent Kemal Ataturk's yacht to be the *venue* for a splendid celebration in Famagusta harbour. Makarios and the amiable Dr Kuchuk were seen hob-nobbing together while their legal experts and those of the two mother-countries were locked in quiet battle. There was however one period of tension between the two communities in the autumn of 1959. On 18 October a British naval patrol intercepted a Turkish motor-boat, the *Deniz*, off the north-east coast of Cyprus. The boarding-party had only time to seize two cases of rifle ammunition before the crew scuttled the boat and sent another seventy-odd cases to the bottom. The crew – three Turkish nationals – were arrested, tried and quickly deported by the Governor. Dr Kuchuk seemed genuinely embarrassed by the incident and condemned the men as 'irresponsible individuals', but the Greek and Greek Cypriot press – especially those elements that hated the Zürich and London agreements – lashed themselves into a frenzy over Turkish perfidy. An official statement from Ankara that the men had merely been 'dolphin-fishing' was treated as an outrageous lie.

Makarios revealed that there had been a previous attempt to smuggle Turkish arms into the island and for a time broke off the constitutional talks. But the moral indignation of the Greeks was less convincing than it might have been; it was barely a month since Makarios had found it necessary to denounce Grivas's supporters for trying to send more arms to Cyprus with which to fight the agreements.

No one had expected Grivas to stay out of politics, as he had promised. At Easter he sent a message to the Cypriot people saying that he had warned the Greek leadership in Athens and Nicosia to make no more concessions to the Turks or the British. When he was not writing his Memoirs he stumped the Greek countryside, delivering impassioned speeches about national betrayal and sacrifices made in vain. Averoff urged Grivas to show restraint while there were difficult negotiations in progress, but it had no effect. For a time Makarios continued to express his regard for Grivas as the hero of the Cypriot struggle and to say that there were no differences between them. But Grivas had a powerful ally in Cyprus in the Bishop of Kyrenia, Makarios's old rival and fellow-exile who now led the faction that openly wanted to continue the struggle for Enosis. As Grivas's statements grew more and more inflammatory Makarios warned him obliquely that the blood of Cypriot youth could not be exploited for the sake of personal ambition. Grivas retorted that he was ready to fight again to smash the dark forces seeking to enslave the island. The Bishop of Kyrenia preached a sermon in which he said he hoped Grivas would soon be Prime Minister of Greece so as to bring a real wind of freedom to the motherland and her daughter, Cyprus.

Throughout the summer there were rumours of plots and counter-plots. Makarios produced copies of an incriminating note from Grivas to the Bishop of Kyrenia. Grivas accused the Greek Government and Makarios of plotting to liquidate him. Later he offered to support the agreements if he were allowed a say in the negotiations. Then he challenged Makarios to a public debate. Eventually, in early October, the Archbishop met Grivas in Rhodes and after three days of private talks succeeded in silencing him. What he promised him can only be conjectured. The reference in the communiqué, issued after the talks, to the need for unity 'during the present brief transitory phase' was a significant pointer.

The Transitional Committee which gradually took over some of the responsibilities of government had a much easier ride than the Constitutional Commission. At the beginning of April Makarios nominated the men who were to hold six of the seven Greek Cypriot portfolios in the first post-independence administration. Four had been leading members of EOKA. Antonis Yeoryiadis, Grivas's chief lieutenant and liaison officer during the last two years of the campaign, was to become Minister of Communications; he was twenty-eight. Polykarpos Yeorkhadjis, a year younger, the man who had once shot his way out of Nicosia General Hospital, killing two people, became prospective Minister of Labour and Social Services. Andreas Azinas, the one-time secretary-general of PEK, the farmers' union, who organised Grivas's first unsuccessful shipment of arms in the *Ayios Yeoryios*, was rewarded with the post of Deputy Minister of Agriculture. Tasos Papadopoulos, a twenty-five-year-old lawyer, who had been summoned by Makarios to attend the London conference as EOKA's representative, was appointed Minister of the Interior for his timely support.[6]

The Turkish Cypriots expressed no surprise that Makarios had chosen EOKA men for his team; they expected nothing less. Sir Hugh Foot accepted the list without demur and began to assign departmental duties. The only strong reaction came from the Greek Cypriot Left. Ziartides, secretary-general of the AKEL-dominated Pancyprian Federation of Labour, denounced the provisional government as completely one-sided. The extreme Right, in spite of its hostility to the agreements, was triumphant. But sober-minded Greek Cypriots were dismayed that the Archbishop had passed over men of experience in public affairs in favour of Grivas's 'boys'. Makarios however had no intention of giving them a free hand; rewarding them with ministerial posts was the best way of detaching them from their former leader.

The presidential elections were not held until 13 December. Ten days earlier, on nomination day, Dr Kuchuk had been declared Vice-President-elect unopposed. The Turkish Cypriots were solidly united in defence of their new rights. By contrast, there was a short, sharp, ugly battle for the presidency, though the result was never in doubt. John Clerides (the father of Glafkos), an elderly, liberal-minded lawyer and QC, found himself pushed to the front as a rival candidate to Makarios. His natural support came from those Greek Cypriots who were appalled at the prospect, as they saw it, of semi-dictatorial rule by the Archbishop, backed by a reactionary Church and yesterday's gunmen. The extreme Right – fanatical Enotists like the Bishop of Kyrenia – quickly rallied behind Clerides. The leaders of AKEL now saw their opportunity. They let it be known that in return for their continued support of the Archbishop they would like fifteen out of the thirty-five Greek Cypriot seats in the House of Representatives, together with the Ministry of Labour. AKEL had no intention of putting forward its own candidate for the presidency; to do so, before the transfer of sovereignty, might have alarmed the three guarantor Powers. When it was clear that Makarios was not prepared to allow the Communists what, with some Turkish Cypriot support could have been a majority in the House of Representatives, AKEL switched its support to John Clerides and his 'Democratic Union'.

Makarios's supporters, now organised as 'the Patriotic Front', made great play with posters depicting the Archbishop and Grivas together as the champions of freedom, while – for contrast – Clerides was shown talking to the former military governor, Sir John Harding. Although there were some clashes between extremist groups during the campaign – as there had been sporadically throughout the summer – election day was quiet and orderly. There was a 91 per cent poll, and women voted for the first time in Cyprus – if you discount the 1950 'plebiscite'. As was generally predicted, Makarios got two-thirds of the votes: 144,501 against the 71,753 for John Clerides. Makarios had overwhelming support in the villages, but Clerides did well in the towns, thanks to the Left.

Two days before the election Grivas issued a statement denying reports that he supported the Archbishop. He repeated that he had no intention of taking part in Cypriot politics.

The stage was now almost set for the proclamation of independence on the planned date of 19 February 1960. By the end of 1959 the Constitutional Commission and its sub-committee had reached agreement on all the main issues except the question of separate muncipalities. The Cypriot ministers were poised to take over their duties. It was the Joint Committee working in London on the international treaties that held up the action, mainly because of disagreement between Makarios and the Macmillan Government over the size of the British bases to be retained in Cyprus and the amount of aid to be given by Britain to the new Republic. Here the Archbishop displayed all his subtlety in negotiation to the point of what looked like dangerous brinkmanship.

But in fact Makarios knew that the British had gone too far to be able to draw back.

The London agreement had not specified the area of the bases; it merely indicated their position by the villages that would be included in them. However, in its summary of the agreements on 28 February 1959 the official Athens News Agency had reported that Britain would keep two enclaves, one of 190 square kilometres at Akrotiri and the other of 250 square kilometres at Dhekelia, under her absolute sovereignty. Together they amounted to 440 square kilometres (about 170 square miles), and this figure was mentioned in the Greek parliament's debate on the agreements.

In April Makarios made a first tentative nibble at the bases through his negotiator in London. He asked that the boundaries should be drawn so as to include no inhabited areas. Over the next nine months the bases originally envisaged by the British Government were 'squeezed, pushed and pummelled' into such odd shapes – to quote the Defence Secretary – that they were reduced from 170 to 120 square miles and their Cypriot inhabitants from some 16,000 to fewer than 1,000. As the British Government strove to meet the Archbishop's arguments that the bases should impinge as little as possible on the sovereignty of the Republic, Grivas joined in with a demand that they must exclude all fertile land and any important water supplies. It was part of his larger attack on the Archbishop for bartering away the rights of the Cypriots, and Makarios was compelled to rebuke Grivas for trying to overturn the agreements. However, he skilfully adopted the EOKA leader's ideas and, pleading the popular pressures against him, made the British Government what he called a 'reasonable' and 'generous' offer of thirty-six square miles for its military purposes.

Makarios had no objection on principle to a British military presence in the island. He had himself offered bases in return for Enosis. He knew that the Communists, for all their denunciation of 'British imperialism', appreciated the fact that the bases would provide employment for thousands of Cypriot workers. However the Archbishop saw that, if the sovereign areas were cut back to the minimum, the British might be persuaded to pay rent for further facilities and the bases would ultimately be less of an obstacle to Enosis. Also, with an eye on the friendship of the 'Third World' and particularly of the Arab countries, Makarios wanted to be able to exercise some control over the purposes for which the bases would be used.

With the Joint Committee still deadlocked at the end of the year over the size of the bases and the amount to be paid by the outgoing colonial power for the other military facilities and in general financial help to the Republic, the British Government invited the Foreign Ministers of Greece and Turkey together with the Archbishop and Dr Kuchuk to another round-table conference in London. It began on 16 January 1960 and lasted for three days but failed to resolve the outstanding difficulties, so the British Government agreed to Makarios's request that independence should be postponed for a month, till 19 March. Early in February Mr Julian Amery, Under-Secretary of State for the Colonies, went out to Cyprus to settle the matter, but returned empty-handed. He went out again and had to stay more than four months, arguing with the Archbishop. For one period of forty-five days there was a complete break in the negotiations. Sometimes they turned on such trivialities as what goods might be sold by NAAFI shops in the bases and whether the British soldier should get his beer and cigarettes cheaper than in the Republic. Makarios's aim was to extract every possible economic concession. Mr Harold Watkinson, the Secretary for Defence, reported to Parliament, much as Lennox-Boyd had done four years earlier, that every concession made to the Archbishop was 'merely a springboard for another demand'; the minister only hoped, wearily, that he would eventually 'claim the prize'.

For a time the Turkish Cypriots admired and enjoyed the finer points of Makarios's haggling. They knew Britain would give way and there was no point in backing the losing side. It was only when Makarios began to seem indifferent about the date for independence that the Turkish Cypriots became restive. On 1 April, the fifth anniversary of the start of EOKA violence, the Archbishop and President-elect was injudicious enough to deliver an impassioned speech emphasising that national struggles never ended – that, though they might change their outward form, deep down they remained the same. The Zürich and London agreements, Makarios said, had not fully realised the hopes and aspirations of the Cypriots, but EOKA had secured for them the bastions from which they would continue the struggle till final victory. Makarios accused the British of delaying independence and said that, if the talks did not end in agreement soon, he would call for civil disobedience and the Cypriots would establish their Republic by themselves.

This brought a strong and immediate protest from Dr Kuchuk. He described the Archbishop's reference to 'Cypriots' as 'grossly inaccurate', since the Turkish community had nothing in common with EOKA which had fought only for Enosis. The Turkish Cypriot leader said that civil disobedience would plunge the island into chaos and probably lead to civil war. He warned Makarios that there could be no cooperation from his community with those who looked upon the agreements as 'a bastion for new campaigns'. Makarios had been unnecessarily provocative, even if his motive was only to put pressure on the British. Eventually the size of the bases was agreed at ninety-nine square miles – little more than half the area originally stipulated. The British Government also gave a pledge that, when it no longer needed the bases, they would be handed over to the Republic of Cyprus and no one else. The sum of £19 million was promised in financial aid with another £1½ million specifically for the Turkish Cypriot community.

There was only one more major question to be settled before independence – the composition of the House of Representatives. Elections were held in both communities on 31 July. The fifteen Turkish Cypriot seats all went to Dr Kuchuk's National Party. Of the thirty-five Greek Cypriot seats AKEL took five unopposed, by agreement with Makarios; the remainder went to the Archbishop's 'Patriotic Front', to the total exclusion of his right-wing opponents. AKEL was satisfied with its own deal. It preferred to keep a low profile because of its ambivalent attitude to the agreements and also because at this date it could not have hoped to win many seats in the House by contesting them. The system of six large electoral districts (taken over from the British) would have allowed the Nationalist vote in the countryside to outweigh any left-wing preponderance in the towns.

The transfer of sovereignty took place on 16 August 1960. After 82 years of British rule the Union Jack at Government House was hauled down for the last time and in its place fluttered the defiant blue-and-white of Greece, the Turkish crescent and star on a menacing red, and between them the pale sun and laurel wreath of the Republic of Cyprus – an emblem irreverently described by one foreign journalist as 'a fried egg surrounded by parsley'.

1. Makarios (Michael Mouskos) as a 13-year-old novice at Kykko Monastery: the earliest photograph

2. The novice-monk goes back to his village for a brief visit

4. Makarios as Bishop of Kitium. This photograph was probably taken not many months after the one on the left

3. Makarios as a post-graduate theology student in Boston, Massachusetts

6. Archbishop Makarios at Ano Panayia with his father and a friend

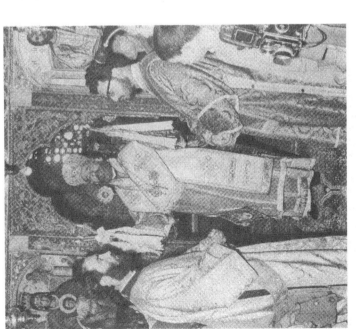

5. Makarios officiating as Archbishop in the full splendour of the Byzantine rite

7.   'Sans Souci' in the Seychelles: Makarios relaxing in exile

8.   After reluctantly signing the London agreements. Behind Makarios his old
     mentor, Abbot Chrysostomos of Kykko, with Kyprianou (his successor as
     President) and Bishop Anthimos of Kitium (a later 'rebel')

9.   Makarios temporarily persuades Grivas to accept the independence
     agreements (Rhodes, 1959). Behind them a smouldering young Nikos
     Sampson

10.   After the breakdown of the constitution and the intercommunal clashes
      Makarios inspects his new 'National Guard', accompanied by his ex-
      EOKA 'Defence Minister' Polykarpos Yeorkadjis

11.   With the great ones. Nasser and Tito listen attentively to Makarios

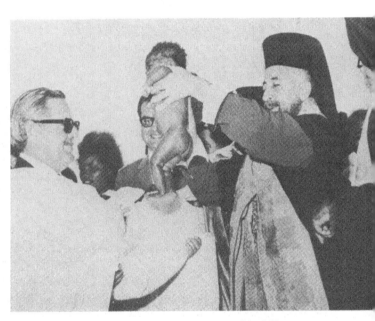

12.   And the small. Makarios baptises a young black Kenyan

13.   The Greek dictator, George Papadopoulos, kisses the hand of the President

14.   Makarios and Denktash meet after 13 years to agree on the 'guide-lines' for
a settlement. Between them the UN Secretary-General, Dr Kurt
Waldheim

15. The lying-in-state. Kyprianou, Makarios's successor as President, kisses the
dead. On the left the man who might have succeeded – Tasos
Papadopoulos, his arm held by his wife, the widow of Yeorkadjis
(presumed author of one attempt to assassinate Makarios)

16. Makarios's tomb on a mountain peak above Kykko. The wreaths are
surmounted by a Greek flag

PART THREE

AFTERMATH

10 The Constitution Breaks Down

The birth had been difficult, but the new Republic seemed a lusty and vigorous infant in spite of its constitutional weaknesses. The island had the second highest standard of living in the eastern Mediterranean; only Israel's was better. The *per capita* income was low according to Western ideas, but it was higher than that of Greece and almost twice that of Turkey. In the first full year of independence (1961) the value of exports from Cyprus, mostly in minerals and agricultural produce, amounted to nearly £18 million. The Emergency had had little effect on the island's productivity and, once the fighting had stopped, tourism soon picked up; under the Republic it expanded quickly. The British bases were a major source of revenue, both directly and from the money that the troops spent in other parts of the island. There was no shortage of doctors or teachers, as there was in many other newly-independent countries, and the new state already had a competent civil service. Cyprus was quickly welcomed to the United Nations and, with Makarios's blessing, it stayed in the Commonwealth. Preferential tariffs and remittances from Cypriots in Britain contributed further to the economy.

Even when the British Government had been most exasperated by Makarios's long haggling over the agreements, it appreciated his skill in political leadership. It realised that the Archbishop might be another in what was to become a long line of colonial rebels – starting with Smuts and going on through Gandhi and Nehru to Nkrumah and Jomo Kenyatta – who, after conflict, imprisonment or exile, graduated into respected Commonwealth statesmen. It was harder for the public in Britain to accept the idea of Archbishop Makarios dining at Buckingham Palace, but it bore no animosity towards the Greek Cypriots in general for the EOKA years.

The Greek Government hoped it had seen the last of the Cyprus problem: Makarios now had enough on his hands to keep him busy and was reasonably satisfied with what he had achieved. Although the Opposition, led by the old Liberal leader, George Papandreou, continued to exploit the Enotist elements in Greece and accuse the Government of having submitted to Turkish blackmail, Karamanlis and Averoff seemed politically secure enough during the early years of the settlement. In Turkey, on the other hand, it was only a dramatic change in the political situation that helped to preserve the fragile agreements. On 27 May 1960 – three months before Cyprus became independent – the Menderes Government was overthrown by a military *coup*. The politicians had completely failed to cope with rapidly-rising inflation. The ruling Democrat Party had been ruthless in its suppression of the popular discontent and in its attacks on the main Opposition, the Republican People's Party. More than 400 parliamentary deputies and members of the Democrat Party were arrested by the military government and charged with corruption and violating the constitution. In September 1961, after long-drawn-out and much-publicised trials, most were convicted. Menderes and his Foreign Minister, Zorlu, were among the fifteen sentenced to death, and both were hanged in public. Their violent end was, in some degree, a condemnation of the policies they had pursued over Cyprus, in quarrelling with a NATO ally and breaching the friendship which Ataturk had established with Greece. The Turkish military regime and the civilian government to which it handed over power after elections in October 1961 – a coalition between the Republican People's Party and the new Justice Party that rallied the former supporters of Menderes – both took a cautious line on Cyprus. The first Turkish ambassador to Nicosia, Emin Dirvana, was instructed to encourage the moderation of Dr Kuchuk rather than the more militant attitude of Mr Denktash, who was now President of the Turkish Communal Chamber. The Turkish Cypriot paramilitary organisation *Volkan* was disbanded on Dirvana's orders, and when Denktash wanted to celebrate one of its more disreputable anniversaries Kuchuk and the Turkish ambassador both vetoed the idea.

In spite of the outward harmony between Makarios and Kuchuk during the early days of independence, the honeymoon period was short; the union of their two communities had, after all, been a shot-gun wedding. Disputes broke out almost immediately, both in Cabinet and in the House of Representatives. The Turks felt from the start that the Greeks were bent on evading those provisions of the constitution which they disliked most. The Greeks were determined not to let the Turks entrench themselves in what they saw as unwarranted privileges. Even though the Joint Commission had spent fifteen months turning the Zürich and London documents into a blueprint for the state machinery, many important functions had only been sketched in lightly at the last moment to avoid further delay. For example, it was agreed after much argument that five months should be allowed from the start of independence for full implementation of the 70:30 ratio between Greeks and Turks in the public service. On 14 October 1960 Vice-President Kuchuk complained to President Makarios that, although the Republic had been in existence for two months, little had been done towards fulfilling this requirement. The Greek Cypriots protested that to give 30 per cent of the public service to Turkish Cypriots, regardless of their qualifications, amounted to ethnic or religious discrimination; in any case, they said, no Greek public servants could be dismissed to make room for the other community since that would infringe their constitutional right to security of employment, while to enlarge the public service needlessly would be unfair to the taxpayer. The Turkish Cypriots maintained that the two communities were equal in status and that the 70:30 ratio was essential if they were not to be completely dominated by the Greek Cypriot majority. During the next three years more than two thousand public service appointments in this small island were contested and referred to the Supreme Constitutional Court, which consisted of a Greek Cypriot, a Turkish Cypriot and a non-Cypriot president.

Makarios tried to keep aloof from these intercommunal squabbles. It was important for him to be seen as the impartial Head of State, though he did little to encourage the idea of a Cypriot nationality. He was more preoccupied with the clash of loyalties inside his own community. Since the ultra-nationalists now looked to Grivas as their real leader, Makarios felt obliged to emphasise his own position as Ethnarch. EOKA anniversaries were celebrated 'officially' by the Archbishop-President and his Greek Cypriot ministers, and this inevitably reinforced Turkish Cypriot suspicions that Makarios saw independence only as a stage on the road to union with Greece.

Apart from the disputed ratio in the public service there were three other major areas of friction – taxation, the armed forces and the municipalities. A full history of the Cyprus problem would require a blow-by-blow account of how the legislators of the two communities provoked each other for three years into mutual and bloody-minded intolerance over these issues. For the purposes of this study a quick synoptic view will be enough to explain Makarios's eventual action and the Turkish Cypriot response.[1]

The question of separate municipalities – in Nicosia, Limassol, Larnaca, Famagusta and Paphos – as provided for in the constitution, probably created the greatest basic fears but it was not, as some have suggested, the ultimate cause of the breakdown in intercommunal relations. Makarios and the Bishop of Kitium had originally thought separate municipalities a good idea, since this would relieve the Greek Cypriots from the expense of bringing the amenities of the Turkish quarters in the main towns up to the level of their own. It was an ungenerous and shortsighted attitude, which Makarios partly atoned for later by extracting £1½ million from the British Government specially for Turkish Cypriot development. The Greek Cypriots generally regarded the Turkish Cypriots, not without reason, as being considerably less productive than they were themselves. Nevertheless the fear of partition made most of them oppose the idea of separate municipalities from the start.

The Turkish Cypriots had, in fact, set up their own municipal authorities, to which they paid their taxes, as early as 1958, at the height of EOKA's divisive campaign. The British colonial government unhelpfully legalised them – if only as a temporary measure – in 1959. The much-fought-over 1960 constitution validated the existing municipal laws for six months after independence, to give time for new legislation, with the added proviso that the President and Vice-President should consider, within four years, whether the continued separation of the municipalities was desirable. As no agreement was reached by the deadline of January 1961, the House of Representatives had to extend the validity of the existing municipal laws for a further three months – and it did this altogether no fewer than eight times.

In March 1962 President Makarios tried to grasp the nettle himself and proposed there should be a single municipal authority in each of the five towns, on which Greeks and Turks should be represented in accordance with the local ratio of population. Vice-

President Kuchuk rejected this outright and insisted on geographical separation. In December 1962 Makarios said that, after his latest talks with the Turkish Cypriot leadership, he saw no hope of a compromise and therefore no reason why the provisional laws should again be extended; repeatedly doing so, of course, was only consolidating the Turkish Cypriot position. However, when the Greek Cypriot members of the House of Representatives voted decisively against a further extension of the old laws, the Turkish Cypriots retaliated by using their Communal Chamber to pass a new law recognising their municipalities. Two days later Makarios countered by getting the Council of Ministers to revive the old colonial law of 1950 which had created 'development areas'. His aim was to bypass the Turkish Cypriot action by creating new unified municipal councils for development, which would be superior to the separate municipalities. The Turkish Cypriots – after consulting Ankara – appealed to the Supreme Constitutional Court, the Greek Cypriots took similar action – though without consulting Athens – and in April 1963 the court, under its president, Professor Ernst Forsthoff of Heidelberg University, ruled that both communal actions were unconstitutional. This left the municipal deadlock complete, since the court had no competence to impose or even recommend a solution.[2]

Another, less obviously divisive quarrel, but one that for a time concealed an increasingly dangerous situation, was the dispute over the armed forces. The constitution said that the Republic should have an army of 2000 men, 60 per cent of them Greeks and 40 per cent Turks, but that there was to be no compulsory military service unless it was agreed by the President and Vice-President. Recruiting began in March 1961, on the initiative of the Minister of Defence, Mr Osman Orek, a genial Turk. Makarios would have preferred to have no army at all, but if there had to be one, he believed it must be on an intercommunal basis with Greek and Turkish Cypriot troops fully integrated. A decision to this effect was taken by the Council of Ministers, even though the appointed army commander, Major-General Pantelides, a mainland Greek, argued that there must be separation at platoon level for practical reasons of language, discipline and cooking arrangements, with Muslims and Christians intermixed. Mr Orek put the Turkish Cypriot view that battalions might be mixed, but that at company level it would be impossible to have Greeks and Turks serving together. The Greek Cypriots were adamant, so in October 1961

Dr Kuchuk used his Vice-Presidential right of veto for the first and only time. Makarios said he considered the reasons for the veto inadequate and he questioned the Vice-President's right to use it at all as he had done. Dr Kuchuk seems to have acted well within his powers, since the constitution gave both the President and the Vice-President the right to reject decisions of the Council of Ministers affecting security. Makarios then resorted to an indirect veto and under his constitutional rights said that he saw no reason why, in the existing circumstances, Cyprus should have an army at all. It has never had a legal one yet.

The failure to create a legitimate internal security force other than the police encouraged secret arming by both communities. The constitutional deadlocks convinced them that sooner or later there must be a showdown. The Greek Cypriots subsequently claimed to have known by the beginning of 1963 that the Turkish Cypriots already had some 2500 men partly armed and trained with the help of the Turkish army contingent stationed in the island. Two ministers, Tasos Papadopoulos (Communications and Works) and Polykarpos Yeorkadjis (Interior), together with Glafkos Clerides, the President of the House of Representatives, were entrusted with the task of preparing the Greek Cypriots for any eventuality. With the help of officers from the Greek army contingent a secret fighting-force was built up around a core of ex-EOKA men. It has been estimated that by the end of 1963 the Greek Cypriots had some 5000 men fully trained and equipped with arms and as many more partly trained. With the Turkish Cypriots also rearming, it needed only a spark between the millstones of two abrasive nationalisms to cause an explosion.

It was the taxation issue and the voting system in the House of Representatives that finally showed Cyprus was not functioning as a unitary state – and indeed hardly as a state at all. The constitution required separate communal majorities whenever the House voted on legislation imposing duties or taxes. Once again, there had been no agreement on a new tax law before independence, and the validity of the old colonial law had been extended until the end of December 1960. Again, as over the question of the municipalities, time ran out, but in this case it was the Turkish Cypriots who thought the Greek Cypriots were deliberately stalling. At the end of March 1961 Cyprus was left without a tax law at all. Glafkos Clerides accused the Turkish Cypriots of trying to blackmail the Greek Cypriot majority over the 70:30 ratio in the public service by obstructing tax legislation. President Makarios then used his executive authority to issue an order requiring the officials concerned to continue collecting taxes and import duties as before. The Vice-President and the three Turkish ministers questioned Makarios's right to do this and the Turkish Cypriot press called for his resignation. The old machinery creaked on for another nine months till there was a major debate in mid-December on a new income tax law. Makarios and his Greek Cypriot ministers wanted a free hand. The Turkish Cypriots demanded that the House of Representatives should review the rates of taxation annually, which the Greeks thought a dangerous idea since any failure to agree on the rates – and this seemed more than probable – would leave the Government unable to raise revenue. Neither Makarios's Bill nor the Turkish Cypriot proposals secured the necessary majority in both sections of the House, so the state was again left without any income tax law. Both communities then resorted to their Communal Chambers. The Greek Cypriots passed a law imposing a 'personal contribution' equivalent to the income tax contemplated. The Turkish Cypriots similarly devised their own legislation. Each side protested about the other's action, but when the Supreme Constitutional Court upheld the right of both Communal Chambers to impose tax legislation, the cracks in the unity of the state were too wide to be concealed.

Yet for much of this period the outside world – apart from Greece and Turkey – seemed unaware that Cyprus was heading for another major crisis. Independence had released a flood of natural energy and self-reliance in the Cypriots, particularly but not exclusively on the Greek side. Trade and tourism began to expand. There was a spurt of building activity in the towns, and in the countryside a drive to intensify the island's agriculture. Complaints were heard at first, some of them justified, that the Cypriot economy was handicapped by the colonial legacy. But in February 1961 the House of Representatives followed Makarios's advice and voted overwhelmingly in favour of staying in the Commonwealth. The Communist-led AKEL did so 'reluctantly', arguing that economic necessity had to override principle for the time being; however it never showed any desire to withdraw.

Makarios attended his first Commonwealth Prime Ministers' Conference in London in March 1961. Both on that occasion and subsequently he made little contribution towards the discussion or solution of Commonwealth problems, but he was well received by the other heads of government and grew in their estimation for his shrewdness and leadership as much as he was liked for his personal charm and affability.

He got on best with other 'Third World' leaders, here as elsewhere, and it was significant that Makarios's first state visit was to Egypt at the invitation of President Nasser, in June 1961. It must have been particularly gratifying to the Archbishop to be welcomed by the most eminent Arab leader as the undoubted Head of State in Cyprus, in spite of the claims of its Muslim community and its Muslim Vice-President to equality with the Greeks. Three months later, in September, Makarios attended the summit conference of Non-Aligned States, held in Belgrade and sponsored by Tito, Nasser and Nehru. Here, as one who had 'graduated' from the earlier conference at Bandung, the Archbishop took an active part in the debate. He also attracted the attention of the West German Government as one of the few political leaders at Belgrade who were opposed to the concept of two German states and advocated a plebiscite under United Nations auspices on the reunification of Germany. In this oblique way Makarios emphasised his opposition to any idea of separate states in Cyprus. His stand at Belgrade was rewarded when he was invited to visit Bonn in May 1962 and given an unusually warm welcome. It was his first state visit to a European country, and it helped to consolidate a substantial offer of development aid to Cyprus from the Federal Republic.

A week later Makarios was in Washington. President Kennedy raised some eyebrows in Britain when he welcomed his visitor as 'a courageous fighter for freedom' and for the independence of his strategically important island. Makarios was in a particularly buoyant mood when he stopped briefly in Athens on his way home from Bonn and Washington. He told journalists he had secured from abroad more than half the money needed for Cyprus's five-year development plan. When he was asked about the political situation in Cyprus he answered that, in spite of some isolated incidents, the Government was firmly in control and there was no danger of intercommunal strife.

Makarios was steadily building up an international reputation for wise and capable leadership. If he looked mainly to the West for economic help, it was in the 'Third World' that he counted on finding political allies when it became necessary to remove the anomalies in the constitution or to resist external pressures on him.

Hence his state visit to India in November 1962, which complemented his earlier trips to Egypt and Yugoslavia. There had also been a state visit to Greece in September and, to balance that, Makarios suggested and obtained a formal invitation to go to Turkey in late November 1962 as the guest of President Gursel. The Turkish Government was outwardly genial, but the press practically ignored the visit and, as Makarios drove into Ankara, Turkish students demonstrated with banners saying 'Respect the London and Zürich agreements' or more laconically, 'Get Out'. The Archbishop pleaded fatigue as a reason for not visiting Ankara University and, unlike other Heads of State, he did not go to Istanbul. That might have aroused unpleasant memories of the anti-Greek riots there seven years before or, even worse, encouraged dangerous day-dreams in a Byzantine priest and politician visiting Constantinople. In private, Prime Minister Inonu urged President Makarios to use his influence to see that the Cyprus constitution was implemented in full as soon as possible.

The Turkish Government was not unduly disturbed by Makarios's ambiguous pronouncements at home. It accepted his need to defend himself against accusations that he had betrayed or abandoned the cause of Enosis. The presence of ex-EOKA men in the Government and in the police force and Makarios's frequent praise of EOKA's achievement were seen as part of the political game. Officially Turkey knew that the Greek Government would give Makarios no encouragement to go back on the Zürich and London agreements, and it believed that without Greek support he would not risk an open violation of the constitution that would force Turkey to intervene.

The Turkish Cypriots put no trust in Makarios. They feared that, even if Turkey was behind them to prevent Enosis, it could not easily check the gradual erosion of their legal rights. There were also economic pressures on them against which they had no constitutional safeguards. Turkish Cypriot businessmen usually found it more difficult than their Greek Cypriot counterparts to obtain import licences or building permits. By the spring of 1962, when Makarios had made it clear that he would not sanction the continuation of separate municipalities and each community had resorted to its own Communal Chamber as the only sure way of effecting legislation, the tensions had become dangerous. Greek Independence Day – 25 March – was marked by the explosion of bombs in two Turkish mosques in Nicosia. A few days later there was an attempt to set fire to a Greek Cypriot school. Makarios denounced the bomb attacks as 'criminal' and Dr Kuchuk appealed to his community not to react to provocation. But EOKA's anniversary, 1 April – when Makarios opened a museum in the old archbishopric commemorating the 'national' struggle – was celebrated with a new enthusiasm and more fervent demands for Enosis than had been heard since independence.

The President's refusal to take a Turkish Cypriot minister with him or to include any Turk in his entourage when he went abroad on official visits did nothing to remove the community's suspicions that Makarios regarded the conduct of foreign policy as entirely his own preserve.[3]

In August 1962, on the eve of the second anniversary of independence, Makarios addressed a large assembly of Greek Cypriots who had gathered at Kykko Monastery to celebrate the Assumption of the Virgin. He made no mention of Enosis but said that the struggle for independence had not yet ended. The Archbishop emphasised the leadership of the Church and told his listeners that it was through religion that they would remain Greeks. The purely secular commemoration of independence the following day was limited to a presidential reception for foreign diplomats and senior civil servants.

When the next emotive anniversaries came round in the spring of 1963 the feeling of frustration in both communities had greatly deepened. In a speech full of ambivalence on the eve of EOKA's eighth anniversary, President Makarios said that the Cyprus created by the Zürich and London agreements had not been the objective of EOKA's struggle 'in any shape or form'. It was a solution demanded by the circumstances of the time. What was desirable was not attainable and those responsible for the fate of the people had to be realists. However, the Archbishop went on, the agreements were a victory, not a defeat. They marked the start of a forward march to conquer the future in the spirit of EOKA.

Earlier, at the same meeting, Glafkos Clerides, the President of the House of Representatives, had appealed for a revival and strengthening of the old friendly relations between Greek and Turkish Cypriots. He said the Greeks had no wish to trample on the rights of the minority but they were not prepared to let it prevent the smooth functioning of the state or override the majority. These moderate words of Clerides were overlooked while the speech of the Archbishop produced a sharp reaction from Rauf

Denktash, who called it 'irresponsible and dangerous'. There was consternation in Athens and anger in Ankara. Some ten days later the Archbishop was asked to clarify his views in an interview with *The Times*. He said that union with Greece had always been the cherished dream of the Greek Cypriots. 'Enosis cannot now be achieved', he went on, but the dream would remain. That 'now' was charged with ambiguity.

By this time both communities were well advanced in their preparations for a show of force. In May 1963 officers of the secret army being organised by Yeorkadjis, Papadopoulos and Clerides, with the help of the Greek mainland unit, set up an 'operations room'. Recruiting went on throughout the summer, and soon several thousand Greek Cypriots had had part-time training in the use of arms borrowed from government stocks. The Turkish Cypriots had to import their arms by caïque from Turkey or get troops from the Turkish contingent to leave weapons behind when their tour of duty in Cyprus ended. All this, of course, was in addition to many of the arms EOKA had not handed in, the weapons stowed away by its Turkish Cypriot counterpart, TMT, and thousands of shotguns in the possession of both communities.

It seems probable that the Turks had no intention of making the first move; they organised primarily for defence against the attack they expected from the Greeks. Greek Cypriot strategy was determined by the so-called 'Akritas Plan', apparently drawn up early in 1963 on the orders of Makarios. The existence of the plan has never been denied; details of it were first published some years later (on 21 April 1966) by the pro-Grivas Cypriot newspaper *Patris* in an attempt to discredit the Archbishop and his aides for their alleged incompetence in dealing with the Turkish Cypriot problem. There is no reason to doubt the genuineness of the *Patris* version.

'Akritas' ('Frontiersman') was the epithet of the original 'Dighenis', the legendary hero who had guarded the outposts of empire in late Byzantine times and whose name Grivas had adopted. In the new context 'Akritas' was Polykarpos Yeorkadjis, Grivas's former lieutenant, who was now Minister of the Interior. The top-secret document sent out under this pseudonym to various 'sub-headquarters' outlined, step by step, Makarios's future strategy in handling the 'National Question'. Satisfactory progress had been made already, the author claimed, in convincing foreign diplomatic missions that the Zürich and London agreements were 'unjust' and had been imposed against the will of the people. Here it was emphasised that the leadership had 'wisely' avoided holding a referendum since, in the circumstances of 1959, the people would definitely have approved the agreements. Now it was necessary to show the world that the aim of the Cypriot Greeks was not to oppress the Turks but to get rid of 'unreasonable' provisions in the constitution before it was too late. The struggle must be based on the claim to self-determination, not on a demand for Enosis.

The 'Akritas Plan' then set out what it described as the only sequence of events that could ensure success. First, the 'negative' elements in the agreements must be got rid of. These involved, apart from certain articles in the constitution, the Treaty of Guarantee and the Treaty of Alliance which inhibited the exercise of self-determination. Once these had gone, no legal or moral force could prevent the holding of a plebiscite and the implementation of the people's will. Since Cyprus would be completely independent, the forces of the state, i.e. the police, and 'friendly military forces' – presumably the Greek army contingent – could 'legitimately' resist any intervention either from within or from outside Cyprus.

The scrupulous regard for external 'legality' and the rather naïve belief that 'right' must prevail were more characteristic of Makarios's thinking than an argument likely to have been advanced by the ruthless Yeorkadjis.

However, the 'Akritas Plan' showed some awareness of the dangers. If Turkey intervened before the Treaty of Guarantee could be got out of the way, such intervention might well seem justified, and this would harm the Greek Cypriot cause internationally and, in particular, at the United Nations. The published text goes on: 'The history of many similar incidents in recent times shows us that in no case of intervention, even if legally inexcusable, has the attacker been removed by the United Nations or by other powers, without significant concessions being made by the party attacked. (This was a warning the Greek Cypriots were to ignore repeatedly until it was too late; even after 1974 they were slow to appreciate the high price they must pay to get rid of the Turkish invasion forces, if they ever could.) The 'Akritas' strategy – again suggesting a precise brief by Makarios – underlined the importance of choosing very carefully the constitutional articles which the Greek Cypriots would propose should be amended, in order to make certain of getting international support. Since there would be no declaration of Enosis until all the previous stages had been completed, the only remaining danger was the risk of intercommunal strife. There must be no provocation of the Turkish Cypriots, but if they tried to create trouble when the amendments were proposed, the Greek Cypriots must counter-attack quickly. If they could get control of the situation within a day or two, outside intervention – it was thought – would not be possible or 'justifiable'. There was a final dash of recklessness that sounds more like Yeorkadjis than Makarios; in the event of widespread clashes with the Turks, all stages of the plan were to be rushed through as quickly as possible to the declaration of Enosis.

Long before Grivas's revelations about the 'Akritas Plan', which were to be such a godsend to the Turks, and only shortly after the outbreak of hostilities – in fact, at the beginning of March 1964 – the Greek Cypriot authorities announced that they had discovered a secret document in the office of a Turkish Cypriot minister, which bore the date 14 September 1963 and carried the signatures of Kuchuk and Denktash. It was said to call for Turkish intervention, the concentration of the Turkish Cypriot community into one area and a declaration of 'partition', if the Greeks tried to abrogate the constitution. Whether the document was genuine or not – and it probably was – neither side took the extreme political steps envisaged when the fighting broke out.

Two external developments favoured Makarios's plan. In Greece Karamanlis had resigned in the summer of 1963, when the pressures against him had proved too strong after eight years in office.[4] A caretaker government took over and elections were not held until November. Then the old Liberal demagogue, George Papandreou, won by too slender a margin to form anything but a minority government dependent upon the support of the extreme Left for survival. After six weeks Papandreou resigned, to win a substantial majority at new elections in February 1964. Karamanlis had already gone off in high dudgeon to his self-imposed exile in Paris, which was to last until he was recalled after the Turkish invasion of Cyprus in 1974.

It was while Greece was uncertainly changing horses at the end of 1963 that Makarios made his move. One of the Guarantor States was in no position nor in any mood to restrain him. Papandreou had denounced the Cyprus agreements as a humiliating defeat for the Karamanlis Goverment and had promised support for the Greek Cypriots in their efforts to achieve Enosis. This alarmed the Turks, but Turkey was in even greater turmoil. In May 1963 officers and cadets at the Ankara military academy mutinied in protest at the revival of Menderes's old Democrat Party under the new name of the Justice Party. Six months later, in that crucial November, the Justice Party made sweeping gains in the local elections, and this show of grass-roots support for hanged and discredited Menderes caused Prime Minister Inonu to resign on 2 December.

On 30 November, when Greece and Turkey were both preoccupied with their governmental crises, President Makarios submitted thirteen proposals – again that 13! – to Vice-President Kuchuk for the removal, as he said, of certain anomalies in the constitution that prevented the smooth functioning of government and the co-operation of the two communities. Makarios proposed first of all to abolish both the presidential and the vice-presidential right of veto on the grounds that they were unnecessary and obstructive; there were other ways, the Greek side argued, of providing political safeguards. However, to compensate for the loss of his veto, the Vice-President – Makarios suggested – should deputise for the President if he were abroad or temporarily unable to carry out his duties. (Under the constitution that right belonged to the President of the House of Representatives, who was always a Greek.) The offer was flattering and paid lip-service to the idea of intercommunal responsibility, but it gave the Turks no new powers in return for the loss of the veto. The same was true of the proposal that the Turkish Cypriot Vice-President of the House should deputise for its Greek Cypriot President, when *he* was absent; and Makarios's suggestion that both should be elected by the House as a whole meant that the Turkish Cypriot would always be the choice of the Greek majority.

Next Makarios proposed to abolish the article in the constitution that required separate majorities for certain legislation; this, it was claimed, was undemocratic and also unnecessary because there could always be an appeal to the Constitutional Court against discriminatory laws. (It was not an argument to cut much ice with the Turks, who had little trust in the Court's decisions.) Then, tucked away in the middle, were proposals to unify the municipalities and the administration of justice. These were such explosive issues that there was no hope of their being considered. There followed a minor proposal about abolishing the distinction between the gendarmerie and the police and a more radical one that the strength of the security and defence forces should be decided not, as the constitution said, by the President and Vice-President in consultation but by a majority of the House – in other words, by the Greeks. Then, as if emboldened by a new access of power, Makarios proposed changing the ratio of Greeks and Turks in the public service and the forces to accord with their ratio of the population; though, out of consideration for the individual, he suggested this change should be gradual so that there should be no victimisation. Finally Makarios proposed to abolish the Greek Communal Chamber but said the Turkish Cypriots might keep theirs if they wished.

According to President Makarios, Dr Kuchuk agreed to study these proposals and give his reply within the month, by the end of December. He may only have been playing for time, though in principle he was not against an attempt to make the constitution more workable. However, on 16 December Ankara, which – like Athens and London – had received a copy of Makarios's memorandum ' as a matter of courtesy', flatly rejected all the proposals as an attempt to breach the constitution. Five days later a night-time incident in Nicosia sparked off the first serious intercommunal violence since independence. In the early hours of Christmas Day Turkey warned the British Government that she would exercise her right to military intervention in Cyprus if there was not swift joint action to protect the Turkish minority. Mr Duncan Sandys, the Secretary for Commonwealth Relations, flew out to Nicosia on the night of 27 December, but by that time the island was already on the brink of civil war.

Greek and Greek Cypriot officials have always maintained that Makarios's proposals were reasonable and, indeed that they had the approval of the British High Commissioner in Nicosia, Sir Arthur Clarke. Sir Arthur, who left Cyprus soon afterwards on health grounds, apparently thought it would do no harm if Makarios set down in a memorandum for Kuchuk the changes in the constitution that he thought desirable. The Greek Cypriots probably read too much into the High Commissioner's sympathy for Makarios's frustration. In the summer of 1963 the British Government had urged Makarios to be patient and not try to change the constitution yet. It is possible that, if he had suggested modifications gradually and offered the Turkish Cypriot community more economic aid, there would have been a dialogue. The Turkish Cypriots might not have objected to some reduction of their onerous share in the public service if this had released men for more productive work for their community. As it was, the proposed changes were too sweeping. Makarios's attempt to remove the Turkish Cypriot veto and claim majority rights for the Greek Cypriots in the name of democracy alarmed the island's Turks and made them look to Ankara for protection. Turkey had no illusions at all about Greek Cypriot aims but she had not expected Makarios to move so quickly. Although she threatened intervention she was in no position then to invade effectively. So the danger of an immediate declaration of Enosis, or at least the overthrow of the constitution, had to be met, as Turkey saw it, by a move towards partition.

In the early hours of 21 December Greek Cypriot police stopped and interrogated some Turkish Cypriots in the red-light district of Nicosia which spanned the two communities. During the altercation that followed a hostile crowd gathered, shots were fired and a Turkish Cypriot man and woman were killed. Other Turks and – according to some accounts – a Greek policeman were wounded. The exact details were made irrelevant by what followed. When daylight came Turkish Cypriots began to collect in the northern suburbs of Nicosia and along the road leading through them to Kyrenia. Greek vehicles were stoned and fired on. During a day of tension President Makarios broadcast a statement that he considered the Treaty of Guarantee – which gave Turkey the right to intervention in certain circumstances – null and void; it was a rash move but a measure of his nervousness at this time. The following day – 22 December – the funeral of the Turks passed off without incident, largely because the Greek police were kept at a distance, but Turkish Cypriot snipers were active from roof-tops and balconies, shooting into the Greek quarters and ignoring Dr Kuchuk's appeal for calm and restraint. That night the Greek Cypriots answered with heavy automatic fire from the roof of the Ledra Palace Hotel, the General Hospital and other buildings overlooking the Turkish part of the walled city. Early the next morning President Makarios broadcast a message to the people, claiming that the Government was in full control and calling on all public servants, Turks as well as Greeks, to go to work as usual.

Had the Turkish Cypriots obeyed, it would have looked like a political victory for the Greek Cypriots. In any case, many Turks were too afraid to go back to work in the Greek sectors. Some of them began to barricade themselves in their houses as bands of irregulars from both sides roamed the streets, taking hostages. The Turkish Cypriot police and gendarmerie slipped away from their posts, taking weapons where they could. Meanwhile President Makarios and Vice-President Kuchuk had met on the morning of the 23rd and agreed to a truce. But the fighting continued and spread to other parts of the island. The following day – Christmas Eve – another cease-fire was agreed by Makarios and Kuchuk at a meeting with the Acting British High Commissioner and the United States ambassador. Makarios was in favour of mixed police patrols to keep order, but when it was discovered that most of the arms available had been distributed to the Greek police and their 'specials' the Turks refused to be less well equipped.

That night Greek Cypriot forces, police and irregulars, launched an all-out attack on Turkish Cypriot positions in the mixed suburb of Omorphita where the Turks had surrounded a number of Greek houses. The irregulars were led by the former EOKA killer, Nikos Sampson, who was later to be foisted into short-lived glory as successor to Makarios after his temporary overthrow by the Greek 'Colonels' in 1974. Sampson had the ingenious idea of using a bulldozer with its excavator raised as an improvised 'tank'. Many Turks were killed, hundreds evacuated or taken as hostages – the distinction was a fine one – and the rest driven out. The Greeks also attacked the neighbouring suburb of Kumsal. The family of a Turkish Cypriot doctor serving as medical officer to the Turkish mainland contingent was brutally wiped out. The bodies of his wife and three small children were found in the bath, riddled with bullets. A woman visitor who had hid in the lavatory next door was dragged out and shot. The Turks did not move the bodies until foreign press photographers had recorded the scene several days later. Afterwards, with a gruesome relish of its propaganda value, they turned this once pleasant little villa into a 'Museum of Barbarism', where for years they pointed out to tourists what they claimed were traces of blood and brains on the bathroom ceiling.

Turkish air force planes flew over Nicosia daily during the next few days but, as yet, this was no more than an empty gesture, as the Greek Cypriots soon realised. The three Guarantor Powers had now called for peace talks and these began on Christmas Day. Makarios readily agreed that British troops from the sovereign bases should supervise a general cease-fire and occupy a buffer zone in Nicosia between the Greek and Turkish quarters. He little appreciated then that what was to become known as the 'Green Line' would – first under British, later under United Nations control – keep the Greek Cypriots out of a major Turkish Cypriot enclave until it was replaced by the Turks' more sinister 'Attila Line' of 1974 which effectively partitioned the whole island.

Knowing that no immediate help was coming from the main-land, the 650-strong Turkish army contingent in Cyprus moved out of camp on Christmas Day and took up positions astride the strategic road-link between Kyrenia and Nicosia. The larger Greek contingent could do nothing to prevent this without precipi-tating a war between Greece and Turkey. Officially both con-tingents were put under British command as part of a joint peace-keeping force, but it was thought wiser to leave this as purely a paper arrangement.

The Secretary of State for Commonwealth Relations, Mr Duncan Sandys, arrived in Nicosia two days after Christmas to strengthen the cease-fire agreement and to prepare the way for talks. Makarios had pointedly asked for British help but not for mediation. Sandys insisted on both sides releasing their hostages – where they had not been killed or spirited away – but his efforts at peace-making received a rude jolt when, on New Year's Day 1964, the Cyprus Broadcasting Corporation announced that President Makarios had abrogated the treaties with Greece, Turkey and Britain. The minister went off immediately to confront the Arch-bishop and get him to retract. At first Makarios refused, but when Sandys warned him that the Turks would now have every justifi-cation to invade, the Archbishop reluctantly gave way. He agreed to issue a 'clarifying' statement that his Government had not abro-gated the treaties but only wished to see them terminated by appro-priate procedures. Makarios apparently told Sandys that the misunderstanding had arisen through faulty translation from the Greek. Kyprianou, the Foreign Minister, who was present at the meeting, then admitted with some embarrassment, on being questioned by Sandys, that the original text of the telegram sent to foreign governments had been in English.

By New Year's Day the deployment of British troops along the 'Green Line' had cut down the killings and hostage-taking in Nicosia but could not prevent them elsewhere, particularly in remote districts. Atrocity stories abounded on both sides and many were substantiated. No reliable figures have ever been given for the total number of casualties, but there can be no doubt that the Turkish Cypriots bore the brunt of the intercommunal violence at this time. They claim that 200 of their community were killed during the Christmas fighting and another 200 never accounted for; these figures may not be far wrong.

Before Sandys left Nicosia he got the leaders of both communities to agree to a new London conference on Cyprus. Makarios did so reluctantly, and only after pressure from some of his own ministers and the Greek ambassador. He wanted to take the matter immediately to the United Nations where his representative, Mr Zenon Rossides, had already protested to the Security Council that Turkey was threatening the integrity of Cyprus. Makarios had no wish to see another London agreement imposed on the Cypriots. He hoped that, with the British keeping the island Turks and his own hotheads under control, he could get the United Nations to recognise the right of the Greek Cypriot majority to unfettered sovereignty and so put an end to Turkish Cypriot intransigence and to the threat from Turkey.

The Turkish Cypriots had now left the Government and abandoned many of their other posts, though they maintained that they had been driven out; to the Greeks they were simply rebels or defectors. But the 'Akritas Plan' had not worked. Even assuming it was to be put into action only if the Turkish Cypriots reacted violently to Makarios's proposed changes in the constitution, the Greek Cypriots had failed to make themselves masters of the situation 'within a day or two'. The uncontrolled attacks on Turkish Cypriots had driven them, and would continue to drive them, into defended enclaves which were not going to be broken up. Although the clashes had been widespread, there had been no immediate declaration of Enosis. In fact Makarios was to say on 11 January that, if Turkey and the Turkish Cypriots were afraid of Enosis, they should ask the Greek Government for guarantees against it. Whether this was a Machiavellian ruse to disarm international suspicion or a sign that the Archbishop was not wholly behind the 'Akritas' strategy and had begun to turn against Enosis as a desirable solution is something we shall probably never know.

The London conference began on 15 January. The Greek Cypriot delegation, led by Glafkos Clerides, called for the removal of the limitations on the independence of Cyprus and its recognition as a unitary state with a parliament elected on a common roll, a Council of Ministers responsible to parliament and minority rights for the Turkish Cypriots, including full autonomy in matters of religion, culture and education. The Turkish Cypriots, headed by Rauf Denktash, demanded the restoration of their rights under the Zürich and London agreements but also claimed it was essential for the two communities to live physically apart. Backed by the Turkish representative, Denktash proposed a federation between a Greek Cypriot majority area and a Turkish Cypriot self-governing canton. This was rejected outright by the Greek Cypriots as tantamount to partition. Here it should be noted that the new Government in Ankara under Mr Inonu was prepared to drop a demand for partition in favour of federation on the grounds that the economy of the island could not be split into two.

Sandys tried hard to reconcile these opposing views and since Clerides and Denktash were personally on good terms he thought there was some chance of finding a basis for negotiation between them. But suddenly Clerides was called back by Makarios, and Denktash was summoned to Ankara. When they returned both sides were completely unyielding.

Sir Alec Douglas-Home, who was then Prime Minister, had no desire to see British troops trapped again between two hostile Cypriot communities or involved in a thankless peace-keeping job on their own. He proposed they should be reinforced by contingents from other NATO countries. Washington agreed, Turkey welcomed the idea and Greece accepted with reluctance. President Makarios rejected the proposal outright. To him it was obvious that a NATO force would take Turkey's views into consideration as much as, if not more than, those of Greece and the Greek Cypriots. The Archbishop said he would accept only a United Nations force authorised by the Security Council.

Meanwhile the situation in Cyprus was rapidly deteriorating. The Turkish Cypriots, with the help of the Turkish army contingent, had enlarged their main enclave to the north of Nicosia to include the old Crusader castle of St Hilarion on a peak in the Kyrenia range of mountains from where they could dominate the coastal plain below and command the pass. At Polis in the north-west five hundred Turks were besieged in a school. At Limassol in the south the Greeks mounted a full-scale attack on the Turkish quarter. Turkey again threatened to invade but Makarios remained unperturbed. The United States Acting Secretary of State, Mr George Ball, flew to Nicosia to 'bully' Makarios into accepting a NATO force before it was too late, but the Archbishop was adamant.[5]

On 15 February the British Government forestalled the Greek Cypriots by a few hours with an appeal to the Security Council; Makarios's 'brinkmanship' had cost him that diplomatic advantage. However, after much argument, mainly behind the scenes, the Security Council adopted a resolution on 4 March which gave Makarios great satisfaction. It called on all states to refrain from any action or threat of action that was likely to worsen the situation in 'the sovereign Republic of Cyprus' or to endanger peace. It urged both communities to show restraint but also asked 'the Government of Cyprus' to take the additional measures necessary to stop the bloodshed and restore order. (Makarios had already demanded a reduction in the size of the British peace-keeping force since it was preventing the Greek Cypriots from dealing with pockets of Turkish Cypriot resistance; he had also announced his intention of creating a police force of 5000 'specials'.) Finally the Security Council recommended the despatch of a United Nations peace-keeping force to Cyprus for three months and the appointment of a mediator who would try to promote an 'agreed solution' of the Cyprus problem ' in accordance with the Charter of the United Nations'. The resolution referred to the need to get the consent of Greece, Turkey, Britain and 'the Government of Cyprus' to all this, but it made no mention of restoring the *status quo*.

It was not until 14 March that the first UN troops – a Canadian contingent – arrived in Cyprus, and almost another fortnight before the international peace-keeping force took over. By then many thousands of Turkish Cypriots had become refugees or been moved from their homes by their leaders. Six months later, as each side tried to impose its will on the other in defiance of the United Nations, it was estimated that between a third and a half of the Turkish Cypriot population had collected in defensible enclaves. The United Nations had no power to prevent it, but it was not what Makarios had wanted.

11 Two Armed Camps

The early months of 1964 had been an anxious time for Makarios. However, as the United Nations Force in Cyprus (UNFICYP) began to build up – it took till June to come near its projected strength of 7000 officers and men – the Archbishop was able to plan his long-term strategy. The UN force, as he saw it, was there primarily to protect the Greek Cypriot community against further Turkish Cypriot attacks and to be a deterrent to any aggression from Turkey. It was also there – as its mandate clearly said – to help the Government of Cyprus restore law and order and bring about a return to normal conditions. Since the Government was now entirely Greek Cypriot, this could be – and was – interpreted as giving the major community the right to call upon UN troops to disarm Turkish Cypriot irregulars or dismantle their road-blocks and fortifications. (The UN force had other ideas about this.) Makarios had furthermore insisted on the Security Council's resolution containing a reference to the clause in the United Nations Charter (Article 2, paragraph 4), which holds the 'territorial integrity' of a member-state to be sacrosanct. The Archbishop saw this as the best guarantee against *de facto* partition until he could get the United Nations to condemn the 1959–60 agreements and affirm the absolute sovereignty of a government elected by a majority of Cypriots. For this he was relying on the support of the Afro-Asian anti-colonial *bloc* at the UN and the anti-NATO vote of the Communist countries. At the same time Makarios had no intention of allowing the United Nations to dictate a solution through its appointed mediator, the former Foreign Minister of Finland, Mr Sakari Tuomioja.

For the Turkish Cypriots there was one simple reason for the United Nations' presence in Cyprus. Its troops were there to prevent their community from being overrun before Turkey was in a position to invade in their defence or they could organise themselves in impregnable enclaves.

UNFICYP failed to live up to either side's expectations. With the limitations upon it to use force only in self-defence it could not prevent Greek or Turkish Cypriots from strengthening their positions or often from attacking each other during those early months. The national contingents making up UNFICYP came from Austria, Canada, Denmark, Finland, Ireland, Sweden and the United Kingdom, the British element being reduced as the others arrived. The force commander was Lieutenant-General Prem Singh Gyani of India. There was also a small United Nations police force, of fewer than 200 men, made up of Austrians, Danes, Swedes, Australians and New Zealanders. Most of these men were completely unfamiliar with Cyprus and its problems. Since their role was restricted, they were often inclined to let armed Greeks and Turks fight it out, so long as civilians were not involved. But the number of casualties fell and the taking of hostages was largely eliminated.

Almost half the Turkish Cypriots now lived in defended enclaves. The main one stretched from the 'Green Line' in Nicosia to the northern mountain range some fifteen miles away, bulging either side of the Nicosia-Kyrenia road like a curled-up foetus. This area contained the new offices of the Turkish Cypriot leadership, some important government buildings such as the Ministry of Justice and the Land Registry, and the Turkish army contingent. There was another less well-defined enclave based on a cluster of Turkish Cypriot villages east of Nicosia. The Turkish Cypriots also controlled the Old City of Famagusta within the ancient Turkish fortifications, but not the harbour immediately outside it or the suburb of Varosha, which was rapidly expanding as a tourist resort under Greek Cypriot enterprise. There were defended Turkish Cypriot positions on the road to Larnaca and in the foothills above Paphos, and some small tightly-controlled enclaves, including beach-heads, in north-west Cyprus. In Kyrenia and Limassol and a number of mixed villages Greek and Turkish Cypriots settled down to living more or less peacefully again, side by side, with freedom of movement between their respective quarters.

The Greek Cypriots had been quick to cut off electricity supplies and telephone and postal services to the main enclaves as soon as the fighting began, but they had to restore the current to the Turkish part of Nicosia in order to get the piped water they needed from that side. The Turkish Cypriots no longer drew salaries or pensions from the Government and many had lost their farms or businesses, but they also paid no taxes to the Greek Cypriot authorities. However, some 50,000 Turkish Cypriots – almost half their population – were soon dependent on relief from Turkey.

In spite of the UN's supposedly deterrent presence both sides continued to arm feverishly. The Turkish Cypriots had established their main bridgehead for the import of arms and supplies from Turkey in the Kokkina-Mansoura enclave on the north-west coast. The Greek Cypriots had control of all the ports and brought in weapons and military stores from Greece under the noses of the UN. They were intended for the new so-called 'National Guard' which Makarios created in March. At first it was simply a fusion of private armies, though some of them continued to operate independently whenever they chose. On 1 April, EOKA-Day, President Makarios took the salute as his 'National Guard' paraded through Nicosia, a few hundred yards from the 'Green Line', with rocket-launchers and armoured cars. Three days later the Greek Cypriots made a determined but unsuccessful attack on the Kokkina enclave. Shortly after this the Archbishop flew to Athens for talks with the Greek Government.[1]

After two days of consultation Prime Minister Papandreou issued a statement expressing Greece's full support for the struggle of the Greek Cypriots and demanding self-determination for Cyprus. He added that the United Nations' presence in the island and the appointment of a mediator proved that the old agreements were dead and that a new political formula had to be found. Makarios welcomed this statement, but he knew that it must increase the danger of Turkish intervention. It was essential for him to have more arms and more experienced leadership for his 'National Guard'. From a military point of view the obvious choice was Grivas but could Makarios take the political risk? The former EOKA leader had kept remarkably quiet throughout the crisis, no doubt enjoying Makarios's discomfiture as much as his own indignation with the Turks would allow. Makarios delayed his return to Cyprus for twenty-four hours to meet Grivas and – according to some accounts – to try to persuade him to accept command of the 'National Guard'. Afterwards he told a press conference that General Grivas 'does not consider the time opportune, probably because he thinks the situation is not serious'. It seems more likely – in the absence of other evidence – that Makarios had to dissuade Grivas from trying to return to Cyprus or at least insisted on political terms that the General could not accept. On 17 April – after the Archbishop had left Athens – Grivas declared that he would go back to lead the armed struggle again if Cyprus was threatened with invasion. A week later it was announced that another retired Greek army officer, Lieutenant-General George Karayiannis, had assumed command of the Greek Cypriot 'National Guard'. The Greek Defence Ministry carefully explained that General Karayiannis no longer had any connexion with the Greek army.

The fighting had worsened while Makarios was away. On his return to Nicosia he offered to dismantle all Greek Cypriot posts and fortifications throughout the island under United Nations supervision, to grant a general amnesty to all Turkish Cypriots and to help in resettling the Turkish Cypriot refugees. He also proposed that the Turkish army contingent should replace the British element in the UN force. The Turkish Cypriots saw this as a cunning move to break up their enclaves and get the Turkish army away from its strategic position on the Kyrenia road; they flatly rejected Makarios's offer.

May was a quieter month, though both sides continued to arm and to get reinforcements. On the 18th there was a semi-official news announcement that the Government of Cyprus was negotiating for the purchase of bomber and fighter aircraft, anti-aircraft guns and other heavy armaments to ward off any invasion from Turkey. On the 27th Makarios introduced a Conscription Bill making all male Cypriots between the ages of 18 and 59 liable for six months' service in the 'National Guard'. Turkey protested that both moves violated the constitution, and Dr Kuchuk went through the motions of interposing his veto. He and Makarios denounced each other for treason.[2]

On 1 June the Turkish Government 'decided' that the only course left open to it was to establish a bridgehead in Cyprus and bring about a complete separation of the two communities. This would have had no more legal justification than the actual Turkish invasion ten years later in 1974, since on neither occasion was there any intention to restore the arrangements created by the 1959–60 agreements. Britain and Greece apparently had no knowledge of the Turkish 'decision' – if it was anything more than another threat – but the information was 'leaked' to the Americans the next day.

The United States could not afford to see two of its NATO allies go to war with each other, and on 5 June President Johnson warned Turkey that she could not rely on American help if the Soviet Union chose to intervene on Makarios's behalf. There was also a sharper warning – to be ignored in 1974 – that American arms must not be used to invade Cyprus. In case the Turks were not bluffing, the American Sixth Fleet discreetly moved into position between Cyprus and the Turkish coast. President Johnson invited Inonu and Papandreou to talks in Washington, but these were unproductive since Papandreou refused to negotiate with Turkey except through the UN mediator. Finally it was agreed that representatives of the Greek and Turkish Governments should meet Mr Tuomioja in Geneva, and that Lord Hood and Mr Dean Acheson, a former Secretary of State, should hold watching briefs for Britain and the United States respectively.

Makarios refused to be drawn into these talks. Both Cypriot communities had already submitted their views to the mediator. Makarios insisted that Cyprus must be a completely independent and unitary state with democratic majority government and communal rights suitably entrenched in the constitution. The Turkish Cypriots rejected full independence as only a step away from Enosis. They demanded a federal system of government incorporating many features of the 1960 constitution but with the island divided into two separate ethnic regions. Significantly, the dividing-line proposed by the Turkish Cypriots ran from the village of Yialia in the north-west, just south of the Kokkina enclave, through Nicosia to Famagusta on the east coast. It was substantially the same as the 'Attila Line' imposed by the Turkish Army after its second thrust in August 1974. The area then seized by the Turks was – with a scrupulous regard Shylock would have appreciated – almost exactly the 37 per cent of the island that the Turkish Cypriots had demanded ten years earlier as their rightful share. They arrived at this figure by claiming to own 30 per cent of the arable land – which the Greek Cypriots deny – and to be entitled to 7 per cent of the state forests, common land, roads, riverbeds and town and village sites.[3]

At the Geneva meeting in July Dean Acheson produced a set of proposals which were quickly 'leaked' by the Greek Government but never published officially. In its original form the 'Acheson Plan' tried to reconcile the main demands of all the interested parties. If most of Cyprus were united with Greece – this was the

American thinking behind it – the Greek Cypriots would achieve their age-old dream of Enosis, Greece would be enlarged and Cyprus would be safe in NATO. However, part of the island – the long Karpass Peninsula to the north-east known as the 'Panhandle' – should be given to Turkey for a military base, to satisfy her supposed security needs. Inside the area that would become part of Greece there should be one or two Turkish Cypriot cantons enjoying local autonomy. Any Turkish Cypriots who preferred to emigrate would receive compensation and, as a further reward to Turkey for accepting 'Enosis', Greece would cede her the small island of Castellorizo, less than four square miles in area but a useful outpost off her southern coast.

Turkey agreed in principle to the 'Acheson plan' but insisted that the sovereign base area assigned to her should be large enough to accommodate most of the Turkish Cypriot population; she did not trust the idea of 'cantons' embedded in Greek territory. Such an arrangement would have amounted to 'double Enosis' or, as the Greeks and Greek Cypriots saw it, partition. Makarios, who had gone to Athens at the end of July for further consultation with the Greek Government, spoke darkly of 'self-appointed mediators' who had worked out 'unacceptable plans' for a solution of the Cyprus problem. A fortnight later Glafkos Clerides, as President of the House of Representatives, confirmed that the Makarios Government had rejected the 'Acheson Plan' since to accept it would have been 'a betrayal of Hellenism'.

During the last days of July Greek Cypriot forces began to mass around the Kokkina enclave. On 4 August President Makarios assured the UN commander that they would not attack, their objective being simply to prevent supplies from reaching the Turkish Cypriot rebels. Two days later, in spite of this promise and, according to some, against the advice of General Karayiannis, the 'National Guard' mounted a full-scale assault on the enclave with mortars and 25-pounders. The order probably came from Yeorkadjis, the ex-EOKA man, 'Akritas' Chief and 'Minister of Defence' since the Turks had left the Government, but the ultimate responsibility for the broken pledge must rest with the Archbishop.

It has been estimated that there were some 500 well-armed Turks and Turkish Cypriots in the enclave, apart from the refugees, but they were outgunned and outnumbered three to one by the Greek Cypriots. On 8 August, as the Turkish Cypriots were being flushed out of their villages down towards the beach-head, thirty Turkish air force jets appeared and attacked the Greeks. The following day more than sixty planes came over and began to bomb and machine-gun Greek Cypriot villages in the area as well as the military target. Swedish troops in UNFICYP did what they could to evacuate women and children from the enclave, but they came under fire themselves and both the local 'National Guard' commander and President Makarios refused to call off the assault. On 9 August the Archbishop threatened to overrun every Turkish village in the island, if Ankara did not stop the air attacks. He also appealed to Egypt and the Soviet Union for military help against Turkey, but neither President Nasser nor Mr Khrushchev showed any desire to do more than send sympathy and express solidarity with the Greek Cypriots. The Greek Government had promised help in repelling an invasion but, in spite of the state of popular arousal in Greece, it had no intention of rushing into a war with a country whose armed forces were three times as large as its own. By now the United Nations Security Council had met – somewhat tardily – in response to an appeal from Turkey and a later one from the Government of Cyprus. When it called for an immediate cease-fire, both Ankara and Makarios agreed to it. Everybody had had a fright, and this was to be the last major clash in Cyprus for more than three years.

A few days later the Geneva talks were resumed and Dean Acheson put forward a revised version of his plan. To make it more acceptable to the Greeks he now suggested that the Karpass base area should be leased to Turkey for twenty or twenty-five years instead of being put under her sovereignty. Ankara promptly rejected this, and it was no more acceptable to Makarios than the earlier version had been, though the Greek Government was willing to consider it. In the middle of all this the official mediator, Mr Tuomioja, had a stroke and died within a month. Washington decided to leave the search for a political solution to a new UN mediator.

Meanwhile General Grivas had returned to Cyprus. Soon after his unheralded arrival in mid-June he made a broadcast in which he declared that he had come to restore unity among Greek Cypriots and to re-establish the old harmonious relations with the Turkish Cypriots. His first public appearance was at a large rally in Nicosia attended by Makarios and his ministers. During the next few weeks Grivas openly proclaimed the need for a referendum to determine the will of the majority. But in private he favoured something like the 'Acheson Plan', with one of the British bases outside the Republic being given to Turkey in place of the Karpass. Grivas's role during the Kokkina fighting is not clear; he may have urged the attack on the enclave in defiance of orders from General Karayiannis and the pledge given by Makarios. But after the cease-fire Karayiannis returned to Athens and Grivas took command of the 'National Guard'.

There can be no doubt that the Greek Government welcomed this appointment and not simply because of Grivas's military ability. His ferocious discipline was needed to keep the Greek Cypriot irregulars under control and so lessen the risk of their provoking a Turkish invasion. But Papandreou also saw Grivas as a useful counterbalance to Makarios. Although he had adopted the Archbishop's slogan of 'unfettered independence' for Cyprus, he had no wish to see Makarios pursue too independent a policy that might endanger Greece's national interests.

Makarios flew to Athens again on 25 August for a four-hour meeting with Papandreou, taking with him Kyprianou and Yeorkadjis, his Foreign and Defence Ministers; their Greek opposite numbers also took part in the talks. Afterwards a communiqué issued by the Greek Government said there was a complete identity of views on handling the Cyprus question, which would be taken to the forthcoming General Assembly of the United Nations. Significantly, there was no reference this time to 'self-determination' for Cyprus. A semi-official Greek comment spoke of the defence of Cyprus being undertaken 'in the name of a united and independent Greece'. Papandreou had evidently begun to suspect that the Archbishop was less committed to Enosis than he had been. The Greek Government was also worried by Makarios's appeal to the Soviet Union for military help. It put out a statement claiming to have received assurances that Mr Kyprianou would not be going to Moscow to negotiate an agreement. Nevertheless, he did, a month later, and a secret deal was concluded on 30 September for the supply of Soviet arms to the Greek Cypriot forces.

Immediately after their visit to Athens Makarios and Kyprianou went to Alexandria to see President Nasser. Diplomatically, the Archbishop's main concern now was to get the support of the 'Third World' countries for a UN General Assembly resolution that would condemn the Treaty of Guarantee and the Cyprus constitution itself as incompatible with the principles of the United Nations Charter. In October Makarios attended the Conference of

Non-Aligned States in Cairo and made a tongue-in-cheek speech denouncing the British sovereign bases in Cyprus, well aware as always of their importance for the island's economy. In return Makarios got two paragraphs in the final conference communiqué, one calling upon all states to respect the independence and territorial integrity of Cyprus, the other declaring that the Cypriot people must be allowed to determine their political future without any foreign interference. The Greek Government became so alarmed that Papandreou felt it necessary to set up an official 'Enosis committee' to campaign for the union of Cyprus with Greece. From now on the hundreds of Greek officers sent to train and command the 'National Guard' were generally chosen for their devotion to the same cause.

The military situation became much quieter. UNFICYP had begun to get to grips with the problem as far as its terms of reference allowed, and when the original three-months mandate was renewed for the second time in September, the troops settled down to the long and largely undramatic business of peace-keeping. Often this meant no more than seeing that villagers of one community could tend their crops without being molested by members of the other. In mid-September Makarios lifted the restrictions he had imposed on the movement of food supplies towards the Turkish Cypriot enclaves, but he still denied them building materials and machinery. He repeated his offer of a general amnesty and help in resettling the refugees but, apart from a few Turkish Cypriots who straggled back to their homes, the offer was ignored.

A new mediator arrived in Cyprus at the end of September – Señor Galo Plaza Lasso, a former President of Ecuador. He had been in the island earlier that year as U Thant's special envoy and had already made an unfavourable impression on the Turkish Cypriots by playing down the hardships they suffered during the siege of the Kokkina enclave.

Meanwhile Soviet arms began to arrive for Makarios's 'National Guard', which UNFICYP had estimated in July numbered about 24,000 officers and men, a large proportion of them from Greece. By December the figure was probably nearer 30,000. There were also 5000 armed men in the Greek Cypriot police force. The Turkish Cypriots had about 10,000 men under arms, some of them mainland Turks, apart from their police force of 1700. U Thant's report to the Security Council in mid-December spoke of an easing of tension, but both sides were preparing now for what they knew would be a long struggle.

Makarios's hopes of getting a favourable vote in the 1964–5 UN General Assembly were disappointed because there was no opportunity to debate the Cyprus question, so much time being taken up – ironically enough – with a long and often acrimonious wrangle over how to distribute the cost of peace-keeping operations.

The new United Nations mediator, Señor Galo Plaza, had long talks with all the interested parties and in March 1965 he submitted his report to the secretary-general. The mediator took the view that there was no going back to the 1960 constitution, which had clearly failed. Like Lord Radcliffe nine years earlier, he declared himself against the physical separation of the two communities, any form of federation, or the equal sharing of political power. Such solutions, he thought, would be unjust as well as socially and economically disruptive, and they would inevitably lead to partition. Galo Plaza suggested that the Greek Cypriots should voluntarily renounce Enosis and that Cyprus should remain an independent, unitary and non-aligned state, with the usual minority rights built into the constitution, as Makarios had proposed. The mediator went on to recommend 'safeguards of an exceptional kind' for the Turkish Cypriots, but in place of veto rights and quotas he proposed only the appointment of a United Nations commissioner who would see that there was no discrimination against the minority. The report as a whole showed an extraordinary naïvety and ignorance of the Cyprus problem. Galo Plaza admitted that there were personal feuds which would outlast any political settlement and that it would be virtually impossible to collect all the arms in private hands. Yet at the same time he played down Turkish Cypriot fears of Greek rule, while pointing out that if Cyprus were fully independent nothing could prevent the Greek Cypriots from declaring Enosis except the Government's obligation under the UN Charter to promote the wellbeing of all its citizens and help preserve international peace and security.

Most of the Galo Plaza report was welcomed by the Greeks and Greek Cypriots as endorsing the rights of the majority. But Makarios had strong objections to renouncing the right to opt for Enosis. He was also persuaded by Yeorkadjis and Grivas that to allow Cyprus to be demilitarised, as Galo Plaza had suggested, would be dangerous unless the island were united with Greece. Turkey's reaction to the report was entirely hostile. Ankara was now in the aftermath of another governmental crisis. Inonu had resigned and been replaced by a caretaker government under Urguplu which had to struggle on until a general election in October 1965. Ankara declared that Galo Plaza had exceeded his brief – as indeed he had done deliberately, though the UN secretary-general, U Thant, refused to accept this.

In October President Makarios submitted a memorandum to U Thant, setting out the fundamental rights and freedoms that his Government was prepared to grant to the minority, and offering, along the lines of the Galo Plaza report, to accept United Nations supervision and guarantees 'for a reasonably (*sic*) transitional period' – a qualification that had an ominous ring for the Turks. In December the newly-elected Government of Mr Suleyman Demirel, the leader of the Justice Party, reaffirmed the Turkish view that Galo Plaza's mission had ended in failure, and a few days later the mediator resigned.

Meanwhile the Government of Cyprus had again appealed to the United Nations General Assembly. Here the Foreign Minister, Mr Spyros Kyprianou, made an all-out effort to win the support of the non-aligned countries by endorsing the main recommendations of the Galo Plaza report – apart from the suggestions that the Greek Cypriots should renounce Enosis and that the island should be demilitarised – and by emphasising the offer of 'fundamental rights and freedoms' for the minority. Turkey was forced on to the defensive and clung to the 1960 constitution which it had previously condemned as unjust and unworkable. On 18 December the UN General Assembly adopted a resolution calling on all states to respect the 'sovereignty, unity, independence and territorial integrity' of Cyprus. It was the United Nations verdict that Makarios had long worked for, since it appeared to cancel the rights of the Guarantor States to intervene and ruled out partition but not Enosis. However, apart from the fact that General Assembly resolutions are not binding on any member-state, this particular one was hardly a resounding victory for the Greek Cypriots. Forty-five countries voted for the resolution and only five against it, but there were *fifty-four* abstentions. These included Britain and other West European states and, even more significantly, the Soviet Union. Moscow had no wish to alienate Turkey by voting against her and no desire to open the road to Enosis, though it supported the idea of 'unfetter d freedom' for Cyprus so long as it remained non-aligned and stayed out of NATO.

The end of 1965 found the Turks bitter and despondent about

the lack of international support for their case on Cyprus. But Greece was in no position to enjoy a diplomatic victory. There had been a prolonged crisis in Athens as a result of a quarrel between Prime Minister George Papandreou and the young King Constantine over control of the armed forces.[4] The Prime Minister accused the King of overstepping his constitutional authority and offered his resignation, which the King promptly accepted before Papandreou could change his mind. The Left-Centre coalition collapsed and a new weak government under the right-wing Stephanopoulos took over. Apart from the fact that Greece was now on the long slide into anarchy that preceded the 'Colonels'' *coup* of April 1967, it meant that Athens was less and less able to exert any control over Makarios. He became confident that neither Greece nor Turkey could interfere with his policy for Cyprus.

The year 1966 was comparatively quiet and uneventful in Cyprus, though both communities continued to import arms and consolidate their positions. The United Nations force was reduced in strength, largely because several contributory countries grew tired of the burden when they saw there was no real effort to reach a political solution. Makarios had refused to allow the appointment of another mediator after Galo Plaza's resignation. The economic blockade of the Turkish Cypriots was intensified. The Greek Cypriot authorities also imposed an extra 30 per cent tax on grain sold by the Turkish Cypriots through the Grain Commission. The Turks reacted by ceasing to deal with the state organisation. Such measures were at variance with Makarios's professed desire to see Turks and Greeks cooperating again. They raised the question of whether the President was completely in control of the Greek Cypriot camp, in spite of his overwhelming prestige.

There were two elements on his own side to worry Makarios. There had been another shift in the attitude of AKEL which, while professing loyalty to the President, began to agitate more and more against conscription and the increasing number of Greek army officers in Cyprus. Makarios tried to placate the Left and counter this disruptive and basically anti-Enosis campaign by proposing to transfer control of the 'National Guard' from Grivas to Yeorkadjis. He wrote secretly to the Greek Government in March 1966, asking that Grivas should be restricted to his command of the mainland troops. The Greek Foreign Minister, Tsirimokos, was agreeable to this but the Prime Minister, Stephanopoulos, and his Defence Minister, Kostopoulos, objected. This disagreement in an already weak Government led to the resignation of Tsirimokos in April. Makarios had to abandon his plan for curbing Grivas under pressure from Athens and so aroused further displeasure on the Left. Grivas proclaimed unequivocally: 'There is only one army in Cyprus – the Greek Army.'

Grivas himself was the other problem for the Archbishop because of his personal intrigues. The Greek Government's enquiry into an alleged left-wing plot in the army, with a cell in Cyprus, uncovered what purported to be a letter from the ex-EOKA leader suggesting that he aimed at supplanting Makarios. Grivas denounced it as a forgery, but in view of their past relations few people were inclined to accept this denial. Makarios believed that, short of a military *coup*, he could always outmanoeuvre Grivas and that, in any case, the popular support for himself as President, Ethnarch and Archbishop far outweighed the little general's following. However, to reduce the danger and because of his own strong personal inclination not to rely upon an army, he had begun early in 1966 to extend the role of the police force – which he thought should make it easier to deal with any possible subversion.

Clerides was instructed to buy rifles, sub-machine-guns and armoured cars from Czechoslovakia for this purpose. The small arms duly arrived – without any protest from the UN secretary-general – but Turkey intervened to stop the shipment of the armoured cars. The Greek Government, now strongly under royalist influence, was alarmed by Makarios's preference for East European arms, especially as it believed there was already a dangerous pro-Communist element in the Greek army.

However, as the months of 1966 went by, the situation in Cyprus appeared to be so static that Makarios felt able to embark again upon the foreign tours that he regarded as all-important to the Greek Cypriot cause and which had been interrupted since 1962. These travels took him, together with his Foreign Minister, Kyprianou, first to Nigeria, Dahomey, the Ivory Coast and Ghana, and later to five countries in Latin America – Panama, Uruguay, Chile, Ecuador and Colombia. There, as at the Lagos conference in January 1967, convened to get Commonwealth backing for British policy on Rhodesia, the Archbishop pursued his campaign for 'Third World' support of the Greek Cypriots. It was all the more necessary to quell some rising doubts since a number of 'Third World' countries – including Ghana and Uruguay – which had voted for the 1965 UN resolution on 'unfettered independence' for Cyprus had since indicated that they were not in favour of this leading to Enosis.

The year 1967 was to prove as disturbing to the Archbishop's plans as 1966 had been uneventful. Early in February the Turkish Government followed up its previous diplomatic success in preventing the importation of Czechoslovak armoured cars by the Greek Cypriots with a warning that, unless Makarios surrendered to UNFICYP the small arms he had already received from the same source, Ankara would send a similar quantity to the Turkish Cypriots. Makarios reluctantly gave in to some discreet pressure from the UN secretary-general's new special representative in Cyprus, the affable Bibiano Osorio-Tafall of Mexico, and agreed to the arms intended for his police being stored in a warehouse where they would be subject to inspection by the UN peacekeeping force.

More doubts about the reliability of 'Third World' support began to enter Makarios's mind when, in March 1967, Turkey's Foreign Minister, Mr Ihsan Sabri, Caglayangil, was warmly welcomed by President Nasser's Government in Cairo. In the same month the Greek Cypriot authorities announced with some embarrassment the uncovering of a Soviet spy network in Nicosia. An attaché of the over-large Soviet Embassy and the Aeroflot representative were both expelled. It seems likely however that at this period the Russians were less interested in Cypriot affairs than in the island's value as a Middle East listening-post; the Arab-Israeli Six Day War was to break out at the beginning of June.

In the meantime Greece had undergone a traumatic experience that was to give a new and vicious twist to the misfortunes of Cyprus. On the morning of 21 April 1967 a handful of Greek officers – all of them colonels – seized power in a bloodless *coup*. They did so by activating the so-called 'Prometheus Plan', devised by NATO against the contingency of an internal (Communist) uprising in Greece. The 'Colonels' claimed at first that they had acted to forestall a Communist takeover. In fact, they may have 'preempted' a similar move contemplated by more senior Greek officers who had the confidence of the King and were afraid that the elections scheduled for May would bring George Papandreou and his Socialist son, Andreas, back to power, with the support of the extreme Left. Since the summer of 1966 there had been a succession of weak governments in Greece, put in office by the King with the backing of the Americans. Their authority had been progressively undermined by paralysing strikes and violent demonstrations organised by the leader of the Opposition, the elder Papandreou. Most Greeks still believe that the Colonels' *coup* was engineered by the CIA, the United States Intelligence Agency. This had certainly helped to shape the operations of its Greek equivalent, KYP – its ill-omened initials also happen to be the first letters of the Greek name for Cyprus! – and Colonel George Papadopoulos, who quickly emerged as the leader of the 'junta', had served prominently in KYP. But the CIA's role in the *coup* – if any – is not proved. The American embassy in Athens was plainly taken by surprise. The Johnson administration had more reason to back a preventive move by generals whose loyalty to the King was not in doubt than to support a *coup* by unknown colonels.

We are not concerned here with the history of the seven-year military dictatorship in Greece except in so far as the Colonels' relations with Makarios and their policy towards Turkey were ultimately disastrous for Cyprus, apart from bringing about their own downfall. For many Greeks, outside political and intellectual circles, the new regime was welcome at first for the relief it brought from near-anarchy. The Greek Cypriots saw a military government in Athens as more likely to stand up to threats from Turkey than previous administrations had done. The Enotists took heart and were jubilant over the discomfiture of AKEL which, according to the pro-Grivas newspaper *Patris*, was preparing to go underground if there was a declaration of union with Greece. Makarios did not appear to be worried by the turn of events. In July the Greek Cypriot House of Representatives passed a Bill regularising the position of the Greek officers in the 'National Guard', whose conscripts already took the Greek army oath and paraded under the Greek flag.[5] When the Greek chief of staff, General Spandidakis, visited Cyprus after the *coup* and referred to it as part of southern Greece there was no protest from Makarios. In September he was reported by *The Sunday Times* of London as saying that, if he had 'any ambition', it was to have his name linked with the union of Cyprus with Greece. It was an equivocal formulation. Makarios must have been aware of the new pressures that might be exerted upon him. But he had no wish to antagonise the military regime in Athens before the direction of its foreign policy became clear.

In August the Demirel Government in Ankara suggested talks with Athens to try to achieve a settlement of the Cyprus problem.

The Turks apparently thought they might get more out of a hard-headed military regime concerned about national security, NATO and the danger of Communism than they had out of weak democratic coalitions. The Colonels equally believed they were strong enough to do a deal with Turkey that would realise the national dream – or most of it – at very little cost. Papadopoulos fell into the trap and, without even informing the Cyprus desk at the Greek Foreign Ministry – much less Makarios – accepted the Turkish offer with alacrity. Together with his puppet Prime Minister and Foreign Minister, Papadopoulos met Demirel and the Turkish government team successively at Kesan and Alexandroupolis, on either side of the Thracian border, on 9 and 10 September. The Greeks immediately offered Turkey a military base in Cyprus in return for the union of the rest of the island with Greece. Demirel countered with the predictable demand for an area big enough to accommodate most of the Turkish Cypriot community – the old idea of 'double Enosis' or, as the Greek Cypriots saw it, partition. For the Greeks it was a major rebuff and Papadopoulos had to fall back on a joint Prime Ministers' communiqué in which they undertook to work for 'a peaceful and agreed solution'.

Shortly before these talks Makarios had eased some of his restrictions on the movement of Turkish Cypriots. This was not to facilitate the Greek-Turkish dialogue, as some have supposed, but rather to persuade the Turkish Cypriots that their best hopes for the future lay in accepting the Archbishop's offer of talks. However, this softer approach, to which Dr Kuchuk seemed ready to respond, was frustrated by other developments, inside and outside the island. Tension began to show itself in Turkey during October as more and more ethnic Turks crossed the border from Western Thrace, complaining that the new Greek regime had replaced their elected officials with its own nominees and was restricting their movements because they lived in what had again become a sensitive area.

Simultaneously a number of Turkish politicians began to demand government action to prevent the creeping annexation of Cyprus. They had seen Archbishop Ieronymos of Athens and two of his bishops launch a campaign in the island in support of Enosis. At the secular level Greek football coaches and sports organisers were being pressed into service by the Colonels to revive the flagging enthusiasm of the Cypriot young for union with Greece.

Rauf Denktash, the most energetic of the Turkish Cypriot

leaders, had spent the past three-and-a-half years in Turkey since Makarios had banned his return to Cyprus after the London conference of 1964. He now persuaded the Turkish Government to infiltrate him secretly into the island with two companions. They were arrested in the Karpass peninsula on 31 October. Makarios, partly under pressure from the UN special representative, Señor Osorio-Tafall, and partly in pursuit of his policy of softening up Turkish Cypriot resistance, had them flown back to Turkey instead of prosecuting Denktash on the 'criminal charges' which still hung over him. Grivas was furious at this and decided to teach the Turkish Cypriots a lesson.

For months there had been friction around the mixed village of Ayios Theodoros just off the main road from Larnaca to Limassol. The Turkish Cypriot Fighters had a strong-point at Kophinou barely a mile away, from which they had been able to prevent Greek Cypriot police patrols from reaching Ayios Theodoros. It was a galling situation in which the UN authorities sympathised with the Greeks but had advised them not to try to reimpose the patrols by force; and after Denktash's release it seemed that the Turks might reconsider their ban. However, on 14 November, the 'National Guard', on Grivas's orders, surrounded the Turks in Ayios Theodoros and the police patrols were resumed. Grivas was photographed by the Greek Cypriot press haranguing the Turkish Cypriots and threatening to 'drown them in blood' if they resisted. Fighting broke out when the 'National Guard' removed a Turkish road-block. The next day the 'National Guard' attacked Kophinou in strength, using cannon- and mortar-fire against the village. The UN authorities appealed to Makarios, but without success, and a British unit of the peace-keeping force which tried to intervene was disarmed by the Greeks. Ankara sent a peremptory ultimatum to Athens, warning that it would bomb the Greek Cypriots if the attack was not called off. The fighting stopped within a few hours, after more than twenty Turkish Cypriots and one 'National Guardsman' had been killed. The 'National Guard' pulled back and the UN troops went in to help the wounded and clear up after the carnage and destruction.

As reports and photographs reached the outside world Turkey quickly pressed home her advantage by demanding the removal of Grivas, the withdrawal of all Greek mainland troops above the number allowed by the 1960 agreements, as well as the disbanding of the 'National Guard' and other illegal Greek Cypriot forces. She also called for an end to all pressures on the Turkish Cypriot community and for payment of compensation for those killed. To back up these demands Turkish air force planes flew daily sorties over the island. Troops began to mass along the Thracian frontier with Greece and on the coast opposite Cyprus, while a fleet of landing-craft built since the 1963–4 crisis was made ready for invasion at the southern port of Mersin. This time there was no mistaking the seriousness of the threat. The Colonels hastily recalled Grivas, who flew to Athens baffled and chagrined at yet another 'betrayal'. On the following day he resigned his Cyprus command. But this was not enough to placate the Turks, who continued their military build-up. The Americans were alarmed at the prospect of a war between two NATO allies in the Mediterranean. Also a Turkish invasion of Cyprus might well prompt Soviet intervention ostensibly in defence of the Republic. With the United Nations powerless to do more than appeal to Greece, Turkey and the Makarios Government to show restraint, President Johnson despatched a former Secretary of State, Mr Cyrus Vance, to all three capitals to mediate. Vance flew to Ankara on 23 November, but hostile demonstrations forced his plane to be diverted to a military airfield. President Sunay warned the world that Turkey meant to solve the Cyprus problem 'once and for all'.

During the next ten days Vance shuttled tirelessly backwards and forward between Ankara and Athens, carrying proposals and counter-proposals and eventually taking a compromise agreement to Makarios. The Colonels, alarmed now that they might have to pit their forces against a country three times as strong, agreed to withdraw all Greek troops in Cyprus above the number allowed by the 1960 agreements, provided Turkey did the same with hers and stood down her invasion forces. Makarios, who remained silent throughout the crisis, had no objection to this. The recall of Grivas had removed the main obstacle to his own plans for the 'pacification' of the island. Provided Turkey dropped her threat to invade, he was happy to contemplate the departure of the 12,000 Greek troops who were more and more likely to be used by the Colonels as a lever against him. With the unauthorised Turkish troops also withdrawn, the Archbishop believed he could rely on his 'National Guard' and his police force for internal security. He had no intention of disbanding them, as Turkey had demanded.

By 1 December it looked as if Vance had secured full agreement between Greece and Turkey on measures to end the crisis. After an almost all-night session with Makarios in Nicosia he believed he had also got the Archbishop's general acceptance of them, in spite of some reservations. But instead of flying home to Washington a few hours before the UN secretary-general, U Thant, was due to announce the terms of the settlement, Vance suddenly returned to Nicosia.

President Makarios was again displaying all his old qualities of 'brinkmanship'. He now claimed – not without some reason – that it would be unsafe for him to disband the 'National Guard' before there were guarantees against a future Turkish attack or threat to invade. At the same time he objected to U Thant's proposal to give the United Nations peace-keeping force wider powers. (The UN troops, of course, had never accepted the Archbishop's view that the Turkish Cypriots were mere 'rebels' to be brought to order.) Makarios had also been genuinely disturbed by a report in the heavily-controlled Greek press that, as part of the agreements, the Turkish Cypriots would be allowed to maintain a police force and have a degree of self-government in their own areas. This was the thin edge of partition and had to be resisted.

During a week-end of talks Vance failed to move the Archbishop. After another brief stop in Athens he returned to Washington. The Colonels, whether prompted by the United States or in their anxiety not to prolong the crisis, now made a declaration of their own in the absence of the expected joint announcement. They said they had reached agreement with the Turkish Government that both would withdraw their national troops from Cyprus, apart from those authorised by the 1960 treaties, and that Turkey would dismantle her invasion forces. U Thant followed this up with an appeal to both Greece and Turkey to take these steps immediately, without waiting for agreement on other points. It was a neat way of circumventing Makarios, but it left the Archbishop still holding his position.

The immediate danger was over. The first Greek troops left Cyprus on 8 December and Makarios saw them off with praise and thanks for their defence of Hellenism. Within the next few weeks an estimated 12,000 mainland Greeks were withdrawn. A much smaller number of Turks left, but only a few hundred officers and men had been infiltrated by Ankara in excess of the 650 allowed by treaty. On both sides some officers stayed to train the opposing Cypriot forces, but Turkey stood down her invasion troops. By Christmas even the Greek and Turkish Cypriots at Ayios Theodoros were fraternising again in spite of all that had happened.

Meanwhile there had been a startling development in Greece. On 13 December King Constantine, badly advised by some of his senior generals and members of his palace entourage – perhaps also by his mother, Queen Frederika – attempted a counter-*coup* against the Colonels. They apparently thought that, after the regime's humiliation by Turkey, popular feeling would turn against it and the monarchy could reassert itself as the true leadership of the country. The King and his family, together – oddly enough – with the puppet Prime Minister, Kollias, suddenly appeared in Northern Greece. A broadcast proclamation called on the Colonels to hand over power and suggested that the King had already won over the army and was about to form a new government. Within a few hours the counter-*coup* was exposed as a complete fiasco. Athens radio announced that the military government was in full control and, later, that 'Constantine' was on the run. He escaped from the country and took refuge in Rome. For a few days there was some bargaining over terms for his return; but the Colonels had already appointed a 'Regent' and Papadopoulos quickly made himself 'Prime Minister'. The 'junta' had found it impossible to stand up to Turkey, but it had no difficulty in imposing its will on the Greek people.

For Makarios the fall of the King was a disturbing event. He had always showed great respect for the monarchy and seen it as one of the three main unifying elements of Hellenism, the other two being language and religion. He had counselled Constantine about the need to keep the cause of Cyprus uppermost and he had come to know the young man at close quarters when they once made a pilgrimage to Mount Sinai together, Constantine riding to the top on a donkey and Makarios leaping agilely from rock to rock with the help of his pastoral staff, like some wise mentor for the young King. Now the Colonels would feel even less inhibited in their attempts to put pressure on Makarios. On the other hand most of the Greek troops were being withdrawn from Cyprus and Grivas had been recalled in disgrace and put under house arrest. The Archbishop could feel freer for that. There were even exciting possibilities over the horizon, though not to be dwelt on at present. Greece now had a 'Regency' and the most distinguished previous holder of that office had also been an Archbishop – Damaskinos of Athens, who had been given the task of uniting the nation after the Communist-led revolt of December 1944.

On 12 January 1968 President Makarios revealed some of his post-crisis thinking in a major pronouncement. He said that the failure of the Greek-Turkish dialogue and the withdrawal of Greek troops from Cyprus created the need for a realistic reappraisal of the way to handle the Cyprus problem. He recalled his earlier statements that the Greek Cypriots had no desire to deprive Turkish Cypriots of their rights as equal citizens, much less to exterminate them. On the contrary, under a new constitution, democratically conceived, there would be a 'Charter of Rights' for the Turkish community. (It was observed that Makarios did not now call them a minority.) He hinted that there could be discussions about these 'rights' with the Turkish Cypriots themselves, within the framework of the 'good offices' tendered by the UN secretary-general.

Finally the Archbishop came to the crux of his message – his 'personal decision', as he called it. Courageous steps were needed to break the deadlock. 'A solution', he went on, 'must necessarily be sought within the limits of what is *feasible*, which does not always coincide with the limits of what is *desirable*'. It was the nearest Makarios had yet come towards admitting that Enosis might be impossible. Before the emotional shock of this could sink in, he declared he would seek a fresh mandate from the people in the form of a vote of confidence in his handling of the Cyprus question. 'If it is the view of the people that my services are inadequate, they may choose another leader. I am ready to submit to the will of the people expressed through elections.'

It was a shrewd stroke. The Greek Cypriots had been shaken by the reality of the Turkish invasion threat and by the abject capitulation of a supposedly strong regime in Athens. If they were now on their own, there was nobody to lead them but Makarios. Those who still yearned for Enosis believed that it must come in time, whatever the obstacles. The word 'feasible' had not yet made its full impact.

There was one ominous portent for the future which even Makarios did not sufficiently appreciate at the time. On 27 December two senior officials of the Turkish Foreign Ministry had arrived in Nicosia and crossed to the other side. On the following day it was announced that a 'Provisional Cyprus Turkish Administration' had been set up, to last until the 1960 constitution was fully restored. Dr Kuchuk was named as head of the new 'Executive

Council', and the three Turkish Cypriot ministers of the original independence Government were among the other ten members. The United Nations was not informed until after the event and U Thant expressed his 'misgivings' about the Turkish Cypriot step, so clearly prompted by Ankara. The Makarios Government declared it quite illegal and warned foreign diplomats not to visit the so-called 'administration' in the enclaves. Later, Makarios withdrew the ban but only after Dr Kuchuk had explained that the change meant no more than a functional rearrangement of the powers the Turkish Cypriots already possessed. In his conciliatory statement on 12 January, hinting that he would no longer be actively pursuing the goal of Enosis and wanted talks with the Turkish Cypriots on that basis, Makarios merely 'regretted' the Turkish Cypriot move as an obstacle to peace. Immediately afterwards he ordered the removal of all Greek Cypriot check-points except for those around the Nicosia and Kokkina enclaves and at certain places on the coast. Otherwise there was to be complete freedom of movement for the Turkish Cypriots throughout the island.

12 Intercommunal Talks

By the end of January 1968 most of the Greek troops had been withdrawn from Cyprus and Makarios felt free to inaugurate his new policy. This was to avoid anything which might again provoke a Turkish threat to invade, while he convinced the Turkish Cypriots that it was in their interests to abandon their 'siege mentality' and to cooperate with the Greek Cypriots in restoring a prosperous unitary state. The new line aroused all the suspicions of the fanatical Enotists, who had seen Grivas, the leader they trusted, outmanoeuvred for a second time. At the Feast of the Epiphany in the New Year the burly Bishop of Kitium – who had once begged Makarios to accept the independence agreements – preached a sermon deploring the growing indifference to the struggle for Enosis and the slanders that had been uttered against the Greek troops in Cyprus. On 25 January Anthimos and two of his fellow bishops, Yennadios of Paphos and Makarios's old enemy, Kyprianos of Kyrenia, waited in a deputation upon the Archbishop and warned him, in the name of the Holy Synod, that he should resign as President rather than accept a solution incompatible with Enosis. Makarios's reply was not published.

There were other voices in the Enosis camp that took on a different tone. The most independent Greek Cypriot newspaper, *Eleftheria*, criticised both Makarios and Grivas for having launched the EOKA campaign without foreseeing the long-term consequences. Nikos Sampson's *Makhi*, not notable for its moderation, accused Polykarpos Ioannides, the Bishop of Kyrenia's secretary, of being too extreme in his passion for Enosis. Yet another newspaper, *Kypros*, thought the only way now to avoid partition was to restore the 1960 constitution, with all its faults.

Makarios appeared little disturbed by these criticisms and indif-

194

ferent to the advice. Preparations went ahead for the presidential election, which had been fixed for 25 February. Only one rival candidate to the Archbishop came forward – a Nicosia psychiatrist, Dr Takis Evdokas, who was nominated by the newly-formed 'Enosis Front'. Makarios made no attempt to campaign but his supporters were active enough on his behalf, some of them even to the point of breaking up one of the rival candidate's meetings. The result was always a foregone conclusion. In a turn-out of well over 90 per cent of the electorate Makarios polled 220,911 votes (95.45 per cent of the total number cast) while Evdokas received 8577 (3.71 per cent) . This was not entirely a vote of confidence in Makarios's tactics, but a proof that all but a handful of Greek Cypriots realised they had no other leader. The Archbishop's massive victory was marred only by the fact that the defeated party was able to claim it meant the death of Enosis, which Makarios had to deny. This naturally confirmed the Turkish Cypriots in their belief that Makarios was only seeking another way to his goal.

Dr Kuchuk had responded to the proclamation of a presidential election by indicating that he would stand for re-election as Vice-President on the same day. A former chief justice made a brief appearance as a rival candidate but withdrew for the sake of Turkish Cypriot unity. Kuchuk was duly proclaimed Vice-President of the Republic of Cyprus unopposed. However he still kept his new title of 'President of the Executive Council of the Provisional Turkish Administration'.

The Turkish Cypriot Vice-President of the House of Representatives (who had not functioned for four years) now asked Clerides to convene a meeting of the House for the double swearing-in ceremony. Dr Kuchuk also offered to send the three Turkish Cypriot ministers to take their seats again in the House. Makarios – somewhat unwisely perhaps – ignored both gestures. If the Turkish Cypriots were going to return to legality, it would be at his timing and on his terms.

Early in March Makarios ordered the removal of all the Greek Cypriot road-blocks and fortified posts around the main Nicosia enclave. The Turkish Cypriots now had almost complete freedom of movement in the island. But, apart from dismantling a few of their own road-blocks as a gesture, their leaders had no intention of lowering their defences or of allowing the Greeks – with certain exceptions – inside their enclaves. They also discouraged their own people from venturing into the Greek areas. This was not so much because they were afraid that Turks might be assaulted as to prevent fraternisation. A number of Turkish Cypriots, attracted by the fuller shops and amenities of the Greek side, were arrested on their return for leaving the enclaves without permission. The Turkish Cypriots were not taking any chances. The display of Czechoslovak arms at the EOKA Day parade on 1 April and the demolition of some abandoned Turkish houses at Omorphita did nothing to encourage them to believe in Makarios's pacification policy. There was some tension during May when two Turkish Cypriots were killed by Makarios's security forces, and the Greek Cypriot police continued to intercept the movement of Turkish arms. But Rauf Denktash had returned from Ankara in April – openly, with the consent of the Makarios Government – and preparations were being made for the start of talks between him and Glafkos Clerides on the shape of a new constitution.

Makarios had already submitted proposals on this to the UN secretary-general, as he had promised in his January statement. They envisaged an independent, unitary state whose structure and government institutions should be approved by the people of Cyprus through any recognised democratic machinery. The Turkish community would be proportionately represented in the House of Representatives and have 'fair' representation in the judiciary, the public service and the police. There should be a ministry of Turkish Cypriot affairs, headed by a Turkish Cypriot minister. There would be autonomy for the Turkish Cypriots in matters exclusively affecting their community, and its other specific rights in the state would be entrenched in the constitution, not to be changed except with the consent of a majority of Turkish Cypriots. Finally Makarios proposed that a United Nations commissioner should be stationed in Cyprus, with an adequate staff of observers and advisers and for as long as was reasonably necessary, to see that Turkish Cypriot rights were not infringed.

Basically these were the same as the Galo Plaza recommendations, which Turkey had rejected outright. Makarios had been careful throughout to refer to the Turkish Cypriots as a 'community', not as a 'minority'. He indicated that he would be willing to discuss counter-proposals. But he still insisted that the future shape of the government must be decided 'democratically' – in other words, by the majority. And he could not commit himself or the Greek Cypriots to renouncing Enosis, as Galo Plaza had suggested. For the Turkish Cypriots the Makarios proposals were a non-starter.

Nevertheless they wanted to talk. Denktash and Clerides, who knew each other well, met first at the house of U Thant's special representative in Cyprus, Señor Osorio-Tafall, on 23 May. Ten days later they began formal discussions on neutral territory, in the Hotel Phoenicia in Beirut. But these were soon moved back to Cyprus, and the two negotiators presently adopted the practice of meeting alternately in each other's houses.

Here it is worthwhile looking at their common background and also at the differences between them, since their negotiations over the next six years were so closely bound up with Makarios's manoeuvring and with the Greek Colonels' *coup* against him in 1974.[1] Clerides and Denktash are both London-trained lawyers, and the former also served as an RAF pilot during the Second World War till he was shot down and taken prisoner by the Germans. Both men are intensely proud of being Cypriots, but still feel the tug of their different ethnic cultures. Clerides impresses by his sincerity but in the last resort he was not strong enough to stand up to the Archbishop in defence of his own convictions. Clerides defended many EOKA men when they were put on trial during the British colonial period. In 1963 he was one of the organisers of the 'Akritas Plan' for action against the Turkish Cypriots if they resisted a revision of the constitution. But throughout the intercommunal negotiations Clerides showed himself flexible, patient and even-tempered. He was the man most capable of reaching an accommodation with the Turkish Cypriots, and through them with Turkey. His dismissal and subsequent banishment to the political wilderness by a combination of the Nationalists and the Communist-led AKEL were directly due to this fact.

Denktash gives – and justifies – the impression of being much tougher than Clerides. Beneath the affability and the plump, rather jolly exterior – which made someone once describe him as looking like 'an ebullient potato' – he can be obstinate and even aggressive. He was ruthless in outmanoeuvring a political rival for the Turkish Cypriot leadership when the easy-going Kuchuk was ready to retire. The Greek Cypriots have always tended to dismiss Denktash as a mere puppet of Ankara. But he has a will of his own, even if he was no longer master in his own house after northern Cyprus was occupied by the Turkish army. Denktash sometimes tries to outbid Ankara in an effort to show his independence. But he is shrewd enough to see the advantages of cooperating with the Greek Cypriots, provided it is on equal terms. He likes to keep all his options open.

The first stage of the intercommunal talks in Nicosia lasted for a month, from 24 June to 25 July 1968. It was mainly exploratory. The two negotiators had already agreed in Beirut that there were unsatisfactory aspects of the 1960 constitution for both communities. Denktash had said that the maintenance of separate munici-palities – on which the Turkish Cypriots had insisted so strongly – would, in the long run, mean a heavy burden for their community. Similarly, to provide 30 per cent of the public service would leave too few young and able Turkish Cypriots available for develop-ment projects to raise their community's living standards. During the first substantive phase of the talks Denktash said the Turkish Cypriots would accept a reduced ratio in the executive, legislature, public service and police, equivalent to their ratio of the popu-lation, provided the office of Turkish Cypriot Vice-President was kept. He even suggested that the vice-presidential veto could be given up. In return for these concessions Denktash proposed a structuring of local government in 'groups of villages' to give the Turkish Cypriots adequate security and a degree of autonomy.

Clerides, on instructions from President Makarios, expressed strong reservations about the retention of the office of Vice-President and said the Greek Cypriots could not accept 'local government', as Mr Denktash had proposed, on the basis of com-munal groups of villages, since this would conflict with the idea of a unitary state and hinder the development of the island as a whole. In any case, Clerides argued, such an arrangement would be unworkable because the Turkish Cypriots were scattered all over the island. (This was somewhat less true than it had been before many of them were brought into the enclaves, which, of course, for the Greek Cypriots had no official existence.) However, the government side was impressed by Denktash's suggestion that the Turkish Cypriots might forgo the vice-presidential veto and the obnoxious 30:70 ratio in the administration. So the talks no longer took the 1960 constitution or Makarios's various proposals for amending it as a basis for discussion. It was an unwitting step in the wrong direction.

At the end of this phase of the talks Denktash flew to Ankara for consultations. When the talks resumed the Greek Cypriots thought they detected a hardening of the Turkish Cypriot attitude, particularly over the question of 'local government'.

Meanwhile Greece and Turkey were continuing their contacts over Cyprus, though they tried to keep them as secret as possible. Mr Panayiotis Pipinelis, an experienced diplomat who had agreed to serve as Foreign Minister under the Colonels and had been largely instrumental in defusing the explosive situation of the Kophinou incident, began talks with his opposite number, Mr Ihsan Sabri Caglayangil. At the end of January Pipinelis somewhat incautiously told a Turkish newspaper that a solution was being found. Subsequently senior Greek and Turkish diplomats met in Athens, Ankara and Vienna. At the start of the intercommunal talks Pipinelis informed the Makarios Government that Greece considered these the best procedure for solving the internal constitutional problem, but that the question of treaties and external guarantees would be discussed at another level. The Greek Foreign Minister said the United States had emphasised in no uncertain way that there must be an accommodation with Turkey for the sake of NATO's eastern flank. This left Makarios even more convinced, if that were possible, that Greece and Turkey, with the Americans behind them, were still trying to settle the Cyprus question over his head.

Yet, as the intercommunal talks continued during 1968 and into the early months of 1969 and as the clashes between Greek and Turkish Cypriots became less and less frequent, Makarios grew confident that he was again master of the situation. Little was leaked from the talks, and the occasional news briefings given by Clerides and Denktash merely said that there was an identity of views on certain points but that other important issues still had to be decided. Outwardly Makarios kept aloof from the negotiations, to emphasise that he was President of all Cyprus. He waited patiently, like an indulgent father, until the 'prodigal son' should see the error of his ways and decide to return home.

Makarios had more time now to concentrate on his image as Ethnarch and his functions as priest. Here he went far beyond the duties normally expected of an Archbishop. Makarios constantly officiated at marriage ceremonies and baptisms with the families of leading Greek Cypriots or of his own entourage. He travelled about the island, preaching in village churches and exhorting the faithful to continue the national struggle as true Greeks. He commemorated the deaths of EOKA heroes and martyrs. He was always accessible to those with petitions and complaints, however trivial or mundane their requests might be. Makarios would accept the homage of the old peasant woman who kissed his hand with the same consideration that he showed to his bishops and ministers or to visiting Greek dignitaries and foreign Heads of State.

The Greek Cypriot sector was now enjoying an unprecedented economic boom. In spite of the troubles, more land had been put under cultivation, dams had been built and irrigation improved, and a rash of new factories had spread round the edges of Nicosia and Limassol. Exports of wine, citrus fruits and vegetables were increasing rapidly. The British bases, the UN forces and the Greek military contingent together brought in a revenue of more than £20 million a year. Apart from what the troops and their families spent, there was a big income now from overseas tourists. New hotels and holiday apartments were springing up along the beaches at Famagusta and around the miniature yachting harbour at Kyrenia. Broad roads and avenues, lined with imposing blocks of offices and smart shops, all glass and chromium, splayed out through the Nicosia suburbs on the south side of the old walled city. Elegant villas crowded the hill-tops. As land prices shot up, much of the profits went to the Church, the biggest landowner in Cyprus. It began to invest heavily in tourism and other development projects.

Little of this prosperity percolated to the Turkish Cypriot side and the tourists who passed through the barbed wire into the Nicosia enclave went mostly to buy cheap bric-à-brac and to gaze at the Turks dozing among their stalls in the narrow streets or performing their ablutions outside a Gothic cathedral-mosque. For many it was where 'Europe' ended and the 'Middle East' began.

The second phase of the intercommunal talks opened in August 1968. Clerides and Denktash now got down to exchanging formal proposals and counter-proposals. Some measure of compromise was reached but this was overshadowed by radical disagreement over the question of 'local government'. Denktash proposed that each group of villages belonging to the same community should be regarded as a local authority area, in which a central community council would be free to legislate in any way that did not contravene state law. This would have given the Turkish Cypriots virtual autonomy in whatever could be regarded as an enclave and so was totally unacceptable to the Greeks.

In the meantime, as the negotiations continued quietly and

almost in secret, there were some major political developments in the broader Greek world. In August 1968 an attempt was made to assassinate Papadopoulos, the leader of the Greek 'junta', by exploding a mine under his car as it passed along the coast-road near Athens. The plan miscarried, and Alexander Panagoulis, an army deserter, was arrested on the spot as the mine-layer; he later became the Colonels' most famous political prisoner. In October the Greek army investigator named some twenty-two persons as parties to an assassination plot; among them were Andreas Papandreou, the son of the former Prime Minister, then in exile, and Polykarpos Yeorkadjis, the Greek Cypriot Minister of the Interior and of Defence.[2] The Colonels called for the dismissal of Yeorkadjis; he denied the allegations and offered his resignation, but Makarios refused to accept it on the grounds that the only link between his minister and the attempt on the life of Papadopoulos was in the statements of persons in custody.

There is little doubt that Yeorkadjis *was* the man behind Panagoulis, in spite of the dubious value of testimony that almost certainly was extracted under torture. Evidence was given at his trial in November that explosives had been sent through the diplomatic bag to the Cypriot Embassy in Athens. It was established that Panagoulis had gone to Cyprus as an army deserter and had been supplied with a false passport on the orders of Yeorkadjis. After the trial, in which Panagoulis was twice sentenced to death, as a deserter and for attempting to overthrow the regime, the Colonels put more pressure on Makarios to get rid of Yeorkadjis. Eventually, in December, Makarios asked him to resign from his two ministerial posts for the sake of good relations between Greece and Cyprus.

Makarios was not sorry to see him go. He showed little interest generally in the capacity of his ministers since he took most of the decisions himself. He had changed his Cabinet frequently over the previous eight years, first replacing some of the young EOKA fighters who had been rewarded with ministries by professional or business men of more experience who would be good subordinates. Even these might be quickly superseded, apparently on the principle of 'Buggins's turn next'. Yeorkadjis had been an exception. His reputation as one of Grivas's most daring sector leaders and his ability to escape from the most difficult situations – the 'Houdini' of Cyprus, people called him – appealed to Makarios. When, at the time of independence, he chose to throw in his lot with the Archbishop rather than with the outmanoeuvred Grivas, Makarios acquired one of the best Greek Cypriot intelligence sources. He found Yeorkadjis invaluable in drawing up the 'Akritas' contingency plan against a Turkish Cypriot insurrection after he had decided that the constitution must be revised. But Yeorkadjis did more than carry out Makarios's instructions; he made decisions himself. Like other Greek Cypriots who were interested in power, he formed his own private army. Men as different as Dr Vasos Lyssarides, Makarios's personal physician, and Nikos Sampson, the EOKA killer turned newspaper editor, did the same. But Yeorkadjis, as Minister of Defence and Minister of the Interior, was the only one who had sufficient inside knowledge and authority to be potentially dangerous. The police force, on which Makarios now relied much more than on his 'National Guard', was entirely Yeorkadjis's creation and used EOKA's strong-arm methods whenever he thought them necessary. Makarios realised that he had put too much power into the hands of one man, and the pressure from Athens over the Panagoulis affair – resisted at first – became a convenient lever for removing him.

For Yeorkadjis his dismissal was a humiliation which he never forgot or forgave. It also left him exposed to his enemies – who were many – and it did not stop him plotting. His ambitions – his desire always to be on the winning side – led him into contacts even with supporters of the regime whose leader he had tried to remove.

In the early months of 1969 a certain political restlessness began to assert itself on the Greek side in Cyprus. There were several reasons for this. The removal of Turkey's threat to invade, the fading of the Enosis dream, the secrecy of the long-drawn-out intercommunal talks and their apparent lack of progress, the abrupt dismissal of Yeorkadjis, all tended to make many Greek Cypriots, of very different political convictions, question Makarios's right to conduct the affairs of state virtually by himself, with docile ministers and a rubber-stamp parliament that had not been renewed for nearly a decade.

Till then the only properly-organised political party with continuous activity was the Communist-led AKEL.

The old 'Patriotic Front' of the Nationalists had long since died of inertia. Its place was now taken by a more compact organisation launched in February 1969 as the Unified (*sic*) Democratic party (*to Eniaion*). This was intended to bring together all the elements of the Right or Centre still loyal to Makarios. Glafkos Clerides, President of the House of Representatives and negotiator with the Turks, was its official leader; Tasos Papadopoulos, a dedicated Makarios man, and Yeorkadjis – in spite of his chagrin over his dismissal from the Cabinet – were both founder-members. The party appealed to the prosperous middle class in the towns and the conservative peasants who would always support the Church and the rest of the Cyprus establishment. Nobody doubted that this was Makarios's own party, although he always tried to present himself, as Archbishop and President, above all parties.

Makarios felt the need for a more organised backing of his Government because his authority and judgement were now being challenged from several different quarters, and new elections to the House of Representatives could not be delayed much longer. AKEL pursued its usual ambivalent course, praising the Archbishop for standing up to fascist, imperialist and NATO plans for Cyprus while it attacked the greed of the great landowners (among them the Church) and the new entrepreneurs who resisted social reform. AKEL, it was generally thought, could still muster about 40 per cent of the Greek Cypriot votes. But other parties were emerging to pare away the Makarios majority.

Slightly to the right of AKEL in the political spectrum was the new Unified Democratic Union of the Centre (EDEK), founded by Vasos Lyssarides, Makarios's personal physician and, for many years, his close confidant. Lyssarides was by conviction a social democrat, in spite of his somewhat flamboyant life-style: a Woodrow Wyatt rather than a Clem Attlee. He had cultivated close links with radical non-Communist elements in the Arab world, particularly in Syria and among the Palestinians, and it was probably from these quarters that he acquired the arms for his private militia which regarded the protection of the President as one of its main duties. EDEK appealed only to the small leftist intelligentsia which disliked AKEL's rigid orientation, in theory at least, towards Moscow. It had no solid inducements to membership like the social benefits that the AKEL-controlled trade unions could offer. Nevertheless Makarios found Lyssarides particularly useful in rallying support for him among the Arabs and in the 'Third World' generally. Lyssarides strongly backed Makarios's policy of non-alignment, but differed from him and the pro-Western *Eniaion* in working to get rid of the British bases, although these were outside the Republic and one of its major sources of revenue.

To the right of Clerides's *Eniaion* two small parties appeared that professed allegiance to Makarios but criticised his policies and method of government. One was the so-called Progressive Front, led by Dr Odysseus Ioannides, the mayor of Nicosia. The other, the Progressive Party, had Nikos Sampson as its founder. Sampson had acquired money and patronage that could not have come simply from the limited success of his newspaper *Makhi*; an Athenian industrialist close to the CIA was said to be behind him. At any rate, he was able to maintain an army of bully-boys who often clashed with those of Yeorkadjis and Lyssarides. During 1969 the weaker Ioannides organisation merged with Sampson's party in what then became known as the Progressive Coalition, with the mayor of Nicosia its nominal leader and Sampson its 'strong-arm' man in the background. The Coalition concentrated almost entirely on challenging Clerides – and, through him, Makarios – in the countryside.

The open opposition to Makarios came only from those who condemned the continued independence of Cyprus and wanted an active pursuit of Enosis, without regard for the consequences. The legitimate part of this campaign was in the hands of Dr Evdokas, the leader of the small and ultra-right-wing DEK (Democratic National Party). But DEK was only the tip of an iceberg that broke surface menacingly from time to time and in various places in the form of terrorist action. During the early part of 1969 warning leaflets and proclamations began to be showered on the public apparently by a number of underground groups, which had adopted such names as 'The Enotist Youth Phoenix', 'Akritas' and 'The Organisation of National Salvation'. It soon became clear that the one that had to be taken seriously was the 'National Front', which appeared first in March 1969.

The 'National Front' was largely recruited from among ex-EOKA men in the ranks of the police.[3] It was another vicious twist of the spiral started by Grivas when he began to subvert the police early in his campaign against the British in the mid-1950s. After independence Yeorkadjis had packed the reorganised force with ex-EOKA men loyal to himself and Makarios. Now many of these were reverting to their old allegiance. The 'National Front' had its base in Limassol where it knew it would enjoy the support of the Bishop of Kitium, the redoubtable Anthimos. It was also encouraged by the more irredentist Greek officers of Makarios's own 'National Guard'. Some of the Front's organising committee even had the nerve to approach Makarios at the beginning and ask for his blessing on a movement with 'national aims'. The Archbishop assured them – no doubt, with an inscrutable smile on his face – that if their aims were truly 'national' there could be nothing wrong with them. Yeorkadjis, now a private citizen, tried to penetrate the movement and get himself adopted as leader, probably because he was a born conspirator and also could not bear to think of his cherished police force being used for purposes outside his control. The Front would have nothing to do with him. It sent an envoy to Grivas in Athens to ask *him* to be its leader, but he reportedly refused.

The 'National Front' quickly made its presence felt with sporadic bombings, raids on police stations and murderous attacks on village presidents or other officials who supported the left-wing parties or even Clerides's *Eniaion*. Makarios was reluctant to take action against any self-proclaimed 'nationalist' organisation for fear of losing even a fraction of his popular support. So it was not until August 1969 that the 'National Front' was proscribed. After that its activity intensified. Makarios turned this to some account in the diplomatic field by pointing to the difference between his own moderate views and those of the extremists, while he could always adduce 'National Front' pressures on him as a reason for not making more concessions to the Turkish Cypriots in the intercommunal talks.

On New Year's Eve, when most Greek Cypriots were off guard, the 'National Front' raided the copper mine stores at Kalavasos and acquired a substantial haul of explosives. Makarios, unperturbed, set off almost immediately for a tour of Tanzania, Uganda, Zambia and Kenya, where he baptised a number of Greek babies, officiated at some Greek weddings and conferred with their Heads of State. On his way back to Cyprus the Archbishop stopped in Athens. There Prime Minister Papadopoulos, presumably after some prompting, denounced terrorism in Cyprus and particularly the activities of the 'National Front'. He further declared that his Government cooperated with nobody in Cyprus but the Government of President Makarios.

By the end of January 1970 the 'National Front's' attacks on the 'National Guard' and on police stations had become so serious that Makarios was obliged to get the House of Representatives to pass a Preventive Detention Bill, allowing suspects to be held without charges being preferred against them for up to three months. He did this reluctantly, since it smacked so much of the former colonial government's measures against largely the same people. Only seventeen of the thirty-five Greek Cypriot members of the House voted for the Bill, seven voted against it and four abstained; another seven were unaccountably absent. The voting reflected the growing public doubt about the Government's attitude to the 'national question'. However, on the day the Bill was debated the 'National Front' announced it was suspending its activities for the time being.

Five weeks later, on Sunday 8 March, Makarios was due to attend a memorial service at Makhairas Monastery on Troodos for Gregoris Afxentiou, the EOKA hero who had been trapped and killed by the British in a cave nearly thirteen years earlier. The presidential helicopter, which Makarios now used regularly for his trips outside Nicosia, had just taken off from the grounds of the new archbishopric shortly after seven in the morning. It was only a few feet above the height of the building when gunmen opened fire from the roof of the library of the Pancyprian Gymnasium opposite. The pilot, a Greek army major, was hit several times and bullets tore through the fabric of the machine. However, with great coolness and skill the pilot managed to avoid power cables and telephone wires and land the crippled helicopter on a tiny vacant plot barely a hundred yards from the archbishopric but out of sight of the gunmen. Makarios was pale and shaken – according to eye-witnesses – but unhurt. The pilot collapsed after a few steps and Makarios tried to help him. People had already rushed out of their houses at the extraordinary sight of their Archbishop's descent from the skies, and he and the pilot were soon whisked off to Nicosia General Hospital in a convenient van. Once there, Makarios insisted on keeping to his programme and went by road to Makhairas Monastery, where he delivered a eulogy on Afxentiou with no hint that he saw the irony of the situation. Broadcasting to his people within a few hours of his escape the Archbishop said that, although the bullets had not struck him, they had deeply wounded his soul. He ended with a prayer that God would forgive the men who had tried to take away his life.

A Sten gun and two rifles were found abandoned on the roof of the school library from where the attack had been made. Ten suspects were arrested the same day, among them the man thought to have driven the escape car; five were soon released. Another four men, including three policemen, were later arrested in Famagusta. Public suspicion fastened immediately on the 'National Front', which promptly disclaimed any responsibility for the attempted assassination of the President. Those conducting the enquiry – the police and Greek officers of the 'National Guard' – concentrated their attention on Yeorkadjis. His flat was searched but nothing more incriminating was found than a pair of revolvers and some ammunition – normal enough when almost every Greek Cypriot was armed. A few days later Yeorkadjis boarded a plane for Beirut, but was taken off it on government orders before it left. He said he believed his life was in danger, but he was told he must remain in Cyprus while the enquiries were proceeding, and he was placed under house arrest.

Most Greek Cypriots were profoundly shocked by the assassination attempt. They realised now that there were forces in the island, unconnected with the Turks but almost certainly backed by outside powers, which were determined to get rid of their national leader. Their aim might be forcible Enosis or a deal with Turkey: in either case it was unacceptable. The fact that Makarios was Archbishop and head of the Church as well as President, added sacrilege to the crime; it was something that even the British or the Turks had never dared to do. At the same time Makarios's escape from a crippled helicopter with scarcely anywhere to land among the narrow streets of the old city seemed to devout Greeks a genuine miracle. The Archbishop knew that his enemies would try again but even he began to share a growing belief in his indestructibility.

Eight days after the attempt against Makarios the body of Yeorkadjis was found, riddled with bullets, in a field a few miles outside Nicosia. The news of his death was given by a police officer, Patatakos, who said he had agreed to go with the ex-minister to a secret rendezvous with a Greek army officer late at night; when the car stopped in a lonely place, Yeorkadjis had been lured away and then killed. In the welter of conflicting evidence from the inquest, the spate of rumours and the alleged revelations some years later in the Greek and Greek Cypriot press, it is still uncertain who killed Yeorkadjis and why he was going to a secret rendezvous. Was he a party to a plot to kill Makarios, as the Archbishop later professed to believe? If so, did he hope to divert attention from himself by threatening to denounce Greek mainland officers who were also implicated? Was he lured to his death by the prospect of finding out who really was responsible for the assassination attempt? We may never know. What seems reasonably certain is that Yeorkadjis knew enough to make him dangerous while he lived. Dead, he could be a convenient scapegoat.

The probability is that the Greek Colonels in Athens were ultimately responsible both for the attack on Makarios's helicopter and for the murder of Yeorkadjis. Many Greeks and Greek Cypriots believe the CIA was also involved. There is no proof. One can only say that the United States Administration saw Makarios as an obstacle to a Greek-Turkish agreement over Cyprus. For that reason and because he might one day be succeeded by an AKEL-controlled government orientated towards Moscow, he was also – in American eyes – a danger to NATO. The CIA may have contemplated removing Makarios from the political scene as it did with Fidel Castro and other 'awkward' heads of state – without actually attempting such a step.

The murder of Yeorkadjis led to suspicion that Makarios himself had ordered it, though nobody said so outright. The Archbishop signally failed to condemn the killing. On the day that six men were charged with the attack on the helicopter (15 April), Makarios told a foreign journalist that he had reason to believe Yeorkadjis had been implicated. Earlier, and immediately after his murder, the policeman Patatakos had handed over to the government what appeared to be a photostat copy of a military operation order marked 'Top Secret'; Yeorkadjis, he said, had told him to give it to Makarios if anything should happen to him (Yeorkadjis). The document purported to be a plan code-named 'Hermes' and originating from the headquarters of a 'National Guard' assault unit, whose commander was a certain Colonel Papapostolou. It was with him – again according to the policeman Patatakos – that Yeorkadjis was to have had his mysterious rendezvous. The 'operation order' was dated 27 January 1970 and envisaged the seizure of all key points in the capital, with help from the 'National Front', on the night of 28 May.[4] Makarios described the document as a forgery, which led to the comment that he did so to avoid incriminating 'National Guard' officers and so worsening relations with the regime in Athens. The friends of Yeorkadjis were convinced that Makarios had at least contributed to his death by preventing him from leaving Cyprus. A number of ex-EOKA men – and Clerides – attended the funeral of the former minister. No one was ever prosecuted for the murder.[5]

The trial of the six men charged with attempting to assassinate

President Makarios took place in November. They were also accused of conspiring with Polykarpos Yeorkadjis and other persons unknown to overthrow the Government. All pleaded 'not guilty'. The widow of Yeorkadjis was not allowed to produce any evidence to try to clear her husband's name and his ghost hung over the courtroom throughout the trial, condemned but unheard. Two of the accused, a police constable and the son of Makarios's fellow-exile in the Seychelles, the Bishop of Kyrenia's secretary, Ioannides, were acquitted for want of evidence. The other four – a businessman, a student, a police inspector and a constable – were found guilty and sentenced to fourteen years imprisonment for the attempted assassination and eight years for the conspiracy, the sentences to run concurrently. As they passed out of their brief limelight, nobody saw them except as the tools of much more powerful interests that would strike again.

The political parties that began to form in or around February 1969 had their eye on early elections to the House of Representatives, but with the emergence of the 'National Front' Makarios still held out against them on the grounds that there might be intimidation. By April 1970 – after the shock of his attempted assassination and the murder of Yeorkadjis – he could no longer resist the demand for a more responsible and representative legislature. He may also have reckoned that, with Yeorkadjis out of the way, there would be less challenge to his authority. Elections were fixed for 5 July.

The campaign was lively but unremarkable. The Unified Party – which, in spite of being officially led by Clerides, was regarded by everyone as Makarios's own faction – won only fifteen of the thirty-five Greek Cypriot seats, in contrast to the thirty previously held by Makarios's Patriotic Front. The Communist-led AKEL took all the nine seats that it contested, thus almost doubling its representation from the five seats allocated to it in its deal with the Archbishop in 1960. It was also widely accepted that AKEL could have won more than nine seats, if it had fielded more candidates; it evidently had no desire to create alarm by pushing itself forward too quickly, and the prize was not so important. The Socialist EDEK, led by Dr Lyssarides, won two seats, and two more went to Independents. The diehard Enotists, represented by Dr Evdokas and his Democratic National Party (DEK), won no seats at all. But the surprise of the elections was the seven seats won by the Progressive

Coalition. It was less a triumph for its nominal leader, Dr Ioannides, than for the 'muscle-man' behind him, Nikos Sampson.

Makarios could still count on a majority in the House of Representatives – for what that was worth – because of the support that AKEL and Dr Lyssarides were ready to give him for standing up to outside pressures. But the election results showed that the Greek Cypriot community was less whole-hearted about the Archbishop's leadership than it had been when it re-elected him President in 1969. Dr Evdokas, who had openly campaigned for immediate Enosis, was imprisoned before the elections for insulting the Head of State by an article in his newspaper headlined 'From Machiavelli to Makarios'. Sampson and Ioannides, more subtly, emphasised the Greek Cypriot right to self-determination in a way which indicated that their aim was still Enosis.

On the very day that the Greek Cypriots held their elections to the House of Representatives, the Turkish Cypriots did the same, though with no intention of trying to take up their seats. All fifteen allocated to them under the 1960 constitution went to Denktash and his supporters.

The groundswell of discontent on the Greek side became noticeable again in August 1970, when some 200 young Greek Cypriots, claiming to represent 6000 Greek Cypriot students at universities in Greece, demonstrated in Limassol and called on Makarios to break off the deadlocked talks with the Turkish Cypriots and proclaim Enosis. They were obviously encouraged by the 'National Front' and some of the Greek officers of the 'National Guard' and the mainland army contingent. During that same hot month there was also a renewal of intercommunal violence, after more than two years of quiet. The worst incident was at Trikomo, Grivas's birthplace, where a 'National Guardsman' killed a Turk and wounded two others who had driven into a restricted area. In return the Turkish Cypriots began to impose tighter road controls in the north.

At the beginning of September Grivas launched a new diatribe against Makarios in the Athens *Estia*. 'No other Greek', he said, 'would agree to be the Head of a State supported at the same time by Greece, Turkey, Britain, the United States and the Soviet Union.' He urged the Archbishop to retire from the political scene. Makarios, still trying to be all things to all men, ignored the attack. Then, in mid-September, he decided it was important to see ex-King Constantine. He met him in Rome. What transpired between them is not known. Afterwards Makarios flew to Athens for talks with the dictator Papadopoulos. On 15 September they issued a joint communiqué, proclaiming once again their identity of views on the Greek Cypriot stand in the intercommunal talks.

The fourth phase of the talks began on 21 September. It was soon interrupted by Makarios's need to go to New York in October for the special ten-day session of the UN General Assembly commemorating twenty-five years of the United Nations Charter. During these months Makarios was frequently absent from Cyprus. Soon after his return from Rome and Athens he had gone to Cairo to attend the funeral of President Nasser – a man he had always regarded as a great political ally. Then came the visit to the United States for the UN celebrations. On the way home he stopped in Japan. On 12 November Makarios found himself unexpectedly in Paris, together with other heads of state, attending the requiem mass for another highly individual leader, the late General de Gaulle. During the second half of January 1971 the Commonwealth Prime Ministers' conference required Makarios to go to Singapore. On all these occasions – and particularly the ceremonious ones – the Archbishop's calm bearing and dignified appearance gave no hint of the turbulence just below the surface of Cypriot politics. When he took part in discussions with other political leaders, whether formally or informally, he would listen gravely and courteously to what they had to say about their own problems but without much real interest or comprehension. At this period he was not even actively drumming up support for the Greek Cypriot case. To be seen constantly at international gatherings as Cyprus's Head of State was enough. He appeared unconcerned by the lack of progress in the intercommunal talks, as though confident that Turkish Cypriot resistance would eventually weaken.

At the end of November 1970 Clerides made a determined effort to bridge the gap between himself and Denktash. In effect, he offered a 'package deal'. If the Turkish Cypriots would abandon their idea of separate 'central authorities' for 'local government', the Greek Cypriots would agree to a number of Turkish Cypriot villages being grouped together in new local government areas. The Cyprus Government would maintain the Turkish Cypriot Communal Chamber and help the Turkish Cypriot local government areas financially. The Greeks, said Clerides, would also be willing to accept the Turkish Cypriot demand for a larger House of Representatives and the continuation of separate electoral rolls, provided the Turkish Cypriots accepted Greek Cypriot views on organising the judiciary.

There were some major concessions here by the Greek side. Denktash took several months to reply and, when he did so by letter in April 1971, after consultation with Ankara, it was virtually to produce a new set of counter-proposals. These aimed at strengthening the powers of the Turkish Cypriot Vice-President – one of 'the two Supreme Heads of the Executive' – and at extending the authority of the Communal Chambers. Denktash now insisted that, apart from what they might agree in a 'package deal', they must return to the main provisions of the 1960 constitution. He also began his letter by arguing the need to reaffirm their terms of reference – after three years of exploratory talks. In view of recent public statements on Greek Cypriot policy – Denktash said – they should make it clear they were searching for a solution based on permanent independence and not an independence which one side or the other could exploit to further 'national aims and aspirations'.

The Turks indeed had reason to think that ministerial statements on the Greek side – and even some by Makarios himself – hardly squared with official Greek Cypriot policy. In private Makarios could say, as he did to the present writer, that the Turkish Cypriots should take comfort from the fact that Enosis would never be achieved while Ankara objected to it. In public the Archbishop would reiterate that Union with Greece, if not attainable now, was still his dream. On one occasion – which Denktash obviously had in mind – Makarios was apparently so carried away during an emotional address to the villagers of Yialousa in the north-east corner of Cyprus that he declared:

> Cyprus is Greek. Cyprus has been Greek since the dawn of history and it will remain Greek. Greek and undivided we have received it. Greek and undivided we shall preserve it. Greek and undivided we shall deliver it to Greece.[6]

Such reported declarations and the plain fact that, after three years, the intercommunal talks were making no real progress began to worry the Greek Colonels in their relations with Turkey. Xanthopoulos-Palamas, another old-time diplomat, who had succeeded Pipinelis at the Greek Foreign Ministry, discussed the situation with his Turkish opposite number, Olcay, at a NATO meeting in Lisbon in May 1971. They said later, in separate interviews, that the intercommunal talks could not go on indefinitely, and Palamas added that, if no agreement was reached soon, Greece and Turkey would consult on how to handle the problem. The Greek Cypriot press began to buzz with stories that Athens was now trying to 'by-pass' Makarios, if not to get rid of him. Papadopoulos wrote to Makarios in mid-June, more in affected sorrow than anger, to say he was 'disgusted' at such 'monstrous rumours'. He referred to recent Greek advice that Makarios had rejected and urged him again to offer the Turkish Cypriots a 'ministry of local government', since this was virtually all that Denktash wanted. Papadopoulos added that, far from weakening the fabric of the Republic, the presence of such a minister in the Cabinet would emphasise the unity of the state. He ended with a warning that, if Makarios insisted on breaking their common front, the Greek Government would have to act in the national interest and the interests of Cypriot Hellenism, however 'painful' that might be. In an icy reply Makarios again rejected the Greek Government's advice about concessions and said that, if the last part of Papadopoulos's letter was intended as a threat, there would have to be some explanations before they could 'continue to cooperate'. The Archbishop is also reported to have enquired what the Greek Government's 'painful' steps might be and to have been told that Papadopoulos intended to withdraw all Greek officers from Cyprus and leave Makarios to the mercy of the Turks.

On 26 June, two days after Makarios's reply to Papadopoulos, Clerides answered Denktash's letter of April. He said he was greatly disappointed at the new Turkish Cypriot stand which widened the gap between them 'by reopening issues agreed upon ... and by raising new ones'. The Greek Cypriots, he went on, had had to consider whether it was better to end the talks or to make one last effort to reach agreement. They had decided on the second course. Clerides now offered new concessions over the judiciary and the police but said the Greek Cypriots could not accept the idea of a 'central local government authority' either for themselves or for the Turkish Cypriots. Denktash replied to this in August with a lengthy exposition of the Turkish Cypriot 'philosophy', that the specific differences between them could be settled only within the framework of political 'partnership' and 'functional federation'. There was one further exchange of letters and then, by September 1971, it was clear to all that the talks had broken down.

Makarios had made one more foreign journey in the past year that had greater significance than the others for his enemies, particularly in Greece. On the eve of the acrid correspondence with Papadopoulos he had spent a week in the Soviet Union. The ostensible purpose of the visit was to attend the enthronement of the new Patriarch of the Russian Orthodox Church, the former Archbishop Pimen, and this undoubtedly gave him much personal pleasure as a churchman. But he and Kyprianou also had an opportunity to discuss the Cyprus question with President Podgorny and Foreign Minister Gromyko. They agreed, in a communiqué, that it was necessary to reach a peaceful solution in Cyprus by negotiation between the communities. The Soviet government also reaffirmed its desire to see all foreign troops leave the island, and here it clearly included those in the British bases.

In September 1971 – the month that saw the breakdown of the intercommunal talks – General Grivas 'escaped' from house arrest in Athens and returned secretly to Cyprus for the fourth time. There were rumours that the Turks or the CIA had arranged his return; there can be little doubt however that it was approved by Papadopoulos, who had taken the 'painful' steps he had threatened. Years later a Turkish newspaper (*Yeni Duzen*) said that Turkish Cypriot 'democrats' had been appalled at the news that Grivas was back in the island. Berberoglu, who had unsuccessfully challenged Denktash's leadership, was reported to have asked him why he had made no protest. 'They've given their word', he is alleged to have answered, 'that as long as Grivas is in Cyprus, no Turk will get a bloody nose'. Perhaps the author of this story was merely being wise after the event.

13 The Bishops Rebel

This time Grivas landed in Cyprus near Limassol, and immediately went to ground in his old haunts there, confident of support from the 'National Front' and the Bishop of Kitium, as well as from a number of mainland Greek officers who were now more and more being hand-picked by Athens. Makarios had no illusions about the purpose of the EOKA leader's return. Papadopoulos had told the Archbishop privately in July that he should be prepared to accept an accommodation with Turkey in the form of 'double Enosis' or else resign as President. Makarios had spoken publicly of pressures on him from outside Cyprus – and everybody knew what he meant. On 20 July Xanthopoulos-Palamas, the Deputy Foreign Minister, had sent a Note to Nicosia, pointing out that, although Cyprus was 'independent', Athens was the 'National Centre' and in a matter affecting the national interest the Greeks of Cyprus must follow the line laid down by Athens. Makarios's reply of 4 August was uncompromising: 'In what concerns its national interest Cypriot Hellenism must have the last word. If there is disagreement between Athens and Nicosia, each must bear responsibility for its own actions.'

Grivas was now seventy-three years of age, mentally alert and as tough as an old walnut in spite of the ravages caused by his years in hiding. He knew he would have more difficulty in organising effective resistance to Makarios than he had had when he created EOKA in the 1950s to fight the British. It is unlikely that he ever contemplated a straightforward *coup*. His aim was to revive the old urgent clamour for Enosis and to put enough muscle behind it to force Makarios to admit the bankruptcy of his policies and resign as President. Backed by the 'National Guard', a new government would then proclaim Union with Greece, while Athens would keep Turkey quiet with the offer of a base in Cyprus and concessions to the Turkish Cypriots. This fitted in well with the plans of the Greek 'junta' and it also suited American policy. Grivas knew that the Colonels would try to exploit him; they had let him down once after the Kophinou incident and he could not forgive them for expelling the King. Some of his more naïve followers even thought Grivas might persuade Makarios to join with him in inviting Constantine to set up a royalist government-in-exile in Cyprus which would eventually replace the Colonels.

For the next few months Grivas stayed in the background, reviving contact with old EOKA members who had not become part of the 'establishment', letting it be known through leaflets that 'Dighenis' would soon be leading his heroic fighters again, and acquiring what arms he could by collusive raids on police stations with the 'National Front'. At the end of October 1971 Makarios publicly warned Grivas that he would be arrested if he persisted in illegal activities. The Archbishop said: 'I do not question the patriotism of General Grivas, but I seriously doubt the correctness of his thinking and his judgment.' Makarios added that he had told successive Greek governments he would unhesitatingly proclaim Enosis if he could be sure that they would support him, but they had always refused to do so. Enosis, he declared, could not be achieved through 'heroic acts of folly'.

Grivas decided he must have a legal cover for his activities. The open political part of his campaign was entrusted to a body calling itself 'The Committee for Coordinating the Struggle for Enosis', or ESEA, from its Greek initials. The committee issued its manifesto on 20 November, attacking Makarios over his leadership and calling for a 'new noble and national struggle for Union'. The committee included a number of well-known Greek Cypriots and it was given an air of respectability by having a former judge and President of the Supreme Court, the amiable and bumbling George Vassiliades, as its chairman. Its offices were in the centre of Nicosia.

The first hint of what a confrontation between the Grivas and Makarios camps might involve came early in 1972. On a dark night in January a Danish freighter unloaded a large number of packing-cases at the little mining-port of Xeros in north-west Cyprus. The cases were stored temporarily in a disused mine and then transported by road to the archbishopric and the main police-station at

Athalassa on the outskirts of Nicosia. The operation was observed by officers of the 'National Guard' and by some of Grivas's men. Subsequently a pro-Enosis newspaper in Athens revealed that Makarios had imported more arms and ammunition from Czecho-slovakia, disguised as explosives intended for industrial purposes. Others besides Grivas had no doubt that the arms were meant for use against a revived EOKA. At first the Cyprus Government denied their existence altogether. Then Makarios issued a state-ment saying that the arms had been ordered partly for the police and partly for the 'National Guard', to help it protect Greek Cypriot villagers from molestation by the Turks. The statement added that the Greek commander of the 'National Guard' knew all about it, but that Athens had advised secrecy to avoid creating an international scandal or alarming the Turkish Cypriots. The Greek Government denied any knowledge of the matter. On 11 February it delivered a sharp Note to President Makarios, calling on him to hand over all the imported arms to the United Nations peace-keeping force. The Colonels reminded Makarios again that Athens was the 'Centre' of Hellenism. They said the time had come to form a government of national unity in Cyprus from all the 'good' elements in society, including representatives of General Grivas. By its use of the emotive word for 'nationalist' (*ethnikofron*) the 'junta' made it clear that AKEL and the small socialist party led by Dr Lyssarides were to be excluded, although these together would account for almost half the Greek Cypriot electorate. The Note was delivered to Makarios by Mr Constantine Panayotakis who, from being Greek ambassador in Nicosia, had suddenly been promoted to the equivalent of Minister of State at the Greek Foreign Office. Panayotakis told Makarios he must get rid of mini-sters who were regarded as hostile to the Government in Athens – in particular, his Foreign Minister, Mr Spyros Kyprianou. The Colonels published their Note in Athens simultaneously with its delivery to Makarios – a breach of normal etiquette. On the follow-ing day Panayotakis gave a news conference in Nicosia, in which he brazenly asserted that there was no question of interfering in the in-ternal affairs of Cyprus and that the Note was not an ultimatum.

Three days later Turkey also called on Makarios to hand over the Czechoslovak arms to UNFICYP on the grounds that their deployment would upset the military balance in Cyprus to the dis-advantage of the Turkish Cypriots. At the same time Turkish forces were ordered south. The Greek Cypriot 'National Guard' was put on alert, but nobody could be sure whether this was to repel Turks or to move against Makarios. The Archbishop was in a difficult position. He could not afford to be seen backing down in the face of such a humiliating Note from the Greek 'junta'. At the same time he could not rely on the loyalty of his 'National Guard' if the Colonels decided to push matters to a conclusion. He decided to play for time and was encouraged by the popular indignation and the massive demonstrations of support for him that followed Panayotakis's news conference. He got Clerides to warn the American Embassy that, if there was bloodshed in Cyprus, the United States would bear a great responsibility. The Nixon Administration urged the Colonels to show restraint.

Then the crisis took a new turn. On 2 March the three Metropolitan Bishops of Paphos, Kitium and Kyrenia met as the Holy Synod of the Autocephalous Church of Cyprus and called on Makarios to resign as President. They had been restive for the past two years. In February 1970 the small bull-like Anthimos of Kitium had roared out a general accusation that those who were now in authority in Cyprus did not 'think Greek' and that even the teachers were trying to create a 'Cypriot conscience'. In May of the same year the bishops had demanded the restoration of the old Ethnarchy Council, so that the Holy Synod could advise on matters of 'vital national interest'. Makarios had appeared to give way to this demand but the idea was quickly scotched when all the political parties and newspapers except those of the extreme Right denounced the proposal as an insult to the people. What self-respecting Cypriot, asked one newspaper, would serve as a minister or a member of the House of Representatives if he knew his decisions would have to be approved by the Church?

Now, in March 1972, the bishops were emboldened by the other pressures on Makarios to claim – somewhat belatedly – that the Archbishop had violated canon law in accepting secular office. With a four-hundred-year-old tradition of the Archbishop being also the Ethnarch, the temporal as well as the spiritual leader of his people, it was hardly a convincing argument. The bishops tried to shore it up with accusations that Makarios had abandoned the struggle for Enosis, that he could no longer lead effectively because his life was in constant danger, and that he had procured Communist arms to fight those who wanted Union with Greece. Of the three bishops only Anthimos of Kitium carried any weight. Kyprianos of Kyrenia, Makarios's one-time rival and fellow-exile, was a shadow of his former self, old and sick. Yennadios of Paphos, the senior bishop, was a frail and foolish 'White Knight' figure, ridiculed even in his own diocese.

It was widely assumed that Athens had prompted the bishops' move but, though it obviously reinforced the diplomatic pressure being exerted by the Colonels, the three elderly clerics had their own reasons for wanting Makarios to step down as President – and they were not the same as the 'junta's'. As Head of State Makarios had to compromise with political realities; as Ethnarch he was free, and even obliged, to pursue the single goal of Enosis, without concessions. Anthimos was also very close to Grivas, physically in Limassol and by temperament. On the day after the Synod's call to Makarios to resign Grivas announced that he had put the three bishops under his full protection. From then on the Limassol bishopric – where Yennadios soon had to take refuge from the fury of his Paphos flock – was always guarded by Grivas's bully-boys.

The pro-Makarios parties and the Panagrarian Union (PEK) – once foremost in the campaign for Enosis – organised immediate demonstrations against the bishops. At the end of a fortnight Makarios replied to his clerics, saying that he could not agree with their 'suggestion' that he should step down as President. His resignation, he argued, would have to be followed by presidential elections, and it was doubtful whether they could be held in the present circumstances. This would mean that Cyprus would have no internationally recognised government, only separate Greek and Turkish administrations. That would open the way to partition. Moreover, the Archbishop went on, the demand for his resignation could only damage the Church. There was nothing either in Holy Writ or in the traditions of the Church of Cyprus that conflicted with his secular office as leader of his people. As if these arguments were not enough, Makarios accused the bishops of irregularity in holding a 'Synod'. Finally he declared that, if they still insisted on his resignation, he would feel obliged to agree to their demand. . . .

It was a masterly letter, calculated to demolish the bishops' case completely and at the same time to alarm the people that he might take them at their word. Yet, in spite of the letter's political astuteness, there is no doubt that Makarios was more disturbed by the assault on his position from within the Church than by the intrigues of the Colonels or the threat from Grivas.

The bishops were unmoved. Eight days later, on 27 March, they renewed their demand for Makarios's resignation. In the meantime the UN secretary-general's special representative in Cyprus, the very able and diplomatic Señor Osorio-Tafall, had had a number of protracted meetings with the Archbishop. Finally he had persuaded him to put all the newly-imported Czechoslovak arms under lock and key at the Athalassa police station, where the UN force commander would have the right to inspect them at any time. Makarios had not surrendered the arms, but the compromise was accepted both by Athens and by Ankara. He could now afford to disregard the bishops.

At the height of the crisis – to be precise, on 26 March, the day before the bishops sent their second demand for Makarios's resignation – the Archbishop had a secret meeting with Grivas in Nicosia. He did not reveal it till a month later, and then said little more than that the meeting had been at his suggestion and that he and Grivas had exchanged views on the situation in Cyprus and possible future developments. What precisely passed between them is not certain. No doubt the Archbishop listened patiently and courteously to the EOKA leader's outpourings on the dangers facing the nation and the way in which they should be confronted. It is likely that Makarios told him the Czechoslovak arms would be under United Nations control – and, by implication, no longer a threat to Grivas's forces. According to the Greek Cypriot journalist, Spyros Papayeoryiou (who was still then in the anti-Makarios camp and had been commissioned by the bishops to draft their second letter to the President), Grivas suddenly sent a message to the clerics that he wanted no more pressure on Makarios. Anthimos's immediate reaction was: 'There! I told you so! The Old Man [Grivas] will mess things up for us.'[1] He was not far wrong. Evidently the Archbishop convinced Grivas again that he must not endanger the unity of Cyprus and so make Enosis impossible by playing into the hands of the Greek Government, the Turks, the Americans and NATO.

Early in May, with memories of the crisis receding, Makarios announced that he would be making changes in his Cabinet during the first fortnight in June. On the following day Spyros Kyprianou, the Foreign Minister, resigned. He made it clear in a public statement that the projected government reshuffle was a delayed but direct response to the demand from Athens in February, in which Kyprianou's dismissal had been specifically ordered. Self-respect, he said, required him to resign immediately. Kyprianou must have felt particularly bitter over Makarios's willingness to sacrifice him, since he had served the President faithfully as Foreign Minister for more than eleven years. Kyprianou had come a long way since he was the Archbishop's London 'office-boy', disseminating Ethnarchy propaganda from a scruffy room near Euston station in the early 1950s. His many foreign trips with Makarios and his frequent appearances as Cypriot Foreign Minister in United Nations debates had given him a standing that his own abilities might not otherwise have secured. The man who was eventually to succeed Makarios as President never gave the impression of great intelligence or political acumen. But he was a stubborn lawyer who could stick to his brief. In spite of the setback to his career Kyprianou had no intention of retiring from politics.[2]

The bishops may have thought that Makarios's resistance to Athens was beginning to break down. At any rate, on 1 June they renewed their demand that he should resign from the Presidency immediately and threatened ecclesiastical sanctions if he did not comply. On 10 June Makarios replied, more curtly than usual, that the current critical situation, his conscience as a Greek archbishop and his Ethnarchic mission would not allow him to abandon and betray his people. One day earlier the clergy in the Paphos diocese announced that they had voted the old and foolish Yennadios out of office and had asked Makarios to arrange for the election of a successor. The ecclesiastical battle was now joined in earnest.

A week later Makarios carried out the promised reorganisation of his Cabinet. Mr John Christophides was brought in from being chairman of the Cyprus telecommunications authority to be Foreign Minister in place of Kyprianou. Odysseus Ioannides, the surgeon and former mayor of Nicosia who had done well in the 1970 elections with Nikos Sampson as the 'strong man' in his Progressive Front, became Minister of Agriculture and National Resources. Other posts were filled by a former chairman of the Cyprus tourism organisation, the director of education, an ex-judge, a senior official from the Ministry of Labour and an engineer. In appointing these ministers Makarios chose technocrats – not necessarily the most appropriate for the job – and men that he knew were loyal to him. He got rid of the more diehard Enotists – Kyprianou himself, in spite of his championship of independence – and men like Komodromos (at the combined Ministries of the Interior and Defence) and Toumazis (at Agriculture and National

Resources).[3] Makarios had made some concessions to the Colonels, but he had saved 'face' and, on balance, manoeuvred himself into a rather better position for dealing with Athens.

Papadopoulos too contrived to come out of the Cyprus crisis with what appeared to be a greater authority. General Zoïtakis, who had been made Regent after the King's abortive *coup* in 1967, found that his relations with the dictator were deteriorating. He disliked the peremptory Note which the Government had sent to Makarios in February, and he did not trouble to conceal it. When it was clear that the Archbishop was not going to knuckle under, Papadopoulos took his small revenge by dismissing Zoïtakis and assuming the post of Regent himself. He was already Prime Minister, Foreign Minister and Minister of Defence.

A week before Makarios's reshaping of his Cabinet the intercommunal talks were resumed in Nicosia after a break of nine months. At the beginning of the year, almost unnoticed in the hullabaloo over the Czechoslovak arms, a senior United Nations official, Dr Roberto Guyer of Argentina, had arrived in Cyprus. The new UN secretary-general, Dr Kurt Waldheim, had taken up a suggestion by his predecessor, U Thant, that some purpose should be injected into the intercommunal talks by broadening them to include a United Nations representative and 'consultants' or 'advisers' – their status was deliberately kept vague – from Greece and Turkey.

Makarios was suspicious of this new approach but by the time he had emerged unscathed from his confrontation with the Greek Colonels and his own bishops he was ready to consider a resumption of the talks according to the UN proposals. On 8 June 1972 Dr Waldheim presided over a formal meeting of Archbishop Makarios and Dr Kuchuk with their negotiators, Clerides and Denktash. They were joined by Señor Osorio-Tafall, the much-respected UN representative in Cyprus, and by two constitutional experts from Athens and Ankara. Dr Waldheim said he hoped the UN peace-keeping mission could soon be concluded since the participating governments were getting worried at the failure to reach a political solution. The eight-year operation had already accumulated a deficit of more than ten million dollars.

The gap between the two sides was made clear at the start. Clerides assured Waldheim that, although he was known as the Greek Cypriot negotiator, his guiding principle was the interests of the Cypriot people as a whole. Denktash insisted that there were two distinct national communities in Cyprus which could live in peace and cooperate only as equals. The new talks started substantively in mid-September. Again the arguments turned mainly around how much and what kind of local autonomy the Turkish Cypriots should have to balance the Greek Cypriot claim for majority rights and a strong central government. Osorio-Tafall, the quiet Mexican, was indefatigable with suggestions and ideas for compromise but progress was slow.

Early in 1973 the three Cypriot bishops made a new threat to invoke canon law against Makarios. Their move was prompted by his announcement in January that he would be seeking re-election as President in the following month after the lapse of the five years prescribed by the constitution for the presidential term of office. ESEA, the Committee for Coordinating the Struggle for Enosis, said it would not put up a candidate unless Makarios stepped down or nominated his choice for successor. In this way the anti-Makarios camp admitted its political weakness. But Grivas and the 'National Front' were in no mood to see the Archbishop score an easy victory. In the run-up to nomination day they sharply stepped up their raids on police stations and other buildings. Apart from arms, ammunition and explosives, they got away with a considerable number of radio transmitters and portable telephone sets as well as with a quantity of police uniforms. At the end of January Makarios publicly accused Grivas of organising a terrorist movement to prevent elections being held. At the same time he ignored ESEA's demand for a popular referendum on Enosis or independence in place of elections just as he had disregarded the fresh fulminations from the bishops.

The campaign of violence reached its peak on 7 February, the eve of nomination day. Some 150 gunmen attacked eighteen police stations in various parts of Cyprus, including three in Famagusta which they dynamited. On the following day Makarios addressed a massive rally of his supporters in Nicosia and warned Grivas that force would be met by force. The people, he said, would not submit to terrorism. The armed bands were trying to undermine the State and promote civil war; instead of furthering the cause of Enosis (as they claimed) they were burying it for good. The Archbishop went on:

As I have declared in the past, all the Greeks of Cyprus are Enotists ... Greek ideals will always inspire our thinking and our conscience ... And if factors and situations beyond our control do not make Enosis possible, this does not mean that we shall cease to be Greeks ... But since we are Enotists, why are we carrying on talks with the Turkish Cypriots and speaking about an independent, unitary and sovereign State? Because this is necessitated by grim reality to which neither the Greek nor the Cyprus Government ... can close its eyes.

By this time even the Colonels had been alarmed by the turn of events in Cyprus. On 1 February Athens radio broadcast a statement from 'a qualified government source', appealing to Greek Cypriots to stop turning their guns on each other when a 'correct solution' of the problem was being sought. Subsequently the Greek Deputy Foreign Minister, Mr Phaidon Kavalieratos, told a press conference that the 'correct solution' envisaged was a constitutional structure 'safeguarding a unitary, independent and sovereign State'. He said the Government's condemnation of violence was addressed to those controlling armed groups in Cyprus – a statement ambiguous enough to include the pro-Makarios private armies as well as Grivas and the 'National Front'.

No last-minute candidate appeared against Makarios and on 28 February he was formally inaugurated as President for a third term. Shortly before that he invited ESEA and the pro-Enosis Democratic National Party of Dr Evdokas to a round-table conference on the divisions within the Greek Cypriot community but the offer was rejected.

Meanwhile the Turkish Cypriots – clinging to their rights under the 1960 constitution in spite of their new demands for equality – had also proclaimed an election for February. As Dr Kuchuk had indicated that he would not seek a new term as Vice-President, the contest was between Rauf Denktash and Mr Ahmet Berberoglu, a socialist who advocated a less militant attitude towards the Greek Cypriots. Denktash was determined to prevent his opponent's election and, after a considerable amount of intimidation, including a period of house arrest. Berberoglu withdrew and Denktash was declared elected 'unopposed'.

Grivas and the 'National Front' had no intention of halting their campaign of violence. During the second half of March and the first week in April there were almost daily incidents. A police sergeant in Limassol led a raid on his own station and got away with a number of guns and more than 7000 rounds of ammunition. Bomb explosions in Paphos damaged several buildings, including a house belonging to the Minister of the Interior and Defence. Several police stations in Nicosia district were blown up after the men on duty in them had been overpowered or forced out and the arms stores raided. On one night in April there were more than thirty explosions in various towns. But most of these, Makarios admitted, were due to government supporters retaliating against Grivas's men. Surprisingly, there were few fatal casualties from these encounters.

On 30 March President Makarios announced that he was setting up a new auxiliary police force under the command of an army officer to combat 'terrorism'. The existing police force – the creation of Yeorkadjis – was clearly too riddled with supporters of Grivas and the 'National Front' to be reliable. Makarios's own 'National Guard' of conscripts could not be used because of its Greek officers who took their orders from Athens and were mostly sympathetic towards Grivas. Even the armed groups organised by Dr Lyssarides and others close to the President could not cope with the widely-dispersed activity of what was now coming to be known as EOKA-B.

The news that Makarios was going to carry the war against them checked some of the 'terrorists' for a time. EOKA Day, 1 April, was celebrated officially but uneventfully, without the *coup* that one Greek Cypriot newspaper had said Grivas would launch on the anniversary, arresting the Archbishop and proclaiming Union with Greece. Grivas was unlikely to move unless he thought that the Archbishop was about to sign an agreement with the Turkish Cypriots ruling out Enosis – and there was little sign of that. On 15 April, when Makarios challenged Grivas to come out of hiding and explain his strategy to the people, the General preferred to remain silent.

Two days later Clerides indicated that he wanted to resign as Greek Cypriot negotiator. A week passed and then he issued a statement setting out his reasons but adding that he had agreed to stay for the time being, after considering a personal message he had received from the UN secretary-general, a categorical statement by the Greek Government and an appeal from President Makarios. Clerides argued that the escalation of violence and counter-violence on the Greek Cypriot side was making his pos-

ition as negotiator untenable, especially when matters affecting
the security of life and property were being discussed with the
Turkish Cypriots. This was a good deal less than the real reasons
for his dissatisfaction. The interference of the Greek Government
in the affairs of Cyprus in the name of a greater Hellenism was difficult to explain away, in spite of Makarios's resistance to it. The
'categorical statement' from Athens that the Colonels believed a
solution of the Cyprus problem was possible only through the
enlarged talks was tempered by the assertion that Hellenism must
remain united. But nothing handicapped Clerides more than
Makarios's continued ambivalence over his ultimate goal: was it
permanent independence or independence only as a stage towards
eventual Enosis? Hardly less embarrassing for the negotiator was
the Archbishop's reluctance to concede any *political* rights to the
Turkish Cypriots *as a community*, in addition to their ordinary
human rights as individuals, in a society where they would always
be outnumbered.

There was a lull in the violence from mid-April to mid-June.
However there was no slackening in the peculiar Cypriot form of
odium theologicum. On 8 March the three bishops announced that
they had met again as the Holy Synod – after Makarios's reinaug-
uration as President – and had decided to strip him of his archiepiscopal titles. They gave him thirty days in which he could appeal
against this decision.

Makarios ordered the bearer of this insolent message to be
turned away. He described the action of the bishops – though
'manifestly inspired' – as the product of 'a dark, mediaeval mentality' which showed utter contempt for the people. He warned those
who had attempted his 'spiritual assassination' that he would take
all necessary measures to protect the people and safeguard the
Church.

The bishops met again on 13 April, in the safety of the Limassol
bishopric, and announced that their decision to depose Archbishop Makarios was now final. In future he would be treated as a
layman and known by his original name of Michael Mouskos.
Parish priests were told to omit his clerical name from their prayers
and letters were sent to banks advising them that Makarios's signature was no longer valid in Church transactions. The old and dod-
dering Yennadios, as senior bishop, was appointed Locum
Tenens.

Makarios fired his first small retaliatory shot by announcing elections for a new Bishop of Paphos, since Yennadios had been voted off his throne by the local clergy almost a year before. Then the Archbishop began to muster the big guns. There was really no need to do this, but Makarios was greatly upset at having his right to administer the sacraments called in question. The constitution of the Church of Cyprus says explicitly that the bishops may convene a Holy Synod only if the Archbishop is incapable of doing so – which plainly he was not. Even the government-controlled Greek press was almost as indignant as the majority of Greek Cypriot newspapers, calling the bishops' intervention 'a criminal act' and 'a stab in the back' for Cypriot Hellenism. Makarios was determined to play the game according to the rules. On 5 July a Supreme Synod of his peers – presided over by the Patriarch of Alexandria and attended by the Patriarch of Antioch, a representative of the Patriarchate of Jerusalem and a good dozen bishops – convened in Nicosia. The only notable absentee was the Patriarch of Constantinople, who was prevented from attending by the Turks. After hearing the evidence the Princes of the Orthodox Church found that the attempt to depose Makarios was contrary to canon law. When the Cypriot bishops refused to appear before the Patriarchs – the anti-Makarios press had called these venerable figures 'agents of Islam' because they came from Arab lands – the Supreme Synod found them guilty of schism, disobedience and contempt. All three were deposed and 'unfrocked'. Yennadios was the first to be replaced – in late July – by Makarios's protégé, Chrysostomos, the Suffragan Bishop of Constantia (the see of Famagusta.) Only four years later Chrysostomos was to succeed Makarios as Archbishop.

Over the next few months Makarios systematically demolished whatever power base the rebel bishops had enjoyed. A new see of Morphou (in north-west Cyprus) was hived off from the diocese of Kyrenia. Kitium was split into two bishoprics, Larnaca and Limassol. This naturally increased the prestige of Paphos, where Makarios's following had always been exceptionally strong. All the new bishops were hand-picked by Makarios and then 'elected' as his nominees. The financial accounts of the bishoprics were closely scrutinised and the flow of money from Kitium and Kyrenia which had once gone to EOKA-B was now diverted to the loyalist cause.

The deposed bishops still had the support of some of the clergy, and for a time they continued to hold services and administer the sacraments in remote or improvised churches which quickly became known as '*katakómbes*'. The clashes between rival political groups around these centres of anti-Makarios propaganda did nothing to enhance the reputation of the Church.

The discomfiture of the bishops stimulated EOKA-B into greater violence. Its most spectacular feat was the kidnapping of the Justice Minister, Mr Christos Vakis, from his home in Nicosia on 27 July. Makarios told a news conference: 'Grivas and his supporters are not going to get the upper hand . . . I will never give in to blackmail'. It was almost a week before the kidnappers made their demands. Leaflets bearing the typewritten 'signature' George Grivas-Dighenis said that Vakis would be released, provided Makarios met five conditions. He must amnesty all 'political' prisoners and reinstate all policemen and other public servants dismissed on grounds of disloyalty. Further, the Archbishop must proclaim new presidential elections, choose for himself between Church and State and allow a popular referendum on the 'National Question'. These were preposterous demands and Makarios refused even to acknowledge them. It was by no means certain that they had emanated from Grivas himself, who was reported to be a sick man.

By this time Makarios's new Tactical Police Reserve was well-armed and well-trained. He had been loth to use it for full-scale 'search and destroy' operations but the kidnapping of his minister called for drastic action. On 9 August the security forces captured some twenty leading members of EOKA-B in Limassol; they included Stavros Stavrou, who had already been identified as Grivas's second-in-command and was probably the originator of most of the attacks. The following day the Government announced that, among the many documents seized, was a plan to assassinate President Makarios by ambushing his car during his early morning drive from the archbishopric to the presidential palace two miles away. The journalist and former confidant of Grivas, Spyros Papayeoryiou, has given a detailed account of several plans for a *coup* allegedly drawn up by the EOKA leader under such code-names as 'Apollo' and 'Flash' (*Lampsis*).[4] Various dates in the summer of 1973 are given for their execution. It is difficult to believe that some of these 'plans' were any more than paper exercises, though probably more than one group was plotting to kill Makarios, who appeared in public so careless of his safety. Any small body of conspirators might have thought that, if it could then seize the radio station and broadcast a rousing call to the nation, there would be the desired response from the 'National Guard' and the Greek army contingent.

Grivas denied the Government's allegations. Meanwhile Makarios kept up the pressure with his Tactical Police Reserve. At the same time he cleverly picked up a suggestion by an Athenian newspaper that he and General Grivas should both go to Athens for talks with 'President' Papadopoulos, as he now was. Grivas refused to fall into this trap, in spite of Makarios's offer to hold a popular referendum in Cyprus if they failed to agree. A fortnight later Papadopoulos called on Grivas to end his campaign of violence and disband his organisation as 'the supreme service' which he could render to 'the national cause'. Two days after this the Justice Minister, Mr Vakis, was released unharmed. Makarios had scored another quiet success. Grivas was still in the island and unlikely to dissolve EOKA-B. But – as the little General had feared – the Colonels had double-crossed him again and rallied behind Makarios.

The rest of the year was comparatively uneventful in Cyprus, though the basic tensions remained and there was another attempt to assassinate Makarios on 7 October. Four mines exploded on a road near Famagusta a few minutes before the Archbishop-President was due to pass in his car on his way to conduct a service. The man who detonated them, a waiter, was arrested near by. Otherwise, Makarios felt confident enough in the political situation to be able to pay visits to Ethiopia and Libya in early November, to meet such ill-assorted 'allies' in the 'Third World' as the Emperor Haile Selassie and Colonel Muammar Gaddafi. Papadopoulos had come to realise that he could not get rid of Makarios without unleashing the forces in Cyprus which would precipitate the very confrontation with Turkey that he wanted to avoid. The Americans too at that time seem to have appreciated the fact that, while Makarios must be 'cut down to size' if there was to be an accommodation between Greece and Turkey, removing him altogether could produce an even more unstable situation on the eastern flank of NATO.

However, Papadopoulos was not to enjoy his 'Presidency' for very long. The worsening economic situation under the dictatorship, widespread discontent, even among former supporters of the regime, and student unrest culminated, in late November, in the bloody affair of the Athens Polytechnic. Some hundreds of students had staged a 'sit-in' and refused to come out. Militant build-ing workers went on the rampage through the streets of Athens and tried to take over banks and government buildings. When the police opened fire, a number of innocent bystanders were killed. As the students and their supporters broadcast their defiance of the regime and called for its overthrow, Papadopoulos panicked and rushed in the tanks. A number of students were killed in the assault on the Polytechnic. Martial law was proclaimed, Papadopoulos appeared on television, visibly shaken, and a week later he was quietly deposed by his fellow-Colonels. The 'strong man' who emerged, Brigadier Dimitrios Ioannides, the head of the military police, was largely an unknown quantity. But he was on close terms with the CIA chief in Athens. He had also served as an intelligence officer with the Greek armed forces in Cyprus in 1964, and he knew most of the personalities there.[5]

By the late autumn of 1973, the enlarged intercommunal talks had made considerable progress, in spite of the uncertainties created by the violence inside the Greek camp. Denktash was confident of his new authority in his own community. The main Turkish Cypriot enclave, based on the northern part of Nicosia, which three years before had looked like becoming a ghetto, now showed a fair amount of prosperity, though it could not compare with the Greek side. Apart from its heavy financial dependence on Turkey, some development projects were simply not possible at com-munity level. But there was an air of relaxation generally, and outside the enclaves Greeks and Turks lived side by side, with only rare clashes. In this atmosphere Clerides and Denktash, helped to some extent by their constitutional advisers from Greece and Turkey and even more by the UN secretary-general's special representative, Señor Osorio-Tafall, had signficantly narrowed their differences on almost all issues except that of 'local govern-ment'.

There was agreement that the powers of the President should be enlarged and those of the Vice-President curtailed, with neither having the right of veto. The two Communal Chambers of the 1960 constitution were to be abolished and instead there would be Greek and Turkish branches of the House of Representatives which could meet separately or together; the ratio would be 4:1. The separate majorities rule was to be abolished for taxation and financial matters and kept only for changes in the electoral law or the constitution and in the case of the Organic Law regulating 'local government'. There was agreement on the ratios in the public service. The Greek side accepted that Turkish villages should be policed entirely by Turkish Cypriots, but it insisted that the police force must be an integrated body: it would not accept the right of the Turkish Cypriot community to have its own police force. But the major sticking-point was still the question of 'local government'. The crucial issue was whether the House of Representatives should have control over the right of the Turkish Cypriot branch to make its own laws.

Suddenly both sides began to harden their attitudes. Early in December Denktash submitted new proposals on 'local government' or, as he now preferred to call it, 'regional autonomy'. There must be, he said, a 'dichotomy of powers' to give the Turkish Cypriots absolute security and allow them to function as partners in a bicommunal state. Denktash argued, in effect, that the Turkish branch of the House of Representatives should have all the powers of the existing Turkish Cypriot administration, except those specifically reserved for the central government. He even claimed the right of the Turkish community to contract directly with foreign governments and international organisations over economic and technical aid. These demands were completely unacceptable to the Greek side.

It is unlikely that Denktash formulated his new concept of 'local government' without prompting from Ankara. Turkey was just emerging from a long political crisis that had lasted for most of 1973. Eventually in the October elections to the National Assembly Mr Bulent Ecevit's Left-of-Centre People's Republican Party had beaten Mr Demirel's Justice Party to first place but failed to get an overall majority. It was not until mid-January 1974 that Ecevit was able to form a viable government with the help of an unlikely partner, the ultra-Right National Salvation Party. However Denktash, keeping in touch with all the politicians in Ankara, may have had a shrewd suspicion that Ecevit would succeed and would be prepared to take a tough line over Cyprus.

On 1 February, when Ecevit presented his Government's programme to the Turkish parliament, he spoke about the need for a 'federal' solution in Cyprus. In Nicosia Clerides protested that the talks would soon be deadlocked again if the Turks aimed at a federal rather than a unitary state, which had been the agreed objective of all the negotiations since 1968. On 27 March Ecevit again called for a 'federal' solution and the Greek Cypriots broke off the talks. They were not resumed till mid-June.

The hardening of the Turkish position seems to have been due to several factors. Ecevit felt confident that his Government was stronger than previous coalitions and therefore more capable of healing the running sore which Cyprus had now become for Turkey. Also, he knew from Denktash that, although the two negotiators had agreed on a number of matters and moved nearer to agreement even on the 'local government' issue, Makarios would always draw Clerides back from any commitment that would give the Turkish Cypriots political rights as a community which would not be subject to government, i.e. majority control. There was probably another factor that influenced Ankara. Ecevit may well have realised that the new 'strong man' in the Athens 'junta', Brigadier Ioannides, would be tougher and more resolute than his predecessor, Papadopoulos.

Meanwhile there was a further development which pushed matters nearer to a confrontation. On 27 January Grivas died of a heart attack; he was seventy-five. He had been in poor health for some time and not fully in command of EOKA-B, though two months before his death he was challenging Makarios to choose between 'war' and 'peace', and even later he was intriguing with Ioannides. Grivas was buried in a tomb prepared for him in the garden of the villa in Limassol where he had had his hide-out for much of his campaign against the British in the 1950s. The funeral service was conducted by the deposed and 'unfrocked' Yennadios of Paphos. The number of mourners was estimated at 70,000 – almost certainly an exaggeration. They included the Greek ambassador to Cyprus, the deputy chief of staff of the Greek armed forces and the Greek commander of the Cypriot 'National Guard', General George Denisis. President Makarios was not represented, but the Cabinet ordered the closing of government offices on the day of the funeral. Nikos Sampson dominated the occasion and in a fiery speech over the coffin vowed that 'Dighenis' would be avenged.[6]

On the day after Grivas's death Makarios released a hundred of his supporters from gaol and promised an amnesty for any wanted persons who surrendered with their arms within five days. In making the announcement the Archbishop praised what he called Grivas's 'inestimable services to the people of Cyprus and the Greek nation'. He said that, although he had often disagreed with the General, he could not ignore his contribution to the 'liberation struggle'. Makarios said he hoped that his amnesty would help to restore the situation in the island to 'normal'.

It failed to do so. There was virtually no response to the offer. Some of those released from gaol went underground immediately to continue the fight against the Government. Grivas had no obvious successor, and EOKA-B now split into a number of rival groups, each of which tried to assert its leadership by being more militant than the others. The attacks on government supporters became too widespread for the Tactical Police Reserve to prevent. Moreover, the anti-Makarios camp now had such support from the Greek officers of the 'National Guard' and even from Cypriots still employed in the government service – policemen and school-teachers in particular – that it was able to launch a campaign of propaganda and intimidation throughout the island, except in the Turkish Cypriot enclaves. Villagers living on the main roads were instructed to fly the Greek flag daily under threat of reprisals. Walls were covered with slogans denouncing 'Mouskos' [the Archbishop] and 'the traitor Clerides'. Eventually at the end of April, Makarios declared EOKA-B an illegal organisation and promised that the full weight of the law would be used against it. It made little difference.

Makarios realised that the mounting pressures on him were weakening his position. His main support now came from the Left, represented by the Moscow-orientated AKEL and the small socia-list party, EDEK, led by Dr Lyssarides. Even here he had suffered some loss of authority and respect for his judgement because of his reluctance to act decisively against EOKA-B, while Grivas was alive, or to purge his government and the public service of elements disloyal to him. On the other hand the more conservative members of the moderate nationalist party led by Clerides – the urban middle class and the industrialists and businessmen – were often worried by Makarios's intransigence in the intercommunal talks and by what they saw as his too great reliance on the Communist-led Left. Even if they condemned EOKA-B and disliked the Greek 'junta', they were also uneasy about the growing rift between Makarios and the politicians in Athens.

Makarios was less concerned about the violence of EOKA-B than by the way in which his 'National Guard' was being steadily subverted to the purposes of the Colonels. When the General Staff submitted a new list of Greek Cypriots selected for training as officers, Makarios's Cabinet rejected a number of them on security or 'loyalty' grounds. The General Staff ignored this and began training its chosen cadets; when the Government protested, the Greek officers claimed the grounds for rejection were too vague. Makarios then had a fruitless meeting with General Denisis, the Greek commander of the 'National Guard', who afterwards went off to Athens. Later, in answer to a buzz of speculation, he said he had made it clear to the commander that Cypriot officers were appointed, not by him or the General Staff but by the Government of Cyprus. Makarios's statement pointed out that Cypriot cadets for the officer reserve were too often the key figures in anti-government activities and had also connived at the theft of 'National Guard' arms by 'the terrorist organisation, EOKA-B'. The President gave warning that he meant to put an end to this. Later he indicated that he planned to reduce the size of the 'National Guard' and to bring it more directly under his own control. He also promised a purge of disloyal elements wherever they were found in government or public service.

A month later, encouraged by the lack of reaction from Athens and by what he saw as popular support for his defence of Cypriot national honour and independence, Makarios decided he could force the Colonels into retreat. On 2 July he addressed a letter to President Gizikis, the obscure General chosen by Ioannides to be the nominal head of state after the overthrow of Papadopoulos. It was a long and detailed communication, and Makarios made it clear it was intended for publication. He began by expressing his 'deep regret' at having to draw the President's attention to a list of anomalies and unfriendly acts against Cyprus for which he held the Greek Government responsible. First there had been the clandestine return of Grivas in 1971, promoted by 'certain circles' in Athens. With the help of Greek officers serving in Cyprus, Grivas had then created an illegal organisation, EOKA-B, allegedly to fight for Enosis but in reality to commit political murders and many other crimes. From the start the 'National Guard' had been the main source of arms and other material for EOKA-B. 'National Guard' camps had been inundated with propaganda against the Government of Cyprus, 'and in particular against me', said Makarios. The pro-Grivas press had been financed from Athens and followed a line laid down by Greek military intelligence and by KYP [the Greek CIA]. The bishops who had created such a crisis in the Church also took their inspiration from Athens.

After Grivas's death Athens had taken over direct control of
EOKA-B – and here Makarios produced what he described as one
of a number of incriminating documents.[7] Finally he came to the
issue of selecting Cypriot officers for the 'National Guard'. The
General Staff, on instructions from Athens, had flagrantly defied
decisions by the Cyprus Government, and this was unacceptable.
In the midst of this catalogue of crimes Makarios declared:

> I have always believed and repeatedly stated that cooperation
> with each and every Greek government is for me a national duty
> ... I cannot say that I feel any special sympathy for military
> regimes, particularly in Greece, where democracy was born and
> cradled. But even here I did not deviate from my principle of co-
> operating. You must appreciate, Mr President, the distressing
> thoughts that tormented me when I realised that persons in the
> Greek Government were constantly weaving plots against me
> and – what was worse – were dividing the Greeks of Cyprus and
> driving them to tear each other apart and destroy themselves.
> More than once before now I have sensed and sometimes almost
> felt an invisible hand reaching out from Athens and seeking to
> cut short my existence.

Makarios went on to say he had decided to change the organisation and structure of the 'National Guard' since under its Greek
officers it had lost the confidence of the Cypriot people. (He had
announced the day before that the period of national service would
be shortened from two years to fourteen months 'to lessen the evil'.)
The Archbishop asked the Greek Government to recall the officers
serving in the 'National Guard' and to send out about a hundred
others simply as 'instructors and military advisers' to help with the
reorganisation. He concluded:

> Meanwhile, I hope orders have been given from Athens to
> EOKA-B to stop its activities ... I do not wish to end my co-
> operation with the Greek Government. You must realise
> however that I am not the prefect of a department [nomarch]
> appointed by the Greek Government, or its *locum tenens* in
> Cyprus, but the elected leader of a large part of the Greek nation,
> and I demand appropriate treatment from the National Centre.

This was strong stuff. Makarios had never before accused the

Greek Government of trying to get rid of him, and by assassination, nor had he dared order it so peremptorily to remove its 'Trojan horse' from Cyprus. There was no immediate answer from Athens; he hardly expected it. Three days later a pro-Makarios newspaper *Apoyevmatini* published details, which had evidently been 'leaked' to it, of preparations for a *coup* said to have been discovered by government intelligence operations. The plot was described as 'a variation of the Apollo Plan' of 1973, envisaging the assassination of Makarios and his replacement by a puppet President within a few days. The *coup* was said to have been planned by 'certain military circles' in cooperation with units of the 'National Guard' and EOKA-B groups, but in such a way as not to implicate senior Greek officers.

That same day Makarios gave a lengthy news conference. He agreed that relations between Athens and Nicosia were 'not harmonious'. When he was asked about the rumours of an Athens-instigated *coup*, the Archbishop replied blandly that he did not attach importance to them. 'I do not think there is any likelihood of a *coup*', he said. 'If there should be one, it has no chance of succeeding.'

This was whistling in broad daylight. The following morning most of the Greek Cypriot press published the full text of Makarios's letter to Gizikis. The London *Times* carried a report from its usually well-informed correspondent in Athens, Mario Modiano, that Ioannides and his inner cabal had decided to use the 'National Guard' to eliminate Makarios. Ioannides was quoted as saying to his colleagues: 'Don't worry. There will be no consequences if the job is done quickly and neatly.'

A week later, Saturday 13 July, Makarios told a correspondent of Britain's Independent Television News that he had not yet had any answer or reaction from Athens. Over the week-end the Greek ambassador in Nicosia informed the Archbishop that the Cabinet had discussed his letter on Saturday and decided to meet again on Monday. General Denisis, the 'National Guard' commander, was already in on the discussions. There was a suggestion that Makarios might care to attend the Monday meeting, but he said he saw no point in going to Athens at that moment.

It was a simple trick, designed to achieve the element of surprise. Early that Monday morning, 15 July, units of the 'National Guard' moved quickly into Nicosia in trucks and armoured personnel carriers. Some of them seized the radio station. A detachment of

Soviet-built T-54s raced to the presidential palace and fanned out along the road in front of the gardens, between the entrance and exit drives. One tank entered the grounds and took up position in the car-park opposite the handsome honey-coloured building that had once been Government House. Then the shelling began.

Makarios had returned from his summer week-end retreat up on Troodos well before 8 o'clock, passing on his way a 'National Guard' barracks from which he must have been an easy target. His first public engagement was to meet some Greek schoolchildren from Cairo. One of the girls was making a little speech when the first shells struck. There was no immediate alarm. It was only when an aide rushed in to tell him the palace was under attack and that all the telephone lines had been cut that Makarios realised what was happening. The children were hustled away into the care of staff and Makarios was then reluctantly persuaded to leave through a french window at the side of the building, without his archbishop's headgear and his formal dress. The palace guard had already engaged the solitary tank in the grounds and apparently put it out of action, but it was joined by another. Makarios, together with his aide – who also happened to be his nephew, Maria's son, Andreas[8] – a bodyguard and a police officer, slipped round to the back when they saw no sign of troops. Here the ground soon fell away steeply through a tangle of bushes to the dried-up river-bed of the Pediaeos. The Archbishop and his companions scrambled down a small dry water-course, crossed the river-bed and reached a small secondary road. It was deserted but almost immediately a private car appeared, a Morris 1500. They flagged it down and the owner readily allowed the Archbishop and his party to commandeer it. After a hundred yards it ran out of petrol. Then, miraculously, but with just a touch of farce creeping in, a Vauxhall came along, driven by a cripple. He was easily persuaded that the Archbishop's need was greater than his own and was left rejoicing on the road-side. The car went straight to the Kykko Metochi, less than a mile away. But the sounds of battle were coming nearer and Makarios decided to head for the mountains. On Troodos they picked up a small radio transmitter from Makarios's summer retreat but could make no contact with the palace, which was now a burnt-out shell. Then, after changing to a third car, they reached Kykko Monastery. There the monks were astonished to see Makarios alive; since eleven that morning the Cyprus Broadcasting Corporation had been starkly announcing his death and playing martial music. But even Kykko was no longer a safe place. Makarios and his party drove across the mountains to Ano Panayia and after a brief stop there went down to Paphos to seek the help of the Archbishop's protégé, the recently-appointed Bishop Chrysostomos.

By now Cyprus Broadcasting Corporation had put out a proclamation from 'the armed forces' which said they had intervened to prevent civil war and to get rid of a government which had usurped power from the people for too long; the statement promised 'a government of National Salvation', elections within a year, a continuance of the intercommunal talks and no change in foreign policy. Later, Greek Cypriots heard with incredulity the voice of Nikos Sampson announcing over the radio that he had been entrusted with the office of President. Makarios was able to get to the small Paphos radio station to broadcast this message:

> Cypriot people!
> You know this voice. You know who is speaking... It is I, Makarios. I am the one you chose to be your leader... I am not dead, as the 'junta' in Athens and its representatives here wanted. I am alive. And I am with you, to fight and carry the flag in our common struggle. The 'junta's' *coup* has failed....

The 'National Guard' was slow in reaching Paphos. By the time it did so the UN contingent there had arranged with the British base at Akrotiri for a helicopter to be sent to pick up the Archbishop. From Akrotiri he was taken by plane to Malta. After a night's rest he flew on to London and then, the following day, to New York, where he presented his case against Greece to the United Nations Security Council on 19 July.

A few hours later Turkey launched her long-threatened invasion of Cyprus by sea and air.

There were many puzzling questions about the *coup*, and not all of them have yet been answered satisfactorily. Why, for example, did Makarios apparently disregard all the warning omens and seem to be taken by surprise? Why did Ioannides stage a *coup* – which was bound to bring in the Turks – instead of merely arranging the assassination of Makarios – which would have delighted Turkey? To what extent, if any, was the American CIA involved? And why was the *coup* so badly bungled? How did Makarios manage to escape so easily?

As far as his own person was concerned, Makarios knew that he lived always 'in the shadow of death', and he was inclined to be fatalistic about it. He was unwilling to take elaborate precautions that a secular ruler might have done. But, like others, Makarios could not believe that the Colonels would be so criminally stupid as to provoke a Turkish invasion. There was an element of naïvety in his character at variance with his long-acquired cunning in dealing with many enemies.

The first serious warnings of an impending *coup* had begun to circulate in February 1974.[9] The United States Embassy in Nicosia reported to the State Department that there was intensified activity among the Greek officers of the 'National Guard' and their EOKA-B contacts. Further, Clerides told the Embassy that the Archbishop's intelligence service had wind of a meeting in Athens in the second week of February between a former CIA chief in Nicosia, Eric Neff, known for his hostility to Makarios, and Nikos Sampson and others. At first, it seems, the Americans denied this. Later they admitted that Neff had been in Athens but maintained it was on private business. By this time the Nixon Administration had begun to find Greece's new dictator, Ioannides, something of a liability – more difficult to deal with than his predecessor, Papadopoulos, more ruthless and more unpredictable. In March the United States ambassador to Greece, Mr Henry Tasca, returned to Washington to testify to what he regarded as the Ioannides danger. He was apparently told by the Secretary of State, Dr Henry Kissinger, not to cause trouble by trying to set Ioannides on a different course. Dr Kissinger may have felt that, if Ioannides was given his head, it would resolve several problems.

In spite of a further warning from the American Embassy the Archbishop felt confident enough to leave Cyprus in May for a week's visit to China. It is difficult to think that either Mao or Makarios penetrated the other's inscrutable exterior, and the exchange of compliments and the warmth of Chinese smiles were hardly worth the risk involved in ignoring the dangers in Cyprus.

In mid-June Ioannides told Washington through his CIA link that something must be done about Makarios. The message was variously interpreted in Washington as signalling Ioannides's own determination to move against the Archbishop or as asking for American backing to do so. Dr Kissinger and his Under-Secretary of State, Mr Joseph Sisco, then instructed Ambassador Tasca to convey to Ioannides Washington's disapproval of any move against Makarios. Tasca made no effort to see Ioannides personally, and tried to justify this later in an interview in *Newsweek* with the argument that it was not the job of an ambassador 'to make diplomatic *démarches* to a cop' – Ioannides being merely Minister of the Interior and head of the military police. Instead, Tasca observed protocol and passed on Washington's message to the Foreign Minister, repeating it for good measure to the Prime Minister and President Gizikis, all of whom lacked any real authority. It could be that Tasca was still interpreting Kissinger's current policy as one of 'non-involvement' with the 'junta' and paying little attention to Sisco's more knowledgeable concern about the dangers of a Greek-Turkish confrontation.

On 14 July, the day before 'Operation Aphrodite', a CIA message from Athens to Washington suggested that Ioannides had begun to have 'second thoughts' about the wisdom of trying to topple Makarios. Was it deliberate 'misinformation' or simply another example of the CIA failing to read the portents correctly?

There can be little doubt that United States policy was operating on at least two different levels in its approach to the 'Cyprus-Greece-Turkey' problem, as in other situations. 'Above the board' there was genuine concern that the quarrel between Greece and Turkey – now further exacerbated in 1974 by Turkey's claim on the Aegean sea-bed – had greatly weakened the eastern wing of NATO. Also the 'junta' had become a liability: it had alienated Greece from Western Europe and America's image had suffered because of Washington's support for it. Makarios was seen as the main obstacle to the improvement of relations between Greece and Turkey, but if he were removed it was important that the 'junta' should not get control of Cyprus or the greater part of it. Here the lines on which many Greeks and others believe Kissinger and the CIA were covertly working begin to emerge. Ioannides could be encouraged to organise a *coup* against Makarios in the belief that the United States approved of it and that Turkey would not intervene. However, after the *coup*, Turkey would exercise her right to send in troops to restore the *status quo*, and the United States would not oppose it. This would create a new balance of forces in Cyprus, tilted in favour of Turkey as a stronger and more dependable member of NATO than Greece. If Ioannides fell, discredited, for provoking a Turkish invasion of Cyprus, so much the better. The stage would be set for a solution of the Cyprus problem.

Such a 'scenario', if it ever existed, was based on a faulty assessment of Turkey's aims and of Greece's reaction. The distinction between the CIA and its Greek offshoot KYP had become so blurred that the local plotters took little account of the international situation, while the makers of policy in Washington were not always aware of what their agents were doing in Greece and Cyprus. Dr Kissinger's reaction to the overthrow of Makarios, the setting-up of a puppet government, Turkey's invasion and her seizure of northern Cyprus strongly suggests that he saw these as a sequence of events essential to a settlement. It does not follow that he planned it this way. Even with his phenomenal capacity for work and for conducting policy on several fronts at the same time, Dr Kissinger had many preoccupations in the summer of 1974. In the Middle East he was trying to clinch a military disengagement agreement between Israel and Syria on the Golan Heights. There were critical SALT talks in Moscow on the limitation of strategic weapons. The Watergate abscess had burst and was poisoning the whole administration in Washington. Kissinger, who never thought of Cyprus as more than an irritant on NATO's under-belly, is unlikely to have foreseen the bitter consequences of the *coup* for American policy.

As for Makarios's escape from his battered palace, the obvious explanation is probably the true one. Through inexperience the 'National Guard' simply overlooked the need to cover the small road at the back beyond the river-bed.

14 A New Turkish Occupation

It took three or four days for the conspirators in the 'National Guard' to get control of Cyprus outside the Turkish Cypriot enclaves. There could be only limited resistance from the Tactical Police Reserve and the pro-Makarios armed bands to a force 20,000 strong, equipped with tanks and artillery. Fierce clashes took place particularly in Limassol and Nicosia, but most Greek Cypriots were stunned by the turn of events, although there had been so much talk of an imminent *coup*. The announcement of Makarios's death, followed by the news that he was alive but a fugitive, together with the sight of the burnt-out presidential palace, brought home to his supporters that the *unthinkable* had happened. The rank-and-file of the Greek Cypriot conscripts in the 'National Guard' were as bewildered as the civilian population. Once the military had taken over the Cyprus Broadcasting Corporation, the Telecommunications Centre and Nicosia airport, the island was virtually cut off from the outside world.

There is still no clear picture of how many people died in the *coup*. Sampson claimed at his press conference on 18 July that it was only 'a few dozen', though reporters suggested to him it was a matter of hundreds. Undoubtedly many old scores were settled in the five days between the *coup* and the invasion, and Turkish Cypriot accounts of the atrocities committed by Greek against Greek should not be dismissed altogether as propaganda. Many government officials were arrested and a number of Makarios's most prominent supporters went into hiding – some, like Lyssarides for part of the time, in a foreign embassy.

Sampson maintained later – in an interview given to a British newspaper after his resignation[1] – that he was surprised at being offered the presidency. He said that he had heard explosions and gun-fire and later had been taken from his home to the 'National Guard' headquarters, believing he was under arrest. There he had been told to find Michael Triantaphyllides, the President of the Supreme Court, and invite *him* to be Makarios's successor. But Triantaphyllides was in Strasbourg, and the next three names on the officers' list also proved to be 'non-starters'. Two were not at home and the third had recently suffered a heart attack. So Sampson – the officers' fifth choice, according to *his* story – agreed to become President on condition that he was not treated as a 'puppet' or expected to deal harshly with supporters of the previous regime. The oath was administered to him the same day by the 'unfrocked' Bishop Yennadios.

In the same interview Sampson denied that he had had any contact with the Greek Government. Yet his friendship with Ioannides was well-known – though the dictator may have seen him more as a ruthless opponent of Makarios than as a likely President. Most Greeks accepted the genuineness of what was later published in the Athenian press as part of a monitored telephone conversation between Sampson and Ioannides on the day after the *coup*. Sampson had spoken of Makarios's escape. 'Nikolaki', said the voice at the other end, 'I want Mouskos's head. You will get it for me. Eh, Nikolaki?'

Sampson announced his political programme when he appeared before the local and foreign press on 18 July, flanked by five of his new 'ministers' and two men with machine-guns. His main emphasis was on rooting-out the alleged corruption of the previous regime and on 'the restoration of human rights', which he said had been trampled upon by 'the self-exiled former President' and the narrow clique around him. As proof of this he paraded a dozen unkempt, bandaged individuals said to have been beaten up or otherwise maltreated in Makarios's gaols. He also produced a collection of whips, chains and other alleged instruments of police torture. Sampson assured the journalists that there would be no ill-treatment of political opponents by his 'government' and that the Turkish Cypriots had nothing to fear from the change of regime. The intercommunal talks would continue with Clerides still as the Greek Cypriot negotiator. When a journalist asked whether the Greek officers of the 'National Guard' would stay in Cyprus, Sampson replied that their position was unchanged. Was this not leading to *de facto* Enosis? Sampson repeated that his 'government' wanted a solution of the Cyprus problem through the enlarged intercommunal talks and added – somewhat surprisingly – that its views on this issue were no different from those of the previous regime.

This did nothing to reassure the Turkish Cypriots. They had watched, fascinated, the drama of events on the other side of the fence. The British High Commission, the UN Force commander and the UN secretary-general's special representative all urged them to remain calm. Denktash at first described the *coup* as an internal affair of the Greek Cypriots. But Sampson had acquired such a reputation with his vicious attacks on the Turkish community ten years before that it expected an onslaught at any moment. Many Turkish Cypriots living outside the enclaves were hurriedly brought in for safety. But it was to Ankara that the community now looked for decisive action.

The Turkish Prime Minister, Mr Bulent Ecevit, immediately denounced the Greek *coup* and hurried off to London the next day to get Britain's agreement to joint military intervention under the Treaty of Guarantee. Mr Harold Wilson's Government, in which Mr James Callaghan was Foreign Secretary, showed no enthusiasm for this. It temporised by inviting the Greek Government to join in three-power consultations in London – a request that, predictably, was rejected since the 'junta' claimed it had no concern with what it said was plainly an internal revolt in Cyprus. Mr Ecevit went away empty-handed and from that moment, if not before, it was clear that nothing was going to prevent a Turkish invasion. Understandably the British Government had no wish to be embroiled again in fighting in Cyprus. Nevertheless, a forthright condemnation of the Greek 'junta' and stronger political support for Turkey's case – with which the British Government sympathised – might have altered the situation or at least bought valuable time.[2]

Events moved rapidly. The UN secretary-general's special representative in Cyprus, Osorio-Tafall, had gone to Paphos to see Makarios even before he was rescued by the RAF, and had been asked by the Archbishop to request an urgent meeting of the Security Council. The Council met formally on the morning of Thursday the 18th and agreed that it would receive Makarios as Head of State. Even the Turkish delegation to the UN told the secretary-general that it recognised Makarios's legitimacy. However the Security Council was obviously divided over what it should do. A group of non-aligned countries wanted an immediate resolution to prevent the Sampson regime from consolidating its position. This move failed because other members, notably the United States, showed no enthusiasm for promoting Makarios's return. Dr Kissinger had seen the Cypriot ambassador on the day of the *coup* and merely told him that Washington would not recognise Sampson before it had a fuller report. There was no condemnation of the *coup*, no expression of regret at the President's reported death or congratulations later on his escape. On the day after the *coup* a State Department spokesman said that, in the administration's view, there had been no outside intervention against Makarios. He added that Dr Kissinger would be seeing him on the following Monday – two days, as it turned out to be, after the Turkish invasion.

By the middle of that fateful week Washington's official view – the Kissinger view – was that Makarios was 'politically finished', that he could not go back to Cyprus unless Ioannides was ousted in Athens – a revealing admission – and that, in spite of the 'junta's' problems, there seemed no likelihood of that at the moment. However, the regional specialists in the State Department did not share the Secretary's views; they wanted him to express support for Makarios as a way of weakening the 'junta'. Kissinger was against this on the grounds that the 'junta' might retaliate by closing the American bases in Greece. The experts also emphasised that, if the administration did intend to recognise a change of regime in Cyprus, somebody less obnoxious to the Turks than Sampson should be found for President. Otherwise they would invade and then it might be impossible to prevent a war between Greece and Turkey.

On the night of 17 July, nearly 72 hours after the *coup*, Dr Kissinger felt obliged to despatch Under-Secretary of State Joseph Sisco, an expert on Cyprus, with instructions to try to 'defuse' what most people now regarded as a highly explosive situation. Sisco stopped briefly in London to see Ecevit, the Turkish Prime Minister, who was still arguing with Callaghan. In Athens he had difficulty in making any contact with Ioannides who refused to do anything to placate the Turks. Then the Secretary of State went on to Ankara.

Meanwhile, during the informal meeting of the Security Council on the 18th, the British delegate had proposed that it should defer adopting a resolution until President Makarios had arrived and could express his views. However he did nothing to lessen Britain's reputation for hypocrisy by saying the Council must take time to decide whether Greece had, in fact, been involved in the *coup*. The Soviet Union and other Communist states, the non-aligned group and a number of Western governments had made it clear they had no doubts on the matter. Makarios arrived in New York on the same day and addressed the Security Council the following evening.

Speaking with controlled emotion he described events leading up to the *coup* and accused the Greek military regime of aggression against Cyprus. He admitted his mistake in trusting the Greek officers of the 'National Guard' – though not the bigger mistake of inviting them to Cyprus in the first place. Makarios appealed to the Security Council to do everything within its power to end the anomalous situation, and specifically to get the recall of all the Greek officers. He rejected the 'junta's' offer to replace those currently serving in Cyprus – another damaging admission – as a mere trick to mislead world opinion.

That was on Friday. Other speakers addressed the Council but no decision was taken. Ecevit was now back in Ankara and Sisco urged him to be patient, but the mediator had come empty-handed from Athens. Sisco saw the Turkish Prime Minister again at four o'clock the next morning, after speaking to Washington, but Ecevit reportedly said: 'We have done it your way for ten years. Now we are going to try it our way'. At dawn a Turkish invasion fleet was heading for Cyprus.

Turkish troops and armour landed on two beaches east and west of Kyrenia and began to converge on the little holiday town and the pass behind it that led into the main Turkish Cypriot enclave north of Nicosia. At the same time planes and helicopters dropped paratroops and equipment inside the enclave while fighter aircraft carried out repeated rocket and bombing attacks on targets in the Greek Cypriot sector of the capital. To everyone's surprise the seaborne invaders met with considerable resistance from the 'National Guard' and suffered unexpected casualties in the first assault. But Turkey quickly threw in more forces, and weight began to tell. The Greek Government had already ordered general mobilisation and began to move armoured units towards the Turkish border in Thrace. President Gizikis declared that Greece had the will and the capacity to defend her national interest in the face of what he called 'unprovoked' aggression against Cyprus. The Turkish Government said it was carrying out a limited police action to restore constitutional legality in the island.

For Makarios the Turkish invasion was the worst blow of all – worse than his own overthrow, worse even than the possibility of war between Greece and Turkey. Ankara had waited for years for just such an opportunity and the Greek 'junta' had played completely into its hands. Makarios at once sent telegrams to all Heads of State except those of Greece and Turkey, denouncing the new aggression and expressing the hope that the Security Council and especially the Great Powers would find a way to end 'this tragic and most dangerous situation'.

It was a vain hope. The Security Council met again on the day of the invasion – 20 July – and, with somewhat more urgency than it had shown the previous evening when the United States delegate, John Scali, had said it would be 'a serious error to rush to judgement', adopted a formal resolution. This *deeply deplored* the fighting and called for an immediate cease-fire. It demanded an immediate end to foreign military intervention which was incompatible with respect for the sovereignty, independence and territorial integrity of Cyprus – an 'escape clause' for Turkey. It merely *requested* the withdrawal without delay of the Greek officers, as asked for by President Makarios. And it called on Greece, Turkey and Britain to negotiate without delay for the restoration of peace and constitutional legality in Cyprus. Forty-eight hours passed before Greece and Turkey agreed to a cease-fire. By that time Kyrenia was in Turkish hands and the invaders had driven a deep wedge into the island.

The delay, which benefited Turkey, was partly due to the fact that the Greek 'junta' had begun to crumble. On the 21st Ioannides had sent a message to the Greek Pentagon announcing his decision to attack Turkey on all fronts, including Cyprus. The chiefs of staff protested: they were ready for a defensive but not for an aggressive war. The next morning they told President Gizikis that they could no longer serve under Ioannides and that a government of the old politicians must be brought back to handle the crisis. Gizikis agreed, but Ioannides confronted the generals and tried to bluster it out. They stood firm; one of them pointedly said he would not go to war on the orders of a subordinate – Ioannides being a mere brigadier. On the 23rd, with a shaky cease-fire now operating in Cyprus, the generals met a group of the old political leaders –

Kanellopoulos, the Prime Minister overthrown by the Papadopoulos *coup* seven years before, Mavros, the leader of the Centre
Union, Averoff, the former Foreign Minister, and several others.
Averoff took the initiative and insisted that only a government
under his old leader, Karamanlis, could adequately cope with the
situation. A telephone call was made to Paris, and Karamanlis,
after eleven years in self-imposed exile, agreed to return as Prime
Minister of a 'Government of National Unity'.

In Cyprus Sampson heard of the collapse of the 'junta' and
threw in his hand. He told his 'War Cabinet' that he was resigning
in favour of Clerides, the constitutional successor to Makarios,
because Athens had let them down. Clerides was duly sworn in by
'Bishop' Yennadios, who was more pleased at his continued recognition as Locum Tenens than at the new choice for President.

For Makarios the dramatic turn of events brought problems as
well as a certain grim satisfaction. At a press conference in New
York on 23 July he expressed his pleasure at the end of military rule
in Greece and at the imminent restoration of democracy there
under such an able and statesmanlike leader as Karamanlis. He
said this would greatly help the situation in Cyprus. But the Archbishop was well aware that Karamanlis would try to exert more
subtle pressures on him than the Colonels had done, to reach an
accommodation with the Turks. Makarios said he expected to
return to Cyprus within the next few weeks and that Clerides had
assumed responsibility as Acting President in accordance with the
constitution and, he emphasised, 'with my agreement'. He also
declared he would be going to Geneva for the tripartite talks
between Greece, Turkey and Britain – though the Security
Council resolution had said nothing about Cypriot participation.
'No agreement', said Makarios, 'will be valid without my approval.'

Then, on the day after the Archbishop's press conference,
Clerides told journalists in Nicosia that he was not an Acting or
caretaker President, but President by virtue of his previous office.
He said he advised Archbishop Makarios not to return to the island
at the moment. It must be left to the people of Cyprus to decide at
elections 'within a matter of months' who would be President.
Clerides announced that he had already seen Vice-President
Denktash and expected there would be further meetings to continue the intercommunal talks. It was a clear hint that he now felt
free of his old master's restraining hand and would conduct his own

policy. Makarios never forgave him for this, and for the hint that he would need to be re-elected as President. The snub from Clerides was only partly effaced by the announcement from Athens the next day that the Karamanlis Government recognised Makarios as still the legitimate Head of State of the Republic of Cyprus.

Makarios had seen Kissinger in Washington and knew he could expect no help there. The Secretary of State had pointedly addressed him as 'Your Beatitude' and not as 'Mr President'. Makarios was plainly dissatisfied with their meeting and told the press afterwards that the United States was pursuing a policy of 'wait and see' which could only make matters worse. Kissinger evidently believed that, after some last-minute manipulation of the crisis, the signals were now set for the solution of the Cyprus problem that the United States had long wanted. The unpopular and dangerous Greek 'junta' had gone – and Washington could and did claim some credit for its collapse. State Department officials said later that Dr Kissinger had been confident at the height of the crisis, between the *coup* and the invasion, that Ioannides and Sampson would both fall through their own folly. Was this proof of some Machiavellian United States plan to push the 'junta' into a suicidal adventure or merely wisdom after the event? Months afterwards, when Ioannides was preparing his defence against his trial, he claimed that he had been seriously misled by the Americans over the possibility of Turkish military intervention. He was also reported to have told Admiral Arapakis, his chief of naval operations: 'If you knew what I knew and had the reassurances that I had before the *coup*, you would have done exactly as I did.' At any rate, the Turks had now gained a major foothold in Cyprus and Ecevit had declared, two days after the invasion, that it would be 'permanent'. There was a responsible civilian government in Athens which must negotiate rather than go to war against a much stronger Turkey. Makarios was out of the way and the moderate Clerides was President of Cyprus. The American 'scenario' was ready; it had only to be acted out.

The Foreign Ministers of Greece, Turkey and Britain met in Geneva on 25 July in accordance with the Security Council's call for tripartite talks. Five days later, after intense round-the-clock argument,[3] they had agreed that the areas controlled by the opposing armed forces in Cyprus should not be extended and that these forces should gradually be reduced. But Gunes refused to give any commitment about the withdrawal of the Turkish army, although Mavros offered an immediate withdrawal of the Greek officers of the 'National Guard' and a limitation of its status to that of a police force. Callaghan managed to get a joint declaration affirming the validity of the 1960 agreements which guaranteed the independence and territorial integrity of Cyprus. But Gunes insisted that there must be a federal system of government, and it was agreed that this would be discussed when they met again in Geneva on 8 August with representatives of the two communities in Cyprus.

However, the fighting continued, in spite of a further call from the Security Council for a cease-fire. Turkey poured more and more armour and men into the Kyrenia sector and began to deploy them eastwards and westwards along the northern coast in what she described as her 'peace operation'. There was bitter resistance from the Greek army contingent and the remnants of the 'National Guard'; many of the conscripts had already fled to their homes. Thousands of Greek refugees began to stream south on either side of the Turkish wedge. At Paphos and Limassol Greek Cypriots took over the smaller Turkish Cypriot enclaves and started another refugee movement. The United Nations peace-keeping force could do little to check the hostilities and, indeed, had no mandate to intervene between Turkey and the Greek Cypriots. Apart from the help it gave to the refugees from both sides, its main achievement was to take over and hold Nicosia international airport in the face of a determined Turkish paratroop attempt to get control of it, which nevertheless put it out of action. One of the more spectacular operations was the Royal Navy's rescue of more than a thousand holiday-makers and British residents from the battle-scarred northern coast of Cyprus.

Makarios flew to London from New York on 30 July and saw Callaghan two days later, after his return from Geneva. The Foreign Secretary could offer him little comfort. By now Turkey had doubled the area in Cyprus that she controlled when the Greek 'junta' collapsed and Sampson resigned. Clerides protested to the United Nations about Turkey's continued aggression, but though the Security Council unanimously authorised the UN peace-keeping force to create a buffer zone between the Turkish army and the Greek Cypriot 'National Guard', it was unable to do so effectively or to prevent violations of the cease-fire by both sides.

The Second Geneva Conference opened formally on 10 August – two days late – with Clerides and Denktash representing their communities; Makarios was not present. There was little in the way of negotiation. Clerides argued, with some support from Callaghan, that the conference could only restore the 1960 constitution, which, he said, he was then willing to revise by negotiation with Denktash. Gunes, for Turkey, insisted that the 1960 constitution was dead and that there were now two autonomous administrations in Cyprus. Mavros, for the Greek Government, rejected the idea that a state which was a guarantor of the 1960 constitution could dictate a new solution by force of arms. Denktash said that Greek and Turkish Cypriots could no longer live together in security, and he proposed a bizonal federation with 34 per cent of the island for the Turkish Cypriots. When Clerides and Mavros dismissed this as unacceptable, Gunes suggested there should be one main autonomous Turkish Cypriot area in the north with five smaller Turkish Cypriot cantons in other parts of the island, the whole still amounting to 34 per cent. Clerides, trying desperately to reach a compromise, asked for an adjournment of thirty-six to forty-eight hours in which he intended to consult Greek Cypriot opinion in Nicosia and President Makarios in London about a plan for 'functional federation' without geographical separation. Callaghan supported the idea of an adjournment but told Clerides that his proposals would not satisfy the Turks. He added that Kissinger – with whom he said he was in constant touch – was not prepared to exert 'further' pressure on Turkey to prevent her expanding her occupation, if the Greek Cypriots would not agree to part of the island – perhaps only 20 per cent – being left under Turkish control. Clerides was even ready to consider this, but Gunes would have no delay. Callaghan urged Turkey not to press her advantage too far, beyond what the Greeks could take; Gunes insisted on his deadline. The conference sat late on 13 August – Makarios's 61st birthday. In the early hours of the next morning Gunes said he considered the negotiations ended since he had had no positive reply to his proposals. At dawn the Turkish troops moved out of their salient and Turkish planes began to bomb Nicosia and Famagusta.

In forty-eight hours the Turks achieved their objective, stopping only when they had driven their long-planned 'Attila Line' from Morphou Bay in the west to Famagusta in the east, slicing off more than a third of the island. Greek villages in the way were overrun and their inhabitants mown down if they offered resistance. In more than one case retreating Greeks massacred Turkish Cypriot civilians, including women and children. The number of Greek Cypriots who fled or were dispossessed eventually amounted to about 180,000 – one in three of their community – though for a time many thousands were trapped in the north. About 50,000 Turkish Cypriots – almost half *their* population – remained south of the 'Attila Line' in Greek-controlled areas or in the British bases where they had taken refuge.

The world watched with seeming impotence. Karamanlis ruled out the possibility of war with Turkey, but under pressure of public opinion withdrew Greece immediately from all military participation in NATO. Turkey declared that her aim in Cyprus was not partition but security and justice for the Turkish Cypriots; she offered a cease-fire and a return to the conference table. Clerides had no option but to accept the cease-fire. The Security Council merely recorded its formal disapproval of the 'unilateral military actions undertaken against the Republic of Cyprus'. The United States Defence Secretary, James Schlesinger, said on 18 August that military aid to Turkey was under review since she had gone beyond what any of her friends or sympathisers were prepared to accept. But this did not prevent the assassination of the American ambassador in Nicosia, Rodger Davies, the next day by a Greek Cypriot gunman during a violent demonstration outside the United States Embassy.

While Clerides and his Cabinet tried to cope with the enormous refugee problem, the loss of the most productive part of Cyprus, the exchange of prisoners and the discussion of other 'humanitarian' issues which was all that Denktash would accept at first, Makarios girded himself in London for a new appeal to the international conscience. He rejected the British suggestion of a simple return to Geneva and also the Soviet proposal of a conference attended by the immediately interested parties and the full Security Council. Instead he proposed that the permanent members of the Security Council – Britain, France, the United States, the Soviet Union and China – together with Greece and Turkey and the two communities in Cyprus should hold talks in New York under the aegis of the United Nations. Makarios said he believed there were good possibilities for Greek and Turkish Cypriot communal autonomy, provided there was a strong central government. The Archbishop gave the impression now that he did not want to return to Cyprus until he had some concrete achievement to offer his people.

He had hopes of meeting Clerides and Karamanlis in Athens to concert action, but there was no welcome for this idea. So in late September Makarios set off on a round of visits to Algeria, Egypt and Yugoslavia to get the support of their 'non-aligned' leaders for his belated acceptance of the concept of 'functional federation'. Lyssarides saw the Archbishop in Cairo and urged him to come back to Cyprus before Clerides became too strong. Makarios promised to return in October, after he had addressed the new session of the United Nations General Assembly. Just before the occasion of this speech there was a huge pro-Makarios rally in Limassol, well-attended by the Left. It prompted Karamanlis to declare the next day that Clerides was the only man who could represent Cyprus and negotiate for it at present. 'The return of the elected President, Archbishop Makarios', the Greek Prime Minister declared, 'is ruled out as long as the crisis continues.'

Clerides however had very little success in negotiating since Denktash refused at first to discuss anything but 'humanitarian' questions – and it was clear that he did not include the return of the refugees in this category. He had already declared northern Cyprus 'autonomous' and threatened to make it 'independent' if the Greek side did not quickly accept 'regional federation'. Ankara said the 'Attila Line' was negotiable, but that Turkey must retain at least 28 per cent of Cyprus to guarantee the security and economic viability of the Turkish Cypriot zone. The Greek Government and Clerides refused to discuss any political solution until the Turkish forces had returned to their positions as they were at the start of the Second Geneva Conference. Turkey said that no forces would be withdrawn in advance of negotiations.

Against this background of deadlock – apart from an agreement between Denktash and Clerides over the exchange of prisoners – President Makarios went to New York and spoke in the UN Assembly's general debate on 1 October. The problem of Cyprus, he said, was not complicated, but very simple. A small member of the United Nations had been the victim of Turkish aggression, and the United Nations must not condone it. Ankara's aim was partition, camouflaged as federation, and this would lead inevitably to 'double annexation' by Turkey and Greece. Makarios rejected geographical federation and declared that a solution of the Cyprus problem must be based on the application of the UN Charter and of previous UN resolutions. He said he was prepared to accept negotiations in a broad international conference held within the framework of the United Nations, but not while part of Cyprus was under foreign military occupation and a third of its people were refugees.

Meanwhile the situation in Turkey had changed. Ecevit had dropped the intractable junior partner in his coalition government – the ultra-chauvinistic National Salvation Party – in mid-September, but he was unable to form another viable adminis-tration. Demirel, his chief opponent, also had no success at first when asked to form a government. With Turkey in the grip of a new political crisis Denktash refused to budge an inch – and could hardly have done so in any case with the Turkish army breathing down his neck.

Clerides was now being sniped at by Lyssarides, the main agi-tator for Makarios's return, as a man who had been prepared to work with the Colonels. This was unjust: Clerides's acceptance that there would have to be some form of federal compromise with the Turkish Cypriots was very different from the 'junta's' aims. Faced with a smear campaign in his own camp, Denktash's stone-walling and Makarios's complete rejection of federation at the United Nations, Clerides threatened to resign. However, on the day after Makarios's speech to the General Assembly, the Arch-bishop had a meeting with Kissinger in New York and was evident-ly subjected to some 'arm-twisting'. Kissinger may have warned him that, if Clerides abandoned the negotiations, the United States would not intervene to prevent the Turks taking over the whole island, if they so wished. At any rate, Makarios issued a statement afterwards, expressing his support for Clerides, and the Acting President withdrew his threat to resign. But two days later Clerides was forced to accept Denktash's view that there could be no political negotiations in Cyprus before they knew the result of the Greek general elections – scheduled for 17 November – and until the Turkish governmental crisis was resolved.

Makarios stayed in America for the United Nations debate on Cyprus at the end of October, briefing Spyros Kyprianou and Tasos Papadopoulos on the conduct of the Greek Cypriot case. On 1 November the General Assembly unanimously adopted a resol-ution urging the speedy withdrawal of all foreign military person-nel from the Republic of Cyprus – apart from the UN peace-keeping force – and calling for the return of all the refugees to their homes in safety. Since it also recommended that the two com-munities in Cyprus should negotiate 'on an equal footing' with a view to reaching a mutually acceptable political settlement,

Turkey felt able to vote for the resolution.

During the next fortnight Turkey withdrew some 5000 troops from Cyprus – out of a total invading force of 40,000 – partly to show goodwill but also to avoid the pressures of the United States Congress for a ban on any further military aid to Ankara. Denktash also agreed to allow about 1600 Greek Cypriots trapped in the north – mostly elderly people – to join their families in the south; it was a 'humanitarian' gesture but also a further step towards the separation of the two communities. Then, after another meeting with Kissinger on 13 November, Makarios announced that he expected to return to Cyprus 'as President' within a few weeks. Whether this was in defiance of advice from the Secretary of State is not clear. It is unlikely Kissinger had been persuaded that a Cyprus settlement was impossible with Makarios 'in exile'. But now that talks 'on an equal footing' had been accepted it was important for the new Ford administration to placate the powerful Greek lobby in Congress which was pressing for the arms ban against Turkey, 'Allowing' Makarios to return to Cyprus may have seemed one way to do this.

Makarios now moved to London and met Clerides there on 21 November in what was officially described as 'a cordial atmosphere'. It was obvious however that Clerides was unhappy about the Archbishop's proposed return and that there was a wide difference in their views of what was now feasible. Clerides had said publicly in Cyprus on 6 November that he thought some form of federation on a geographical basis was inevitable. Makarios had already ruled this out in his speech to the UN General Assembly, though he said later in an interview that he was willing to discuss administrative federation; for him the cardinal point was that there must be no compulsory transfer of populations and that the refugees must be able to return to their homes.

Clerides and Makarios agreed to meet again in Athens at the end of November for talks with Karamanlis, whose New Democracy party had now emerged from Greece's first post-dictatorship elections with a handsome parliamentary majority. Ostensibly the meeting was to coordinate Greek and Greek Cypriot policy on removing the Turkish threat from Cyprus. In fact, Makarios and Clerides were each seeking the endorsement of the Greek Government for their own divergent policies. Clerides said before leaving Nicosia that he still hoped Makarios would not return yet. Denktash had uttered repeated warnings about the effect the Archbishop's presence would have on the intercommunal talks, and the caretaker Government in Ankara had echoed this pessimism, though neither had made any concessions to Clerides. Karamanlis had his own reservations about the wisdom of Makarios's decision but he did not feel he could oppose it.

Makarios drove once again in triumph from Ellinikon Airport to the centre of Athens and addressed a large welcoming crowd in Constitution Square. He made no reference to Clerides, but in a moderately-keyed speech said he was going back to offer the Turkish Cypriots an olive-branch – though not 'earth and water' (the ancient Greek symbols of submission).

In the two days of talks that followed Clerides tried but failed to get a clear 'blueprint' from the Archbishop – which Karamanlis would have endorsed – for negotiations on the basis of geographical federation. Makarios thought the Turks might agree to the system of cantons they had once proposed at Geneva, and that this could be devised so as to preserve a unitary state. Clerides was sure it was too late for that: Turkey would be satisfied now with nothing less than a bizonal federation. In his turn Clerides refused to commit himself to continuing as negotiator unless he had a precise mandate. The joint communiqué issued by Makarios and Karamanlis said they had agreed on a common line which would be the basis for detailed written instructions to Clerides – a phrase that all too clearly revealed the lack of agreement.

On 7 December Makarios was flown to the British base at Akrotiri – Nicosia airport still being closed – and was taken from there, appropriately enough by RAF helicopter, to Nicosia. An estimated 100,000 Greek Cypriots lined the streets to give him a rapturous welcome that recalled his first return from exile in 1959. The refugees waving flags and banners saw him as the champion who would restore them to their homes and lands rather than as the leader whose policies had so much contributed to their tragedy. There was no trouble from EOKA-B. It did no more than scatter leaflets before the Archbishop's arrival, warning him that he must not repeat the mistakes of the past or there would be bloody civil strife again. It was an illusion, the leaflet said, for Makarios to think that he could end the Turkish occupation and secure the return of the refugees. He should speedily withdraw from politics and devote himself to healing the wounds in the Church. In fact, Makarios had already seen two of his 'unfrocked' bishops – Yennadios and Anthimos – in Athens and had agreed in principle to their recovering their former dignities – though as retired rather than incumbent Metropolitans – provided they instructed their followers to support the Archbishop.

There were wild emotional scenes in Greek Cypriot Nicosia as Makarios drove first to the Church of St John in the old walled city to conduct a service of thanksgiving a few hundred yards from the 'Attila Line' and the nearest Turkish machine-guns. Then he walked next door to the archbishopric and addressed the crowd from a balcony. In moderate, restrained terms the President assured his people that he would not accept the *fait accompli* of the Turkish invasion. He said he was ready to seek a settlement that would include 'self-government' for the Turkish Cypriots and lead to peaceful coexistence between the two communities. Makarios gave no more precise indication of the solution he envisaged, but he again ruled out any transfer of populations which would amount to partitioning of the island. The Archbishop also gave a warning against 'outdated chauvinistic tendencies and prejudices of any kind' but he promised he would not persecute his old enemies or try to bring to justice those who had been involved in the *coup* against him; on the contrary, there would be a general amnesty for the sake of Greek Cypriot unity.

Denktash held a press conference the next day for the many foreign journalists who were in Cyprus. He noted with approval that there had been no mention of Enosis in the Archbishop's speech and no calls for it from the crowd. Denktash said he hoped that, when Makarios had seen the 'bitter reality' of the situation, he would be ready to accept the present geographical separation as the basis for negotiations, though there would be room for some Greeks in the Turkish region. The Archbishop and he would negotiate as the leaders of the two communities, not as President and Vice-President.

The 'bitter reality' was soon borne in upon Makarios as he toured the Greek Cypriot sector. Nearly 40 per cent of the island was in Turkish hands: almost all the cereal-growing plain of the Mesaoria, the dense citrus groves around Morphou, the tobacco-fields of the Karpass, the industrial estates north-east of Nicosia and the two most important tourist towns, Famagusta and Kyrenia, with dozens of luxury hotels and apartment blocks. Almost every house in the south had its refugees. For the less fortunate there were vast tented camps, turned into quagmires by the winter rains. And the fate of some 2000 Greek Cypriots, missing since the *coup* and the invasion, was still unknown.[4]

A week before Christmas Makarios tried to make contact with the Turkish Cypriot refugees in the British base area of Akrotiri, but the road was barricaded against him and some of the cars in his convoy were stoned. Denktash and the Government in Ankara both denounced the Archbishop's action as a political manoeuvre; they were then pressing hard for the Turkish Cypriots to be sent to the north. By contrast with the indignation of the Turkish Cypriot refugees – which was probably not spontaneous – the majority of Greek Cypriot refugees continued to show, even months and years later, an extraordinary lack of bitterness towards the Turkish Cypriots who had taken their homes.

Early in January 1975 Makarios announced the formation of a new nine-man Cabinet. A number of the old faces were there, but again there was no one to represent AKEL or Lyssarides's EDEK, though both the left-wing parties had demanded a government of national unity. Makarios was determined to keep the direction of policy firmly in his own hands, though he realised he had little room to manoeuvre. He was careful to warn the refugees that they must be patient and that he could not work miracles. But the smile that still lit up the deepening sadness of his expression often seemed to belie this.

Clerides had resigned the Presidency with a good grace and gave no sign that he saw his hopes frustrated. But he knew he was back again on a short leash as negotiator and the written 'guidelines' he had been promised never materialised. His first formal talks with Denktash after Makarios's return took place on 14 January. They had agreed in the preliminaries to tackle the constitutional issues, beginning with such matters as the powers and functions of the central government on the assumption that there would be some form of federation. When Clerides tried to raise the question of the refugees as a matter of extreme urgency on humanitarian grounds, Denktash insisted that this was a political issue which must be left till there was agreement on a bizonal federation. The talks were further jeopardised by the British Government's announcement the next day that it had agreed to allow the 8000-odd Turkish Cypriots in the British base areas who wanted to go to Turkey to be evacuated there. Britain, which had been under strong pressure from Ankara, argued unconvincingly that the arrangement might help to break the deadlock over the refugees and encourage Turkey to allow some Greek Cypriots to return to the north. Makarios's

Government was furious; it had wanted to use the Turkish Cypriot refugees as 'hostages' for the proper treatment of the 20,000 Greek Cypriots still 'enclaved' in the north. It is difficult however to see what else the British Government could have done. It was impossible to keep the Turkish Cypriots in the bases indefinitely or to guarantee their safety if they were released into the Greek Cypriot sector, though Makarios would have tried, for obvious political reasons, to have made them feel secure. Also, thousands of Turkish Cypriots had already made their way north, often with the help of Greek Cypriots who were anxious to see them go and to take over their property. But Britain's actions seemed like collusion with Turkey for an official transfer of populations. Before the end of January the Turkish Cypriots evacuated by Ankara from the British base areas were being installed in Greek Cypriot property in the north.

Makarios's attitude hardened appreciably. On 26 January, at a memorial service in Phaneromeni Church for those who had been killed during the Turkish invasion, he declared – echoing the words he had spoken in that place twenty-two years before during his Enosis campaign – that he would look East or West for help to preserve the independence and integrity of Cyprus. 'Go to Moscow' came the cry from a congregation whose fathers, a generation earlier, had sung the 'Internationale' in the same church.

The pressures built up. On 5 February the embargo on arms for Turkey called for by the United States Congress – in spite of protests from Dr Kissinger – came into force because by that date Turkey, still under a caretaker government, had made no move towards solving the Cyprus problem. Denktash – clearly prompted by Ankara – called off the next meeting with Clerides, scheduled for the 10th. Three days later he announced the setting up of a Constituent Assembly to reorganise the administration of northern Cyprus 'on the basis of a secular and federated state' until such time as a biregional Federal Republic could be established with the Greek Cypriot community. In proclaiming unilaterally what was now described as 'The Turkish Federated State of Cyprus' Denktash, with Ankara's backing, ruled out any discussion of the Greek Cypriot proposals for a multi-regional federation which Clerides had sent him on the 10th.

Makarios at once called for an emergency meeting of the UN Security Council to denounce this move as a flagrant violation of international treaties and a defiance of the United Nations. He also said he would 'turn to Moscow' for help in fighting this further step towards partition. But when the Security Council adopted a resolution by consensus on 12 March, it did no more than 'regret' the proclamation of a 'Turkish Federated State of Cyprus', as tending to compromise free negotiations, and call upon the UN secretary-general to get the parties to the conference table again 'under new agreed procedures'.

It was another set-back for Makarios and further proof that, even if some Western governments genuinely deplored Turkish intransigence and the well-substantiated reports of the ill-treatment of Greek Cypriots still in the north, they were not pre-pared to apply sanctions against Turkey. At the same time the Archbishop could not seek Soviet political help, whatever he might say at rhetorical moments. There were strong rumours that Kara-manlis had warned him that he could not rely on continued Greek support if he went to Moscow to invite Soviet intervention. Makarios's use of the 'Moscow gambit' was primarily to keep the support of Lyssarides and AKEL, who were excluded from his Government though not from consultation.

The 'new agreed procedures' suggested by the UN secretary-general, Dr Kurt Waldheim, and accepted by the two Cypriot communities led to six rounds of talks over the next two years, five of them in Vienna and one in New York. They were hardly negotiations. In the first round, which opened in the Austrian capital on 28 April 1975, with Waldheim in the chair, Clerides and Denktash agreed to set up a joint committee to discuss a federal constitution. Denktash insisted that there must be a 50:50 ratio in the central government and promised to submit precise territorial proposals at their second meeting. This began, again in Vienna, on 5 June, but Denktash refused to make any proposals about the amount of territory the Turkish Cypriots should retain since the Greek Cypriots had not yet conceded the principle of a bizonal federation. The negotiators came together for a third round at the end of July. Some 800 Greek Cypriots had recently been sent south from the Karpass area and Denktash had threatened to expel the remaining 10,000 Greek Cypriots in the north unless the similar number of Turkish Cypriots in the south were allowed to go to the 'Turkish Federated State'. Clerides reluctantly agreed to let them go in return for a commitment from Denktash that the Greek Cypriots in the north could stay if they wished and enjoy a normal life. Denk-tash again promised to produce a comprehensive plan for a settlement before the next meeting.

The fourth abortive round was held in September in New York, where Waldheim had to be for the UN General Assembly. It was abandoned after only one session because no formal proposals had been tabled. It needed strong pressures from Greece and Turkey to get a fifth round of talks in Vienna in February 1976. Again there was no progress beyond an agreement that both sides would submit proposals before a sixth round of talks scheduled for May.

In the meantime the Greek Cypriot position had considerably worsened from most points of view. The seven-month political crisis in Turkey had ended in April 1975 with the formation of a new government under Mr Demirel, whose willingness to make concessions over Cyprus – if he had any – was completely inhibited by the two chauvinistic ultra-right-wing parties in his coalition. Denktash's stalling appeared to be mainly a device to gain time to change the demographic character of northern Cyprus. In spite of his promise to respect the rights of the Greek Cypriots still living there, they were subjected to outright intimidation – often from the Turkish army – as well as to the psychological pressures of being restricted in their access to churches and schools. In the summer of 1976 they were crossing to the south at the rate of forty a day. By then many thousands of mainland Turks had been shipped to Cyprus, ostensibly as seasonal labour but in reality to take over Greek Cypriot property and bring the population of the north nearer to the desired figure of 200,000.

From time to time Denktash threatened to declare the 'Turkish Federated State' independent, if the Greek Cypriots refused to accept federation on his terms. It never seemed likely that Ankara would let him do so, since this would have made a settlement impossible. In any case Denktash was shrewd enough to realise that he could not make his 'state' viable. Cooperation with the Greek Cypriots on equal terms was infinitely preferable to being absorbed into Turkey as an off-shore province. The grandiose development schemes envisaged by Ankara at the beginning of the occupation had not materialised. The Cyprus pound – a relatively strong currency – had quickly disappeared from the north and been replaced by the frequently-devalued Turkish lira. There were virtually no tourists – except Turks – and these brought in no hard currency. For Makarios there was a certain grim satisfaction in hearing of Denktash's difficulties: his inability to maintain the prosperity of the north, the restrictions on his authority imposed by the Turkish army, and the clashes between his own people and the unpopular mainland Turks, who were often uncouth Anatolian peasants or members of unwanted minorities. By contrast Makarios's Government had worked 'miracles' in rehousing and rehabilitating the refugees. The economy of the south was soon booming with new enterprise as the resilient Greeks developed Limassol, Larnaca and Paphos to replace the loss of Famagusta and Kyrenia. But this very achievement and the economic weakness of the north only encouraged Makarios to believe that he could still play for time.

He expected little help from the United Nations. The General Assembly passed another basically pro-Greek resolution in November 1975, which only Turkey opposed, though there were nine abstentions. It stood no more chance of being implemented than any of the previous resolutions. However, in February 1976 Clerides and Denktash agreed to exchange written proposals on the constitutional and territorial issues within six weeks and before they met again in Vienna. Denktash privately persuaded Clerides to undertake to give him the Greek Cypriot proposals ten days before he would submit his own. To Clerides it seemed a harmless procedural concession and one that might even incline Denktash to be more reasonable in his opening bid, once he had seen the Greek Cypriot proposals. However, it was officially stated that the proposals would be submitted simultaneously – which was what Makarios wanted. Denktash then broke the confidentiality when he announced that the Greek Cypriot proposals, particularly on territory, were 'unacceptable' and 'not serious'. Immediately there was an uproar on the Greek Cypriot side, especially from the Left – AKEL and the small but vocal EDEK led by Lyssarides. They had long regarded Clerides as a 'traitor', the man who had tried to prevent Makarios's return in order to reach a settlement with the Turks that would legitimise their possession of a large part of Cyprus. Makarios affected ignorance of the Clerides-Denktash arrangement, though some people believe it was no secret on the Greek side. Since Denktash had scored a tactical victory, Clerides felt he was obliged to resign as negotiator. After eight years in this position, with no chance now of having a free hand, he was not loth to go. In his place Makarios appointed Tasos Papadopoulos, who could be trusted to keep in step with him.

The proposals submitted by Denktash some ten days later called for a biregional republic in which two federated states should exercise full powers and authority separately in their own territories while sharing equally in the limited powers reserved to the central government. This was what the Turkish Cypriots had proposed at Vienna a year earlier and the Greek Cypriots had totally rejected. Denktash produced no proposals on territory on the grounds that the Greek Cypriot offer of 20 per cent of the land was 'unreasonable'. He had already said there could be only minor modifications of the existing demarcation line.

There can be no doubt that Makarios welcomed the opportunity to get rid of Clerides, if he did not actually help to engineer it. Their approaches were no longer compatible. Clerides had reluctantly come to accept that no force was likely to shift the Turkish army and that, since the two communities were now effectively separated, the only negotiable issues left were the powers of the central government, the size of the territories to be 'federated' and some freedom of movement between them. An early agreement on a 'package deal' was essential, in his view, to prevent complete *de facto* partition. Makarios still insisted publicly on a unitary 'federal' state in which the Turkish Cypriots' share of the land and of powers in the central government should be proportionate to their ratio of the population. He also required the withdrawal of the Turkish army 'without further delay', an end to the Turkish 'colonisation' of the north and complete freedom for Cypriots of either community to travel or reside in any part of the proposed 'Federal Republic'. Makarios frequently spoke of the 'long struggle' that lay ahead before there could be a just settlement. In private he showed that he was prepared to concede more than he would put on paper, and he saw the 'long struggle' partly as necessary to accustom his people to the bitter truth that many of the refugees would never return to their homes. To the Turks it still sounded like the old arrogant Greek claim to a dominant role in Cyprus.

Makarios had now entered upon the most static phase of his political career, apart from his exile in Seychelles. The mental and physical drive was still there, but the gears could not engage: there seemed no way forward or backward out of the *impasse*. At the same time the Archbishop found himself preoccupied again with maintaining his position as undisputed leader of the Greek Cypriot community.

Shortly before the dropping of Clerides, he had been forced to order the arrest of Nikos Sampson, who had been included in the general amnesty proclaimed by Makarios on his return in December 1974. Sampson had gone back to edit his two newspapers and, after lying low for a time, felt bold enough to begin a new anti-Makarios, pro-Enosis campaign. In January 1976, on the second anniversary of Grivas's death, he made an impassioned speech in justification of the *coup* that had brought him to the Presidency for eight inglorious days. Despite the amnesty an investigation was ordered, and on 17 March Sampson was arrested and charged with complicity in the *coup*. At the end of August he was sentenced to twenty years imprisonment, specifically for aiding warlike activities against the state and usurping the office of President.[5] During the intervening months AKEL and Lyssarides tried hard to persuade Makarios to purge the government and public services, including the police, of some 2000 persons who, they alleged, had supported the *coup*. Makarios refused to stir up a hornet's nest and lose the support of the Right, but Sampson had to be silenced.

The Greek Cypriot Left then concentrated on getting new elections to the House of Representatives, which had been unchanged since 1970. Makarios too was keen to have endorsement of his firm stand against the demands of the Turks. During the longest and liveliest run-up to elections that Cyprus had yet known three parties made common cause to support the policy of the 'long struggle' and drive Clerides into the wilderness. AKEL and EDEK were joined on the Right by a large section of the old nationalist *Eniaion* which was loyal to Makarios rather than to Clerides; it emerged now as the new 'Democratic Front' under the leadership of Spyros Kyprianou, the former Foreign Minister, who had returned to active political life after a long period of ill-health and more than one heart attack. Clerides opposed this odd alignment with a 'Democratic Rally' created from those who accepted with him the need for realistic negotiations with the Turks before it was too late. Unfortunately for Clerides he also had the support of EOKA-B elements which were still ready to make territorial concessions to the Turks in order to achieve the union of the rest of Cyprus with Greece. In the elections of 5 September the 'triple alliance' swept the board. Kyprianou and his Democratic Front won twenty-one out of the thirty-five seats, AKEL took nine – again having limited the number of candidates it put forward to this figure as it had done in 1970 – while Lyssarides and EDEK gained four places. The combination of parties against Clerides in an election organised on the 'simple majority' system left him without a single seat in the House of Representatives, though his Democratic Rally received 24.1 per cent of the votes. Tasos Papadopoulos, the new negotiator, stood as an Independent with the backing of the three anti-Clerides parties and won the remaining seat. Makarios now appeared to have solid backing that stretched from the Nationalist Right to the Communist Left, leaving out only EOKA-B, the disgraced Clerides and those 'misguided' enough to share his views.

Denktash had held elections in the north in June. His National Unity party won 30 out of the 40 seats in the Turkish Cypriot Assembly with only 54 per cent of the votes, which reflected a measure of discontent both with his internal policies and with the lack of progress towards a settlement. But he was returned as 'President' of the 'Turkish Federated State of Cyprus' unopposed.

The Turkish Cypriots had expressed great moral indignation at Makarios's appointment of Tasos Papadopoulos as the new negotiator. They recalled his original links with EOKA, his part-responsibility for the 'Akritas Plan' to suppress Turkish Cypriot resistance in 1963–4 and subsequent statements that he made in support of Enosis. Denktash quickly seized on the opportunity to downgrade the talks by appointing Mr Umit Suleyman Onan as *his* negotiator. No further meetings were scheduled, and when Makarios offered to meet Denktash himself in June – though not to negotiate on equal terms – the offer was refused.

The annual United Nations debate on Cyprus in November 1976 gave Makarios no encouragement but by the beginning of 1977 there were indications that both sides in Cyprus were moving towards a resumption of their dialogue. The pressures were greater on Denktash. Although his community professed to feel secure at last from Greek oppression, it was not happy with the influx of mainland Turks, the reluctance even of Islamic countries to recognise the 'Turkish Federated State' and the prospect of its being sucked further into the depressed Turkish economy. Denktash had also noted an interview which Makarios had given to *The Times* a week before Christmas. The Archbishop had then tacitly accepted the idea of a bizonal federation, as distinct from a cantonal system or 'functional federation', and had said that, once the amount of territory to be administered by the Turkish Cypriots was agreed, there should be no difficulty in drawing a new map of Cyprus. He still argued that they should have not much more than 20 per cent of the island, though when he had attended the Helsinki Conference on European Security in 1975 he reportedly told several Western heads of government that he would accept a bizonal solution if the Turks would reduce their claim to 25 per cent.

On 27 January 1977 Makarios had his first meeting with Denktash for thirteen years. The approach came from the Turkish Cypriot side and, after some sparring over Denktash's designation, they met on the neutral territory of the United Nations peace-keeping force headquarters at the Ledra Palace Hotel in the presence of the UN special representative, Señor Xavier Perez de Cuellar of Peru. Denktash said he was prepared to cut back the Turkish Cypriot zone to between 32 and 33 per cent of the island's territory in return for the right settlement. Makarios replied that the offer was not good enough, whereupon Denktash said the figure was 'negotiable'. They met again on 12 February, this time with the UN secretary-general, Dr Waldheim, present. They then agreed to resume the intercommunal talks, which had lapsed for almost a year, and – in what seemed to be a major advance – worked out mutually acceptable 'guidelines' for the negotiations. The leaders of the two communities declared they were seeking 'an independent, non-aligned, bicommunal federal republic'; that the territory to be administered by each community should be 'discussed in the light of economic viability or productivity and land-ownership'; that questions of principle like freedom of movement and freedom to settle were open for discussion, 'taking into consideration the fundamental basis of a bicommunal federal state and certain practical difficulties which may arise for the Turkish Cypriot community'; and, finally, that the powers and functions of the central federal government should be 'such as to safeguard the unity of the country, having regard to the bicommunal character of the State'.

The first round of talks – or the sixth since the Turkish invasion – began in Vienna on 31 March and lasted for eight days. It had been decided, in agreement with Waldheim, that the Greek Cypriots should put forward the first territorial proposals while the Turkish Cypriots took the initiative with a constitutional plan, on the understanding that each side would discuss the other's offers in a 'meaningful' way. This was a tactical error on Makarios's part, and repeated the mistake made by Clerides. Tasos Papadopoulos produced a map showing the 'Attila Line' pushed back so as to restore much of the citrus-growing area around Morphou in the west, a bulge north-east of Nicosia, half the Karpass Peninsula, all

Salamis Bay and the modern part of Famagusta (Varosha) to the Greek Cypriots. The area to be left to the Turkish Cypriots was no more than the 20 per cent proposed by the Greek side a year earlier – in spite of Makarios's previous hints of 25 per cent or more.[6] Papadopoulos also emphasised that the territorial offer was part of a 'package deal' and could not be separated from recognition of the principles of freedom of movement and settlement and the right of all refugees to return to their homes.

This was unrealistic even as an opening bid and Onan, the Turkish Cypriot negotiator, rejected the territorial offer as contrary to the 'guidelines' and 'totally unacceptable', without producing any counter-proposals. On the constitutional side the Turkish Cypriots demanded equal sovereignty with the Greek Cypriots. The Federal President, they said, should have only representational powers and be alternately a Greek and a Turk. Each 'federated state' should have its own constitution, its own armed forces and its own reserve bank and customs regulations. Papadopoulos promptly rejected this Turkish Cypriot 'outline' as falling short of substantive constitutional proposals and also as being incompatible with the 'guidelines' which were for a unitary, if bicommunal state. The talks ended with no agreement except that the negotiators would meet again in Nicosia about the middle of May.

The lack of progress, even after the supposed 'breakthrough' of Makarios's meetings with Denktash, caused no great surprise. It was a bigger shock for the Greek Cypriots to learn from a laconic government announcement on 4 April, during the talks, that Makarios had experienced what was described as 'a mild coronary episode' the previous day. He had been taken ill after officiating at a Sunday morning service. Lyssarides was quickly with him, as his personal physician, and heart specialists were called in. The government spokesman said there was no cause for alarm, though the President would have to 'slow down' for a time. It was just before Easter, a particularly onerous time for Greek Orthodox clergy, and Makarios always carried a full load of religious duties. But he was only sixty-three. His health had always been good. He had never had any serious illness. He ate sparingly and seldom drank wine, but he was – in private – a heavy smoker of cigarettes, like most Greeks.

Makarios believed he had gone as far as he could in concessions to the Turks. He had accepted that there should be a Turkish Cypriot region. It meant that many thousands of Greek Cypriots would not be able to return to their homes, since few would want to live under a Turkish Cypriot administration and, in any case, their numbers would have to be limited so as not to upset the ethnic make-up of the region. But Makarios was adamant that the central government must be strong enough to hold the two regions together, and he was not prepared to concede equality in this to the other community. He also insisted on the right of any Cypriot citizen to own property or work anywhere in the Republic; to the Turkish Cypriots this carried the threat of again being dominated by the more thrusting, businesslike Greek.[7]

Although Ankara had encouraged Denktash to seek agreement with Makarios, Demirel's coalition government was too weak to make any concessions over Cyprus. In the hope of getting a stronger government capable of tackling Turkey's worsening economic situation and the growth of political violence, elections were brought forward from October to June. Ecevit emerged from them as the leader of the largest party in the National Assembly but with no overall majority. After a month of trying to govern without resorting to another coalition he abandoned the attempt. On the last day of his premiership, 20 July, he loosed a Parthian shot at his jubilant successor, Demirel, evidently with the intention of embarrassing him over Cyprus. It was time, said Ecevit, to open Varosha (the modern Greek Cypriot part of Famagusta) to settlement.

The announcement created great consternation among Greek Cypriots. Varosha, with its dozens of tourist hotels and restaurants, had been sealed off by the Turkish army immediately after its capture in August 1974. It was now an eerie, deserted 'ghost town'. The United Nations peace-keeping force had reported systematic and apparently 'official' looting of the town by the Turkish military. No Turkish Cypriots – not even members of Denktash's administration – were allowed into it. The belief had grown that Ankara was keeping Varosha for eventual use as a bargaining card in the negotiations; with the minimum sacrifice of territory the Turks could offer to let some 40,000 Greek Cypriots return to their homes and businesses in return for a settlement. This may have been an ulterior motive, but the Turks' prime reason for keeping Varosha unoccupied was that they had not got the trained staff or the experience to run it as a tourist resort.

Ecevit's statement coincided with the third anniversary of the

Turkish invasion of Cyprus. It extinguished any Greek Cypriot expectation that Turkey was ready to give back territory even in exchange for a 'federal' solution. The following day Makarios held a press conference at the archbishopric for a party of journalists who had just finished taking part in an international symposium on Cyprus. He said, in answer to a question, that, if the Turks carried out their 'threat' to open up Varosha for settlement, it would 'eliminate any hope of solving the Cyprus problem in the near future'. It was the answer of a tired man with his back to the wall who will not admit that all hope is lost.

It was also one of Makarios's last public appearances; within a fortnight he was dead. On Sunday, the last day of July, he felt indisposed but did not tell his entourage. It was not until late on the following Tuesday evening – according to the official announcement after his death – that he 'appeared to be suffering from a major cardiac crisis'. Doctors were summoned and Karamanlis sent a heart specialist to Nicosia during the night in the plane normally reserved for the President of Greece. There was little that could be done. Makarios died at a quarter past five on the morning of Wednesday, 3 August – ten days short of his 64th birthday.

There had been no warning that the end was near until the last fatal seizure. The Archbishop appeared to have recovered completely from his earlier heart attack in April, though it was known that this had been more severe than was admitted at the time. He had given up smoking and was even more careful about his diet. The only thing his doctors could not persuade him to do – Lyssarides told the present writer in the week before Makarios's death – was to lighten his work-load. Yet whatever private strains he felt, he seemed relaxed and calm; his courtesy and consideration for others remained to the end.

The news of Makarios's death stunned the Greek world – and shocked many others who had almost come to believe that the Archbishop was 'indestructible'. In the Greek sector of Nicosia the 'National Guard' and the police were put on immediate alert in case there were armed clashes between the remnants of EOKA-B and the extreme Left. There were no disturbances. But every Cypriot, Greek or Turk, and every government involved in the Cyprus problem realised that with the death of Makarios the future of the island was again unpredictable. For seventeen years as President and for ten years longer as Archbishop and Ethnarch he had been the one constant factor in an ever-variable equation.

The Greek Cypriot Cabinet and the 'National Council' that had largely superseded it met jointly at six o'clock on the morning of Makarios's death and decreed forty days of public mourning. Spyros Kyprianou, as President of the House of Representatives, automatically became Acting President of the Republic. The constitution prescribed that, on the death of the President, elections for his successor should follow within 45 days. However, for the sake of their precarious national unity and to have time to adjust to the new situation, the Greek Cypriot political leaders agreed that Kyprianou should stay in office until the following February, when Makarios's term would have ended. The fact that Kyprianou was known to be in poor health and had indicated his intention of retiring from politics only a week or two before Makarios's death added a new spice to the political brew that was soon fermenting.

Makarios's body was laid in state in full canonicals of gold and purple in the Church of St John, next to the archbishopric. Thousands of Greek Cypriots filed past the open coffin and paid a tribute of tears and kisses to the man who had been their leader for so long. Messages of condolence and eulogies of the dead President poured in from around the world. Karamanlis urged the Greek Cypriots to rally around the national ideals for which Makarios had given his life when he was so much needed. Ecevit, now leader of the Opposition in Turkey, sent his not entirely tongue-in-cheek sympathy to the Greek Cypriots; he knew at least that Makarios could have made an agreement stick. Queen Elizabeth II, who had last met Makarios at the Commonwealth Prime Ministers' Conference in London two months before, said he would be missed for his 'valuable contribution' to Commonwealth councils. Mr Callaghan, as Prime Minister, said Britain would 'continue to strive' for 'a just and peaceful solution to the tragic problem of Cyprus' which would be 'the lasting memorial he [Makarios] would most desire'. President Carter called him 'a great world statesman' but was even wider of the mark than the customary indulgence of the occasion would allow when he described the Archbishop as 'leader of the Cypriot nation'.

Makarios had carefully chosen the site of his tomb and ordered its unusual design, though all this was kept secret till after his death. He wanted to be buried at a spot high above Kykko Monastery, from where his own village of Ano Panayia is visible in the distance across the valley. The place is known as Throni, the Throne [of the Virgin], and Makarios must have come to know it well during his long novitiate. Bulldozers worked night and day to clear a road to the chosen spot, just modestly below the peak, and the tomb itself had to be scooped out of the rocky mound like the top of an egg. Then a dome was built of polygonal stones, open both to the East and the West, and the approach was made like the entrance to a Mycenaean 'beehive' tomb.

Early on the morning of 8 August the formal funeral service was held in Nicosia, with all the subdued splendour of the Byzantine rite, in the presence of the representatives of more than fifty countries. Kyprianou delivered the funeral oration, addressing Makarios as one of the greatest leaders of all time who now passed into the pantheon of the immortals. All the people, all Hellenism – he declared – took an oath that day to continue the struggle faithfully along the road Makarios had charted till his vision was realised. Then a long procession set out on the sixty-mile journey to Kykko. Almost the whole Greek Cypriot population lined the route. Women in their peasant black sobbed and cried: 'Why have you abandoned us?' Banners proclaimed: 'Makarios lives. He will be with us always.' For the first half of the journey the route ran close to the 'Attila Line'; then it swept up into the mountains through forest-land which had seen some of the fiercest encounters between EOKA and the British. Suddenly, on that August day, the sky darkened and there was torrential rain till Kykko was reached.[8] The last mile of rough road to Throni was strewn with laurel and myrtle. Kyprianou, his ministers, the political leaders and the bishops crowded into the small vault and the old Abbot of Kykko, Chrysostomos, pronounced a benediction. The coffin was lowered into the grave draped in the Greek and Cypriot flags. Then the high dignitaries and afterwards the common people threw earth into the grave until it was filled.[9]

Epilogue

Clerides and most of his party wanted elections for Makarios's successor as President to be held early in September, within the time-limit laid down by the constitution. He argued that any uncertainty about the leadership would create yet more troubles for the Greek Cypriots, and he obviously thought his own chances of securing it were good. To head him off, the other three parties – AKEL, EDEK and the right-of-centre Democratic Front, representing virtually the whole House of Representatives, or the Greek Cypriot part of it – came to an agreement that Kyprianou should be confirmed as President until February 1978, when Makarios's term would have expired. Clerides had to accept this but he made it clear that he would still be a candidate, and there was every prospect of a bitterly-contested election in the spring. However, Clerides subsequently withdrew, after the temporary kidnapping of Kyprianou's son by EOKA-B in December had rallied much sympathy for the sitting President and his handling of the affair and reduced Clerides's chances because of the suspect support *he* had from the extreme Right. In the event Kyprianou was proclaimed President unopposed for a full new term.

Meanwhile Bishop Chrysostomos of Paphos, the Locum Tenens and Makarios's protégé, was elected Archbishop without opposition. A big bluff man in middle age, he declared he had no political ambitions, but he soon made it apparent that, as Ethnarch, he was wholly opposed to any compromise with the Turks and Turkish Cypriots and was in favour of a 'long struggle'.[1]

President Kyprianou showed that he too had no inclination to resume the dialogue with the Turks, although Ecevit had become Prime Minister again and there were expectations that he would make new proposals if the American arms embargo against

272

Turkey were lifted. Kyprianou indicated that he had moved away from Makarios's acceptance of a bizonal republic – in submitting a map showing a proposed territorial division – and he now insisted that 'federation' was incompatible with the idea of a unitary state.

The assassination of a well-known Egyptian editor and friend of President Sadat by Palestinian gunmen while he was attending a conference in Nicosia led to a disastrous clash at Larnaca airport when an Egyptian anti-terrorist commando unit was mown down by the Greek Cypriot 'National Guard'. This did nothing to enhance President Kyprianou's international reputation, and Egypt broke off relations with Cyprus.

Ecevit's eventual offer in Cyprus envisaged leaving the Turkish Cypriots still in control of about 35 per cent of the island and included a demand that the two 'federated' states should each have its own assembly, its own defence forces and the right to conclude treaties with other countries. The Greek Cypriots rejected this as not even a basis for discussion. When Denktash subsequently made a proposal that Varosha, the modern part of Famagusta, might be returned to Greek occupation on certain conditions, Kyprianou turned it down immediately, but was persuaded by Greek Cypriot hotel-keepers and restaurant-owners to think again. However, his counter-proposals on Varosha were unacceptable to the Turkish Cypriots and the idea lapsed.[2]

In the summer of 1978 Kyprianou claimed to have discovered a Greek Cypriot plot against him, which he later said he could not reveal for security reasons; nobody took it very seriously. At the same time he dismissed the negotiator in the intercommunal talks, Tasos Papadopoulos, with a letter in which he accused him of being blinded by sick ambition. Papadopoulos was not accused of being involved with the 'conspiracy' but he waived his parliamentary immunity so that, as he said, he could refute the ridiculous charges against him. He declared there was a government attempt to smear him because he had said Kyprianou intended to abandon the intercommunal talks.[3] Significantly no new negotiator was appointed.

In the autumn Kyprianou tried to get the UN Security Council to order sanctions against Turkey until she withdrew her army from Cyprus, but predictably the attempt failed. Then, after many months without any sign of forward movement, Kyprianou and Denktash were brought together in May 1979 in the presence of the UN secretary-general, Dr Waldheim, and they agreed on a ten-point formula for resuming talks. The framework was to be the Makarios-Denktash 'guidelines' of February 1977, together with the UN resolutions on Cyprus. The two men promised that their negotiators would meet continuously in Nicosia with the aim of reaching a settlement based on the concept of an independent bicommunal and non-aligned Cyprus. The talks broke up after the first meetings in June because Denktash insisted that bicommunal must mean bizonal and Kyprianou refused to continue negotiations on that basis. Archbishop Chrysostomos was against the idea of talks altogether. Two years after Makarios's death the prospect of any real dialogue between Greek and Turkish Cypriots looked very remote. The fact that the Greek Cypriots still missed Makarios so much was an unspoken comment that they did not like the continuing deadlock.

Dr Kissinger is reported as saying of Makarios that he was 'too big for such a small island'. That judgement was probably correct. But in another sense Makarios was also perhaps too small for the responsibilities of a role thrust upon him when he had very little experience of the world. The narrowness of his education – the village school, the seminary at Kykko, the Greek gymnasium, the theological and law schools in Athens and the post-graduate studies at Boston – had left him, at the age of thirty-five, with little more than an academic training to be a priest, a teacher or a lawyer in a purely Greek environment. His sudden appointment to the see of Kitium was less a recognition of outstanding talent in any general sense than proof of the limited field for recruiting to the Cypriot hierarchy. Years of political wrangling between the bishops, a feeble but disastrous revolt against colonial rule, repressive British laws and the growth of a strong, left-wing anti-clericalism under AKEL had created a situation where few Greek Cypriots of ability thought of the Church as a career. Moreover, the Church of Cyprus had a secular mission which not every Greek Cypriot felt he wanted to promote.

Makarios had shown no particular interest in the politics of Enosis as a student and, though he must have accepted the goal of Union with Greece as unhesitatingly as he believed in heaven, he chose not to return to Cyprus at the end of the Second World War when there were hopes that the British might be ready to realise Greek Cypriot dreams. It has been argued – unconvincingly – that Makarios's experience of the sufferings of wartime Greece channelled his thoughts towards Enosis. It is more likely that his admiration for metropolitan Greece and a sense of being a somewhat despised Greek Cypriot cousin fused in him a passion for integration – but only when he felt the power of the Ethnarchy under him, first as bishop and then as Archbishop.

For years Makarios was detested by a large part of the British public and regarded as a most sinister figure because, although he was a churchman, he condoned and sometimes even instigated violence. Gradually people came to understand the role of the Orthodox Church in the Greek struggle for freedom, and it was not for a Western bishop who would bless a 'just war' to cast the first stone. Much more relevant to any assessment of Makarios is the *kind* of violence he condoned. He could not have prevented Grivas from launching his EOKA campaign, short of denouncing him to the British. He tried to limit him to sabotage, which he thought would be helpful. Apart from the occasions when, as Grivas said, the Archbishop advised him to throw a grenade or two among the Turkish Cypriots to discourage them from demonstrating, Makarios never approved of violence against persons. But his praise of EOKA after Grivas's main thrust had turned against so-called Greek Cypriot 'traitors' and the Turkish Cypriot community inevitably damaged his reputation.

Makarios must also be judged by the way in which he interpreted the will of the people who chose him as their Ethnarch. If the clamour for Enosis was a genuine political demand of the majority of Greek Cypriots, why did they accept independence – with Enosis ruled out – so easily in 1959? Dr Evdokas, who stood against Makarios for President on an 'Enosis' platform in 1968, got a miserable 3.71 per cent of the votes. Was this because most Greek Cypriots then accepted a Turkish veto on their Union with Greece or because they preferred independence which they have insisted on since?

Makarios's political judgement was often at fault. As Archbishop he rejected every British offer of a constitution – even the Radcliffe proposals which would have given the Greek Cypriots immediate control over a large area of self-government with built-in security for the Turkish Cypriots. Such a constitution could have been a sure step to independence along the inevitable road for all viable British possessions, in spite of a Hopkinson 'never'. It would almost certainly have been more durable than the 1960 model. Again, Makarios's 'thirteen points' for amending the constitution were too obviously designed to remove Turkish Cypriot obstructiveness for them to be acceptable to Ankara. In the tense situation of 1963 it needed only a casual spark to set off the explosion.

On one occasion, in a BBC television interview, President Makarios confessed he had made a number of mistakes in his career. When he was invited to mention some, he replied with a disarming smile that he would not like his people to know about them. Asking for Greek mainland officers to staff his 'National Guard' – instead of merely to train it – was certainly one cardinal mistake, as he later admitted. But the letter to President Gizikis demanding their withdrawal – and touching off the *coup* against him – was to be another.

How did a political leader who made so many wrong decisions survive in elected authority to the end and die mourned by his whole people? It was not that he lacked enemies or critics. To some extent it was the pressures on him from many different sides that kept him at the top. But he gave the Greek Cypriots a new sense of purpose which they had lacked before, even if for much of the time he led them through a wilderness of mistaken directions.

At the same time, because of his early pursuit of Enosis instead of the more rewarding independence, he failed to distinguish between the legitimate interests of the Cypriot Turks who had so much in common with his own community and the demands of a Turkey which was growing in strategic importance. By refusing at the outset to make any political concessions to the Turkish Cypriots *as a community* and subsequently making them too late, Makarios let himself become enmeshed in Great Power politics which were too strong for him.

He was a deeply religious person, without in any way being 'saintly'. His spiritual convictions gave him an inner serenity which, in spite of haunting political doubts and the outward contradictions in his behaviour – the ambivalence towards violence, the moments of indecision, the tactical shifts and manoeuvrings – earned him respect.

Since his death there has been some harsh Greek Cypriot criticism of Makarios. He has been described as a power-hungry tyrant, a megalomaniac who identified himself with Cyprus and behaved as if he would live for ever. This seems as far from the truth as the much more frequent fulsome praise of him as the inspired leader who always led his country forward towards freedom and justice.

Makarios was essentially a simple man, for all the deviousness that his public role forced upon him. He had great natural dignity, which was accentuated by the Archbishop's dress, not due to it. He was very accessible, and courteous and considerate to the least important visitor who came to see him. Few could resist the charm and the twinkling smile that was never far away, except on the most serious occasions. With those he knew well – such as his ministers – he had a teasing sense of humour, but it never appeared to be unkind. He had no real intimates, and that must have been one of the greatest burdens of his secular office.

He left no political testament and no heir-apparent. Clerides had been groomed originally as his successor but disappointed him later by seeming too soft towards the Turks. Kyprianou had been a favourite son, but often irritated him with his humourless approach and his lawyer's habit of arguing a subject into the ground; he was about to be sent abroad as ambassador when Makarios's death left him, as President of the House of Representatives, the constitutional stop-gap. Tasos Papadopoulos was probably nearest to the Archbishop in the last years; he followed his ideas closely and he is still an ambitious man.[4]

If Makarios had lived a few more years he might well have solved the problem he so largely helped to create by persuading his people to accept a painful but constructive compromise. There is no sign of his successor being able to do that. Makarios fell short of being a statesman but he was undoubtedly the only leader of his people for nearly thirty years. It was his tragedy that he had to fail them in the end.

Notes and References

CHAPTER I

1. There were plans in 1979 to restore the house and refurnish it as it was, making it a place of pilgrimage.
2. Doros Alastos (pseudonym of Evdoros Ioannides), *Cyprus in History* (Zeno, London, 1955) pp. 309–10.
3. See Panos Myrtiotis, *President Makarios of Cyprus* (Nicocles' Publications, Nicosia, no date) for a colourful, sentimentalised account of the Archbishop's early years. This is one of several short illustrated paper-back tributes to Makarios published soon after his death. The family details given by the present writer are confirmed by Makarios's sister, Mrs Maria Hadjicleanthous, and from visits to Ano Panayia.
4. Rupert Gunnis, *Historic Cyprus* (Methuen, London, 1936) p. 366.
5. These and other anecdotes are given by Myrtiotis, op. cit.
6. Myrtiotis, op. cit., pp. 11–12.

CHAPTER 2

1. The reminiscences that follow were recorded for the author by Abbot Chrysostomos in 1974, when he was in his late eighties. Makarios broadly accepted them as true.
2. Myrtiotis, op. cit., p. 13.
3. See Sir George Hill, *A History of Cyprus*, vol. IV, ed. by Sir Harry Luke (Cambridge University Press, 1952) for the fullest account of relations between the Archbishop of Cyprus, the Turkish Governor and the Sublime Porte in the eighteenth and early nineteenth centuries; also, for an analysis of this relationship, the present author's *Cyprus and Makarios* (Putnam, London, 1960) chap. I.
4. See Hill, op. cit., and Doros Alastos, op. cit., for typical British and Greek Cypriot assessments of the significance of this episode.
5. Makarios was unusually old to be a 'middle-school' gymnasium student even under a system that is not strict about age-levels. It points to the limitations of his Kykko education and suggests that Makarios's success at the Pancyprian was partly due to his maturer mind. His age also made him less inclined to join in the activities of his fellows, apart from debating.

5. The class registers and mark-books of this period have been preserved at the Pancyprian. Incidentally, they say mistakenly that Michael Mouskos was born in 1914 (instead of 1913).

CHAPTER 3

1. Recalled by Mrs Margaret Le Geyt from her conversations with the Archbishop during his stay in Seychelles. See Capt. P. S. Le Geyt, *Makarios in Exile* (Anagennisis Press, Nicosia, 1961).

2. Ibid. Origen's independence of thought obviously appealed to Makarios.

3. The evidence for this visit comes from Makarios's sister, Mrs Maria Hadjicleanthous, and from Andreas Azinas. Most accounts of Makarios's early life make no mention of it. H. D. Purcell says in *Cyprus* (Ernest Benn, London, 1969) p. 252, that Makarios told him he had spent a month in Cyprus while he was a student at Boston and had delivered a number of speeches and sermons and made contact with persons of influence in the Church. Makarios's own 'archivist', Mr Patroclos Stavrou, can find no record of a later (i.e. 1947) visit and it seems unlikely that Makarios could have afforded the fare. But see note 8 below. The Archbishop died before this important detail could be cleared up.

4. Charles Foley (ed.), *The Memoirs of General Grivas* (Longmans, London, 1964), note on p. 17.

5. See Capt. Le Geyt, op. cit., for his wife Margaret's account of Makarios's voyage to America and his experiences there.

6. Makarios's personal physician, Dr Vasos Lyssarides, the Socialist leader, told the author that the Archbishop's life had been 'monastic' during the time he had known him as a patient (since 1959). Makarios disliked being touched, in spite of enduring thousands of handshakes and hand-kissings every year, according to another in his confidence. Certainly there has never been any hint of sexual scandal, even from the bishops who later denounced Makarios or from the Turks.

7. Andreas Azinas, in a personal communication.

8. Capt. Le Geyt, op. cit., p. 95. This conflicts with a letter to the author from Mr Walter G. Muelder, Dean Emeritus of Boston University School of Theology, in which he says that he remembers Makarios coming to him in the spring of 1947 to say he had been elected a bishop. The Dean asked him whether he could postpone taking up his duties for a year or two, and he says Makarios later told him he had received permission to stay abroad another year, but thought that would be the limit. If one allows for the difficulty of remembering the exact words of a conversation of more than thirty years ago, Makarios may only have said that he was being pressed to accept a bishopric after the British restrictions on Church elections in Cyprus had been lifted towards the end of 1947. Mr Muelder concurs.

CHAPTER 4

1. Similar principles apply even more to the election of an Archbishop of Cyprus.

2. Dr. P. N. Vanezis, *Makarios: Pragmatism v. Idealism* (Abelard-Schuman, London, 1974). From the foreword by Lord Caradon, pp. xiii–xiv.

3. Myrtiotis, op. cit., pp. 30–1.
4. Doros Alastos, op. cit., p. 360.
5. Nikos Kranidiotis, *I Kypros eis ton Agona tis Eleftherias* (Cyprus in the Struggle for Freedom) (Athens, 1958) p. 64 ff.

CHAPTER 5

1. General George Grivas-Dighenis, *Apomnimonevmata Agonos E.O.K.A. 1955–1959* (Memoirs of EOKA's Struggle 1955–59) (Athens, 1961) p. 21 ff. Also Foley, op. cit, p. 18 ff.
2. Grivas-Dighenis, op. cit., 17, Foley, op. cit., p. 18.
3. From the official Greek text.
4. Foley, op. cit., p. 18.
5. Makarios's love of rhetoric encouraged such symmetrical phrases and gestures but he was obviously playing for AKEL's support here. Many Nationalists had decided to boycott the rally.
6. Sir Charles Peake, the British ambassador, thought he had persuaded Papagos not to mention Cyprus but to wait for the official visit to London which Eden was going to offer him.
7. From the official Greek text.
8. *Terrorism in Cyprus: The Captured Documents* (HMSO, London 1956).

CHAPTER 6

1. Other writings usually refer to these broadcasts for Cyprus as 'The Voice of the Fatherland'. But since Greece is always a 'Mother' to her children and as the Greeks often qualify *patrida* (lit. 'fatherland') with the word for 'mother' (thus: *mitera patrida*), I prefer 'The Voice of the Motherland'.
2. This exploitation of youth through 'a patently irreligious oath', as the British authorities called it, was used to good propaganda effect in Britain. However, it overlooked the fact that many Greek Cypriot boys and girls leapt at the chance of continuing the Greek tradition of resistance, with all the excitement of defying parents and teachers (or some of them) and running great risks.
3. The rigours of Orthodox Lent can produce a great sense of exaltation and disorientation even in ordinary people.
4. *Terrorism in Cyprus*, op. cit., p. 32. Makarios met Grivas again in August, on the eve of the Tripartite Conference. Later in the year, on 8 November 1955, he told an audience in Crete that he did not know 'Dighenis' personally. It was one of the few occasions when the Archbishop is known to have resorted to an outright lie.
5. Sir Anthony Eden, *Full Circle* (Cassell, London, 1960) p. 366.
6. Ibid. p. 401.
7. Ibid. p. 409.
8. Charles Foley, *Island in Revolt* (Longmans, London, 1962) p. 63.
9. Grivas records for the day of the Abbot's murder only that two British soldiers were killed and at least two more wounded. *Apomnimonevmata*, p. 11 of appendix.

CHAPTER 7

1. Capt. P. S. Le Geyt, (Margaret's reminiscences), and a conversation with Makarios's sister, Maria Hadjicleanthous; she normally packed for him.
2. Capt. Le Geyt, op. cit. Part I of this charming and now almost unobtainable little book gives a rambling but detailed account of the exiles' daily life and ends with brief character sketches. Part II consists of Margaret Le Geyt's recollections of her English lessons and conversations with Makarios. In Part III Capt. Le Geyt adds his impressions of Seychelles and mentions earlier deportees.
3. The internees refused to sign a written parole on the grounds that, as three of them were priests, their word was sufficient bond. The authorities finally accepted their initials as a compromise.
4. Grivas was generally referred to in the letters captured with the diaries as 'the Leader' or 'Uncle'. Father Papastavros was indicated by a diagonal cross. The Bishop of Kyrenia's younger brother, Renos Kyriakides, who took part in many EOKA operations until he was captured in December 1955, was identified as 'Romanos'.
5. Foley, op. cit., p. 103.
6. Stanley Mayes, *Cyprus and Makarios* (Putnam, London, 1960) p. 213.
7. Doros Alastos, *Cyprus Guerrilla: Grivas, Makarios and the British* (Heinemann, London, 1960) p. 9.
8. Among other widely different figures admired by the Archbishop were George Washington, Mahatma Gandhi and Frederick the Great. Margaret Le Geyt discovered he was also interested to know more about Winston Churchill and Billy Graham.
9. Makarios continued to have an affection for Seychelles all his life. He paid a return visit as President during one of his African trips and his memory is still kept alive in the islands where it is said that at least 250 children have been baptised Makarios.

CHAPTER 8

1. Grivas-Dighenis, op. cit., p. 170.
2. The Menderes Government's increasingly repressive measures against its opponents and critics led to a new polarisation of Turkish politics which was to have an adverse effect on Cyprus for many years.
3. Makarios stayed first in Psychiko, then in Ekali, with his sister Maria and her family. She had not been permitted to return to Cyprus after his deportation, though she had gone to Athens only for medical treatment. She was obliged to stay in Greece for three years until the Archbishop was allowed back in the island after the Zürich and London agreements.
4. The Greeks also failed to appreciate the difference between the powers and role of Labour's National Executive and those of the Parliamentary Labour Party.
5. This is a view shared by many mainland Greeks, especially since the Turkish invasion of Cyprus. They argue that, if Greece were lost to the West, Turkey's strategic importance would disappear.
6. Grivas-Dighenis, op. cit., pp. 304–5.
7. Ibid, pp. 305–6.

8. In spite of the over-reaction of British troops many Greek Cypriots were shocked by the murder of Mrs Cutliffe. Dr Dervis, the mayor of Nicosia, who had once said 'We are all EOKA now', offered a reward of £5000 for information leading to the arrest of those responsible; nobody was ever charged.

9. See Stephen G. Xydis, *Cyprus Reluctant Republic* (Mouton, The Hague; Paris. 1973), for a very full and informed account of the contacts behind the scenes in 1958 that led to the Greek-Turkish dialogue. Also François Crouzet, *Le Conflit de Chypre 1956–1959* (Bruylant, Brussels, 1973) vol. ii. Dimitri S. Bitsios, *Cyprus The Vulnerable Republic* (Institute for Balkan Studies, Salonika, 1975) gives the impressions of a Greek diplomat involved in the contacts.

CHAPTER 9

1. Xydis, op. cit.

2. Grivas says in his *Apomnimonevmata*, p. 354, that he had a letter from Andreas Azinas in Athens (undated but on internal evidence written just before Christmas 1958) which was 'quite enlightening'. Greek government circles – Azinas is quoted as saying – were worried by the Archbishop's 'fear of responsibility' (*efthinophovia*), which they attributed not to any doubts about the verdict of history but to his dread of the situation being exploited against him by the Greek Opposition and the Greek Cypriot Left.

3. Xydis, op. cit., p. 456.

4. Grivas-Dighenis, op. cit., p. 403.

5. See Xydis, op. cit., for the most detailed account of the long and tortuous negotiations.

6. Some of these appointments were changed before independence. Yeorkadjis took the important Ministry of the Interior, with far-reaching consequences. Papadopoulos was switched to Labour and Social Services.

CHAPTER 10

1. Stanley Kyriakides, *Cyprus Constitutionalism and Crisis Government* (University of Pennsylvania Press, 1968) and Thomas Ehrlich, *Cyprus 1958–1967* (Oxford University Press, 1974) both give good accounts of the breakdown of the 1960 constitution. A more legalistic and schematic analysis of the problem and the attitudes of the two communities is to be found in Polyvios Polyviou's *Cyprus in Search of a Constitution* (Nicosia. 1976).

2. Prof. Forsthoff resigned from his unenviable job in May 1963 after he had been abused by the Greek Cypriots as a 'Nazi' and his assistant had received anonymous threats to kill him because of his friendship with Rauf Denktash, then President of the Turkish Cypriot Communal Chamber.

3. Spyros Kyprianou, the former Ethnarchy representative in London and Makarios's eventual successor as President, was given the Foreign Ministry portfolio at independence when he was only twenty-eight. He frequently accompanied Makarios on state visits and was the faithful interpreter of his policies for the next twelve years.

4. Karamanlis's position had been undermined by Greece's growing economic

difficulties and by his too obvious determination to hold on to office. The immediate cause of his resignation was his dispute with King Paul, whom he advised to cancel the projected royal visit to London in view of the hostile reception Queen Frederika had met with from left-wing demonstrators there during a private visit in April and because of the international outcry the following month when a left-wing member of the Greek parliament, Gregory Lambrakis, was deliberately knocked down and killed in Salonica by a motor-cycle combination on the orders of the Greek police. This was the basis of the film '*Z*'. King Paul refused to take his Prime Minister's advice but Karamanlis could not survive the scandal of the Lambrakis affair.

5. According to Lawrence Stern in *The Wrong Horse: The Politics of Intervention and the Failure of American Diplomacy* (Quadrangle, New York, 1977) Ball was particularly fierce with Makarios and said to him: 'Your Beatitude, you can't turn this beautiful little island into your private *abattoir*'. He thought Makarios would be angry but the Archbishop only said: 'Mr Secretary, you are a very hard man', and stood his ground. Some years later, in 1969 – again according to Stern – Ball said in front of colleagues: 'That son of a bitch [Makarios] will have to be killed before anything happens in Cyprus'. Nevertheless Makarios indicated to the present writer in the summer of 1976, during the run-up to the American presidential elections, that he would be quite interested to see George Ball as Secretary of State.

CHAPTER 11

1. As soon as UNFICYP had become operational Makarios had written to the Prime Ministers of Greece and Turkey, asking them to move their national contingents back to camp since they were no longer needed. Inonu refused, whereupon Makarios accused Turkey of violating the Treaty of Alliance and announced that it was terminated. Ankara warned Athens that it would regard any Greek Cypriot move against the Turkish contingent as an act of aggression against Turkey. Makarios felt he had urgent need of Greek support.

2. The Turks were on firmer legal ground.

3. The Greek Cypriots have always maintained that the Turkish Cypriots own less than 18 per cent of the land – their ratio of the population. It is difficult, if not impossible, to get at the truth between the conflicting claims but it is known that many Turkish Cypriots were persuaded to sell land to the Greeks in the early years of this century, much as Arabs in Palestine were persuaded to sell land to the Jews.

4. In January 1965 Grivas had sent the Greek Government reports of an alleged conspiracy among left-wing Greek army oficers in Cyprus belonging to a larger group known as *Aspida* (the 'Shield'). Right-wing newspapers in Greece began to identify the Prime Minister's son, Andreas Papandreou, as its political leader; he was then Minister of Coordination in his father's Government and thoroughly feared by the Right for his radical views, though in the United States where he had been a professor of economics he was regarded as a fairly orthodox academic. The elder Papandreou was obliged to order an enquiry into the *Aspida* affair, but when he tried to dismiss his Minister of Defence and take the portfolio himself over another issue the King objected because the *Aspida* case was still *sub judice*.

5. Greek Cypriots saw nothing incongruous between this and their claim that Cyprus must be a united, independent state. The author once asked Makarios

why the Greek blue-and-white was flown over his own palace and most public buildings instead of the Cyprus flag. He agreed it was damaging internationally, but said he would encounter much opposition from certain quarters if he tried to change the practice.

CHAPTER 12

1. See Polyvios Polyviou, op. cit., for the fullest account.
2. There was nothing to connect Papandreou with the assassination attempt.
3. There is much information on the 'National Front' in Spyros Papayeoryiou's *Makarios: poreia dia pyros kai siderou* (Makarios: through fire and sword) (Ladias Publications, Athens, 1976). Papayeoryiou, an anti-Makarios Cypriot journalist and close confidant of Grivas for many years, changed sides and revealed his inside knowledge of the plotting against the President that culminated in the 1974 *coup*.
4. Papayeoryiou, op. cit.
5. Tasos Papadopoulos subsequently married Yeorkadjis's attractive and wealthy widow.
6. The evidence for this is Turkish Cypriot, but the statement was not repudiated and attempts by the author to get the text of the Yialousa speech from Greek Cypriot sources met with coy evasiveness.

CHAPTER 13

1. Papayeoryiou, op. cit., p. 120.
2. He turned for the first time to making a living as a lawyer for which he had trained at Gray's Inn in London.
3. Komodromos especially had been something of a political embarrassment through his forthright pronouncements on Enosis.
4. Papyeoryiou, op. cit.
5. The Italian journalist Oriana Fallaci says Makarios told her in an interview that Ioannides once came to see him in 1964, accompanied by Nikos Sampson. Ioannides reportedly suggested that the whole Cyprus problem could be settled for ever if the Greek Cypriots only made a concerted attack on the Cypriot Turks.
6. Stern, op. cit., pp. 77–9.
7. This purported to be a copy of a letter from an EOKA-B lieutenant, L. Papado-poullos (*sic*), code-name 'Thunderbolt', to Ioannides, the 'junta' leader, ident-ified as Cadmus, in which he compained that the organisation had received none of the help promised from Athens after the death of Grivas. The text is given in Papayeoryiou, op. cit., p. 270 and there is no reason to doubt its genuineness. It suggests that Ioannides was not relying much on EOKA-B.
8. This account is based on detailed information about the escape and the journey to Paphos given to the author by Andreas Neophytou, the nephew, who was with Makarios throughout. (Neophytou dropped his surname Hadjicleanth-ous when the family was in 'semi-exile' in Athens). The Archbishop did not escape through a secret underground passage, as some versions have said.
9. Stern, op. cit., pp. 94–5.

CHAPTER 14

1. *The Sunday Times*, 28 July 1974.
2. When Mr Callaghan, as Foreign Secretary, gave evidence in February 1976 to a House of Commons select committee on Cyprus he defended the British Government's 'masterly inactivity' after the *coup* against Makarios with a denial that he had foreseen the imminence of a Turkish invasion. Earlier Mr Roy Hattersley, the Minister of State, had told the committee that Britain had not got the manpower in the bases for military intervention and that, in any case, the Government would not have thought such a step 'appropriate' in the circumstances of 1974.
3. See Polyviou, op. cit., for a detailed account of the Geneva negotiations.
4. Probably the majority of these were killed during the Turkish invasion and the second thrust to the 'Attila Line'. Some certainly died during the Greek *coup*. But a small number were identified, through photographs or Turkish broadcasts, as being alive after the fighting stopped. The Turkish Cypriots have refused to co-operate in any joint enquiry into the question of the missing persons unless the Greek Cypriots also agree to an investigation into the deaths of Turkish Cypriots in 1964. The subject is a highly emotional one for Greek Cypriots but it has also been exploited politically.
5. Makarios's successor, President Kyprianou, reduced the sentence in the context of clemency towards former EOKA-B elements. In 1979 Sampson was sent to West Germany for medical treatment.
6. It was a tactical mistake to go back to the smaller figure but Makarios *had* conceded the principle of a *bizonal* federation. President Kyprianou subsequently moved away from this position.
7. The difference in temperament between members of the two communities became one of the biggest obstacles to a settlement. Appropriate legislation in the Turkish Cypriot region could set a limit on Greek Cypriot enterprise there, but would be regarded by the Greek Cypriots as damaging to the island's economy as a whole.
8. There were reports that Makarios's laying to rest was greeted with majestic thunder and lightning from the heavens. His detractors denied there was any bad weather that day. The writer has checked the facts, as given here, with persons who travelled in the funeral procession.
9. There is now a permanent military guard on the tomb. The authorities have sensibly left the last part of the approach in as natural a state as possible. A simple Byzantine chapel, open to the four winds, has been built on the very peak, some two hundred yards away, and the place attracts many visitors.

EPILOGUE

1. During his prolonged visit to the United States in 1979 to get support from the Greek lobby there Archbishop Chrysostomos criticised the eventual Kyprianou–Denktash agreement to resume talks as 'untimely'.
2. The ten-point formula for a new dialogue agreed on by Kyprianou and Denktash in May 1979 included a decision that they would negotiate over Varosha independently of the main talks and might reach a separate solution on this issue first.

3. Kyprianou plainly regarded Papadopoulos as the main political challenge to his prestige as President.

4. Tasos Papadopoulos had come to accept the need for a territorial compromise with the Turkish Cypriots.

Bibliography

There was little published material for a biography of Makarios outside general political works on the Cyprus problem. The two books by Dr P. N. Vanezis of the Cyprus High Commission in London, *Makarios: Faith and Power* and *Makarios: Pragmatism v. Idealism,* are somewhat uncritical studies of the Archbishop's pursuit of Enosis and his acceptance of independence, with only a sketchy account of his early life. Spyros Papayeoryiou, in *Makarios: poreia dia pyros kai siderou* (Makarios: through fire and sword), gives a frank inside account of the plotting that led to the *coup* against the President from the viewpoint of one who was close to Grivas and the rebel bishops but later repented and changed sides. Grivas's own Memoirs, especially in the fuller Greek version, are invaluable for their comment on the tortuous manoeuvring of the Archbishop both before and during the first EOKA campaign and while he was resisting the Greek and British pressures on him to accept a compromise with the Turks. The Archbishop emerges as a warm, human personality mainly in the artless account of his internment in Seychelles given by Capt. P. S. Le Geyt and his wife, Margaret, in their *Makarios in Exile*; they refused to allow their disapproval of his political 'crimes' poison their liking for him as a man. Otherwise there are only some highly-sentimentalised short illustrated biographies of the Ethnarch published in Cyprus soon after his death – for example, *President Makarios of Cyprus* by Panos Myrtiotis and *Tora Yia Panda* (Now for Always) – and a much longer part-work by A. Pavlides published weekly in Nicosia under the simple title *Makarios*.

In writing this biography I have relied heavily on conversations and interviews over a number of years with Makarios himself, members of his family, his advisers and ministers, his political opponents in both communities in Cyprus, the Church hierarchy – bishops, priests and monks – and Greek politicans and diplomats. I have also drawn upon some hundreds of talks on the Cyprus problem which I wrote for the BBC between 1955 and 1977, though I often found my opinions had changed with the years. Of the many books on the general subject of the Cyprus problem those by François Crouzet, Stanley Kyriakides, Polyvios Polyviou, H. D. Purcell, Robert Stephens and Stephen Xydis which I have listed below proved most useful for the depth of their analysis. Nancy Crawshaw's book, *The Cyprus Revolt*, detailed and well-documented for the period before independence, less adequate in its Postcript for the years since, appeared only when my own work was nearly complete. It has the most comprehensive bibliography, of both official and unofficial publications, and I would recommend this to anyone who wants to supplement the following list.

Alastos, Doros (pseudonym of Evdoros Ioannides), *Cyprus in History* (Zeno, London, 1955).
——, *Cyprus Guerrilla: Grivas, Makarios and the British* (Heinemann, London, 1960).
Bitsios, Dimitri S., *Cyprus: The Vulnerable Republic*, 2nd edn (Institute for Balkan Studies, Salonika, 1975).
Cobham, C. D., *Excerpta Cypria: Materials for a History of Cyprus* (Cambridge University Press, 1908).
Crawshaw, Nancy, *The Cyprus Revolt* (Allen & Unwin, London, 1978).
Crouzet, François, *Le Conflit de Chypre 1956–59*, 2 vols (Bruylant, Brussels, 1973).
Eden, Sir Anthony, *Full Circle* (Cassell, London, 1960).
Ehrlich, Thomas, *Cyprus 1958–1967* (Oxford University Press, 1974).
Foley, Charles, *Island in Revolt* (Longmans, London, 1962).
——, *Legacy of Strife: Cyprus from Rebellion to Civil War* (Penguin Books, Harmondsworth, 1964).
——, (ed.) *The Memoirs of General Grivas* (Longmans, London, 1964).
Gunnis, Rupert, *Historic Cyprus* (Methuen, London, 1936).
Grivas – Dighenis, General George, *Apomnimonevmata Agonos E.O.K.A. 1955–1959* (Memoirs of EOKA's Struggle 1955–59) (Athens, 1961).
Harbottle, Michael, *The Impartial Soldier* (Oxford University Press, 1970).
Hill, Sir George, *A History of Cyprus*, vol. IV ed. by Sir Harry Luke (Cambridge University Press, 1952).
Kranidiotis, Nikos, *I Kypros eis ton Agona tis Eleftherias* (Cyprus in the Struggle for Freedom) (Athens, 1958).
Kyriakides, Stanley, *Cyprus Constitutionalism and Crisis Government* (University of Pennsylvania Press, Philadelphia, 1968).
Le Geyt, Capt. P. S., *Makarios in Exile* (Anagenissis Press, Nicosia, 1961).
Macmillan, Harold, *Riding the Storm 1956–1959* (Macmillan, London, 1971).
Mayes, Stanley, *Cyprus and Makarios* (Putnam, London, 1960).
Papayeoryiou, Spyros, *Makarios: poreia dia pyros kai siderou* (Makarios: through fire and sword) (Ladias Publications, Athens, 1976).
Polyviou, Polyvios, *Cyprus in Search of a Constitution* (Nicosia, 1976).
Purcell, H. D., *Cyprus* (Ernest Benn, London 1969).
Stavrinides, Zenon, *The Cyprus Conflict: National Identity and Statehood* (Stavrinides Press, Nicosia, 1976).
Stephens, Robert, *Cyprus: A Place of Arms* (Pall Mall Press, London, 1966).
Stern, Lawrence, *The Wrong Horse: The Politics of Intervention and the Failure of American Diplomacy* (Quadrangle, New York, 1977).
Storrs, Sir Ronald, *Orientations* (Nicholson and Watson, London, 1949)
Vanezis, Dr P. N., *Makarios: Faith and Power* (Abelard-Schuman, London, 1971)
——, *Makarios: Pragmatism v. Idealism* (Abelard-Schuman, London, 1974).
Xydis, Stephen G., *Cyprus: Conflict and Conciliation 1954–1958* (Ohio State University Press, 1967).
——, *Cyprus: Reluctant Republic* (Mouton, The Hague-Paris, 1973).

I have not thought it necessary to try to list the vast number of official documents, propagandist pamphlets and newspaper articles relevant to the Cyprus question that have been published in Britain, Greece, Turkey and Cyprus and at the United Nations over the past thirty years; the most important are given in Nancy

Crawshaw's bibliography. I would only draw attention to the following, given in chronological order, as deserving careful study in any assessment of Makarios's motives, the pressures on him and his reaction to events.

Greek Irredentism and Cypriot Terrorism (Cyprus Government, Nicosia, 1956).

Terrorism in Cyprus: The Captured Documents, Grivas Diaries (HMSO, London, 1956).

Constitutional Proposals for Cyprus, Lord Radcliffe's Report, (HMSO, London, 1956).

Cyprus, Independence Constitution and the Treaties (HMSO, London, 1960).

The Cyprus Problem, Akritas Plan, (Turkish Cypriot Administration, Nicosia, 1971).

The Cyprus Problem: Historical Review and Analysis of Latest Developments (Greek Cypriot Public Information Office, Nicosia, 1975).

Report from the Select Committee on Cyprus (HMSO, London, 1976).

Index

290

Printed in Great Britain
by Amazon